NOT GAY

T0355560

SEXUAL CULTURES

General Editors: José Esteban Muñoz and Ann Pellegrini

Titles in the series include

For a complete list of books in the series, see www.nyupress.org.

NOT

SEX BETWEEN STRAIGHT WHITE MEN

GAY

Jane Ward

NEW YORK UNIVERSITY PRESS

New York and London

NEW YORK UNIVERSITY PRESS
New York and London
www.nyupress.org

References to Internet websites (URLs) were accurate at the time of writing. Neither the author nor
New York University Press is responsible for URLs
that may have expired or changed since the manu-
script was prepared.

Library of Congress Cataloging-in-Publication Data
Ward, Elizabeth Jane.
Not gay : sex between straight white men / Jane
Ward.
pages cm. — (Sexual cultures)
Includes bibliographical references and index.
ISBN 978-1-4798-2517-2 (pb : alk. paper) — ISBN
978-1-4798-6068-5 (cl : alk. paper)
1. Men—Sexual behavior. 2. Gay men. 3. Hetero-
sexual men. 4. Homosexuality. I. Title.
HQ28.W37   2015
306.70811—dc23   2015004665

New York University Press books are printed on
acid-free paper, and their binding materials are
chosen for strength and durability. We strive to use
environmentally responsible suppliers and materials to the greatest extent possible in publishing
our books.

Manufactured in the United States of America

10 9 8 7 6 5 4 3 2 1

Also available as an ebook

For Kat

CONTENTS

ACKNOWLEDGMENTS

SEVERAL years ago I took myself on a writing retreat to a little cabin in Joshua Tree National Park, with the goal of starting this book. On the second day in the cabin, as I was typing away, I slowly started to cry—a rarity at this stage in my life. It took me by surprise that I was crying, but I also knew why it was happening: I was *really* happy. In contrast with my first book, a revision of a dissertation that never fully felt like my own project, this book unfolded with ease, urgency, and clarity. Some sections made me worried I would lose my job or meet some other unfortunate fate if I dared to publish them; others made me laugh out loud. Writing a book about sex practices—a subject generally devalued in academia despite its high political and ethical stakes—was not only intellectually energizing, but a vital counterbalance to my sleep-deprived existence as a new parent. I am grateful for the pleasure this book has brought to my life, and for my new awareness of what the writing process can be.

This project has been shaped by many friends, colleagues, reviewers, and conference interlocutors to whom I am indebted: Karl Bryant, Salvador Vidal-Ortiz, Mark Broomfield, Jack Halberstam, Amin Ghaziani, Carol Tushabe, David Halperin, Stephen Valocchi, Rachel Luft, Lisa Jean Moore, Margaux Cowden, Peter Hennen, Kate Frank, Jennifer Doyle, Ann Cvetkovich, Melissa Dase, Beth Schneider, Steven Zeeland, Tristan Taormino, Chrys

Ingraham, Hélène Frohard-Dourlent, CJ Pascoe, Merri Lisa John-son, Tracy Fisher, Piya Chatterjee, Tamara Ho, Christine Gailey, Mike Chavez, and the women's studies students and faculty at the University of California Riverside. I am especially thankful to Rod-erick Ferguson and Paisley Currah for their careful reading and extensive feedback; the book is much better as a result.

I am also incredibly fortunate to have received the generous support and incisive comments of my comrades in "Lezerati," the long-running queer women's writing group in Los Angeles. Deep thanks to my friends and mentors in the group: Jeanne Cordova, Lynn Ballen, Talia Bettcher, Judith Branzburg, Robin Podolsky, Dana Marterella, Claudia Rodriguez, Jacqui Meisel, and Raquel Gutierrez. Extra thanks goes to the lesbian feminist icon Jeanne Cordova, who, despite being initially flummoxed by my decision to write an entire book about "white dick," found it in her heart to embrace this project. Lezerati members kept me on track even when writing was the last thing I wanted to do.

This book was given new life when José Esteban Muñoz and Ann Pellegrini welcomed it into New York University Press's Sex-ual Cultures series. José died before he could offer much guid-ance, but his enthusiasm for the project and his dazzling legacy have been profound inspirations. I could not be more grateful to Ann Pellegrini for her brilliant and extensive engagement with this project, and for modeling how to take on complex questions with an eye to accessibility. Ann pushed the work in new and rich directions, challenging me to think more deeply about the theo-retical stakes at hand. Her influence runs through every chapter of the book. My gratitude, also, to Ilene Kalish, Eric Zinner, and New York University Press for their excitement about this book. This work was also supported by grants from the Wayne F. Placek Foundation and UC Riverside's Queer Lab. Thanks are due to both for supporting the writing retreats so essential to the book's completion.

My love and appreciation also go to my beloved friends and family who sustained and grounded me as I fell into the rabbit hole of this project or down the spiral of new parenthood: Felix Solano Vargas, Layla Welborn, Margaux Cowden, Rachel Luft, Melissa Dase, Macarena Gomez-Barris, Beth Schneider, Leanne Southhall, David Arnn, Lisa Lowmann, Joshua Arnn, Beck Bailey, Kikanza Ramsey-Ray and all the folks at Village Playgarden, Molly Sadeghi, Lauren Dinaro Veca, Rebecca Prediletto, Rachel Pedroso, Jesse Cripps, Reese and Elliott Cripps, Maren Ross, Steven Ross, Peter Ross, and especially, my brother, Alex Ward, my sister-in-love, Laurie Gow, and my mother Shirley Ward. Sweet thanks and tickles go to the little Yarrow "Pickles" Ross-Ward, who isn't allowed to read this book for a few more years. Thank you, Yarrow, for always keeping it silly.

Finally, this book is dedicated to my partner, Kat Ross, whose own delicious embrace of the unexpected, the discordant, the feminist, and the queer is the fuel that kept this project in motion. Without her rare and generous capacity to cheerfully take care of our child while I worked—and somehow be impossibly sexy at the same time—this book would have been dead in the water. I can't wait for our next adventure together.

1

Nowhere without It

The Homosexual Ingredient in the Making of Straight White Men

ABOUT fifteen years ago, in the late 1990s, I was a young dyke who would occasionally date boring straight men, especially after a difficult queer breakup. I am not proud of this time in my life, but it is where this story begins. On one such date, one of these men sheepishly agreed to tell me some of the details of his experience in a fraternity at a Southern California university he had attended a few years prior. Looking for something—*anything*—to shift our conversation to my newfound queer feminist rage, I probed him for the most damning information about fraternity life at his notorious party school. I waited to hear contemptible stories of violations committed against drunken young women. I imagined that what he would tell me would offend my feminist sensibilities, that I would get angry, and that this would push me to stop seeing him and get back into the more personally meaningful and high-stakes terrain of queer life. I do not doubt that he had tales of women and Rohypnol to tell, but when asked for the most confidential details about fraternity life, his response surprised me. He offered instead a story about a fairly elaborate hazing ritual called the "elephant walk," in which young men inserted their fingers into each other's anuses. Participants in the elephant walk were required to strip naked and stand in a circular formation, with one thumb in their mouth and the other in the anus of the young, typically white, man in front

Figure 1.1. 1970s elephant walk, Indiana University (Roger Dorn, totalfrat-move.com, http://totalfratmove.com/in-defense-of-the-elephant-walk/?page=0#comments).

of them. Like circus elephants connected by tail and trunk, and ogled by human spectators, they walked slowly in a circle, linked thumb to anus, while older members of the fraternity watched and cheered.

At first I was a bit shocked, but then his story prompted me to recall another experience, one of watching a video in a senior seminar on Sexual Politics that I took while I, too, was an undergraduate in college. There were nine students in our course, and our final project was to produce a multimedia presentation that would creatively explore the complexities of "postmodern sexuality." My presentation—basically a fanatical ode to Madonna—did not receive a warm reception from the graduate student teaching the seminar, but all of us *were* impressed by an ethnographic film submitted by the only male student in the course. The video, a compilation of chaotic footage he had shot exclusively inside the bedrooms and bathroom of his fraternity house, showed nude white boys laughing and holding down other white boys whom they mounted and "pretended" to fuck on top of a bunk bed. I recall the small frat-house bedroom packed wall to wall with shirtless young white men wearing baseball caps, screaming hysterically, playfully pushing and punching their way through the crowd of bodies to obtain a better view of the "unfortunate" boys underneath the pile of their naked fraternity brothers. The boys on top were laughing and calling those underneath fags; the boys on the bottom were laughing, too, and calling the aggressors fags as they struggled to switch the scenario and get on top. None of these boys seemed like fags to me. The student who shot and edited the video, himself a member of this fraternity, had remarkably little to say about the meaning of these images. "We're just fucking around. It's a frat thing. . . . It's hard to explain," he told us.

As a young feminist, I was repelled by the heteromasculine culture of abjection and aggression in which these encounters were embedded, and I believed that this way of relating to sexuality was not unrelated to homophobia and misogyny. Both of these men—the date who reported to me about the elephant walk and my classmate who had filmed his fraternity brothers engaged in "pretend" sex—seemed to take for granted that these were scenes of power and humiliation, not sex. These encounters can be read as humiliating or disgusting precisely because they involve normal, heterosexual young men behaving like fags, or being subjected, ostensibly against their will, to homosexual contact. And yet, despite the homophobia of the participants, I was also captivated and excited by the existence of this kind of contact between straight men. The budding queer critic (and pervert) in me was impressed by the imagination required to manufacture these scenarios, the complex rules that structured them, and the

Figure 1.2. "Members of a fraternity displaying their new heart brands" (Wikimedia Commons, released into public domain October 2, 2006, http://en.wikipedia.org/wiki/File:Hearts.jpg).

performative and ritualistic way that straight men touched one another's bodies or ordered others to do so.

I also sensed that the men involved believed they were doing something *productive*—something fundamentally *heterosexual, masculine,* and *white*—as they fingered each other's anuses. Consider, for instance, this quotation from a currently popular website by and for young men in fraternities (also known as "bros"), which explains the purpose of the elephant walk as follows:

> The rule of thumb is the heavier the hazing, the stronger the bros [brothers]. By doing things like forcing your pledges/rooks to eat human shit or do an elephant walk you are basically saying, "Hey, by learning what your fellow bros' shit tastes like you will be better bros," and I have to say—I really respect that. . . . War builds amazing bonds. Hazing is basically war, only instead of freedom the end goal is getting hammered constantly with bros who are cool as shit and banging hot slam pieces [women]. It's still up in the air which goal is more important, but one thing is for sure, bros would be nowhere without hazing.[1]

Is it possible that straight white men would really be nowhere without the opportunity for intimate contact with one another's anuses? Before I answer that question, I will say that what *is* clear is that when young white men grope one another, they believe they are getting work done. They are, as the straight dude quoted above suggests, engaged in something urgent and powerful—a form of bonding comparable to what soldiers experience during times of war, and a kind of relief and triumph comparable to freedom.

To the extent that sexual contact between straight white men is ever acknowledged, the cultural narratives that circulate around these practices typically suggest that they are *not gay* in their identitarian consequences, but are instead about building heterosexual men, strengthening hetero-masculine bonds, and strengthening the bonds of white manhood in particular. This book does not argue against this premise. In fact, in the chapters that follow, I am going to amplify this premise by suggesting that homosexuality is an often invisible, but nonetheless vital ingredient—a constitutive element—of heterosexual masculinity. Taking sexual contact between straight white men as my point of departure, my aim is to offer a new way to think about heterosexual subjectivity—not as the opposite or absence of homosexuality, but as its own unique mode of engaging homosexual sex, a mode characterized by pretense, disidentification, and heteronormative investments. In particular, I am going to argue that when straight white men approach homosexual sex in the "right" way—when they make a show of enduring it, imposing it, and repudiating it— doing so functions to bolster not only their heterosexuality, but also their masculinity and whiteness.

Why focus on white men? All heterosexual practices—indeed, all sexual practices—are embedded within gendered and racialized circuits of meaning. For instance, as Chrys Ingraham demonstrates in the book *White Weddings*, the whiteness of weddings is not simply a matter of white bridal gowns, but a description of the white women who appear disproportionately in bridal magazines, the whiteness of Mattel's bridal-themed Barbies, and the racial hierarchy of the wedding industry itself. Idealized white femininity is central to the construction of weddings as special and perfect, and the wedding industry in turn reinforces the normalcy and legitimacy of whiteness. Similarly, this book attends to what whiteness *does* for white heterosexual men as they come into homosexual contact, and what homosexual contact does for white hetero-masculinity. While much attention has been paid to the ways that race and culture crosscut the sex practices of men of color, including and especially straight men of color who have sex with men "on the down low," the links between whiteness and male sexual fluidity are mostly unacknowledged. Most accounts of the down low suggest that straight-identified men of color who have sex with men are doing so because they are actually gay, but cannot come out due to elevated levels of homophobia in their ethnoracial communities. I'll return to this story later, but for now I raise it to point out that, in contrast, the links between whiteness and white male sexual fluidity have been largely ignored, as if white men's sex practices have nothing to do with their racial and cultural location. By focusing on straight white men, I want to think about the ways that whiteness and masculinity—as a particular nexus of power—enable certain kinds of sexual contact, sexual mobility, and sexual border crossing that are not possible, or at least don't carry the same cultural meanings, when enacted by men of color.

I begin this book with the example of the elephant walk not because it is my most convincing piece of "data"; regrettably, I have never witnessed it (though it has been well documented by other scholars[2]). Instead, I begin here because it marks the beginning of my own journey into this terrain, one that started not with the media frenzy over "straight girls kissing" in the late 2000s, but a decade earlier, with images of straight white boys kissing in front of other cheering straight white boys. Hearing the story of the elephant walk first introduced me to an evolving cultural narrative about the circumstances in which straight dudes might, for various reasons, engage in homosexual sex. This story set in motion my curiosity about why so little attention is given to the sexual fluidity of straight white men, why this subject elicits so much denial, and what all of this reveals about the heterosexual/homosexual binary.

Research psychologists have long been concerned with the reasons that straight men engage in homosexual sex. The sheer number of terms invented by U.S. psychologists in the 1950s to describe such practices—"deprivational homosexuality," "facultative homosexuality," "functional homosexuality," "situational homosexuality," "opportunistic homosexuality," and so forth[3]—provides a window into the amount of effort researchers have expended to distinguish "false" homosexualities from their authentic, or truly gay, counterparts. A considerable body of twentieth-century psychological research on sex between straight men suggests that this sex most often results from desperate circumstances, such as in situations of heterosexual deprivation that occur in prisons and the military. According to this logic, a man with a heterosexual constitution may engage in homosexual sex acts (and presumably, vice versa), but if his homosexual encounters are *situational* (i.e., occurring only in prison, or while at sea, in military barracks, and so forth), these encounters are a blip on the otherwise static sexual radar screen. They signal nothing particularly meaningful about his sexuality.

Still today, the dominant mode of thinking within the disciplines of psychology and sexology—and arguably within the broader culture—is that the sexual content of male heterosexuality is fundamentally different from that of male homosexuality. When heterosexual men *do* engage in homosexual sex, and if they are not immediately presumed to be in the closet, these practices are treated as momentary aberrations, and a good deal of work goes into explaining why they occurred and why they are misrepresentative of, or discordant with, the true sexual orientation of participants.

In contrast, this book is based on the premise that homosexual contact is a ubiquitous feature of the culture of straight white men. Many other studies have demonstrated that straight men engage in acts of kissing, touching, jerking, licking, and penetrating men, typically in specific institutional environments and under particular circumstances. But little attention has been paid to the aggregate finding of these studies: namely, that white straight-identified men manufacture opportunities for sexual contact with other men in a remarkably wide range of settings, and that these activities appear to *thrive* in hyper-heterosexual environments, such as universities, where access to sex with women is anything but constrained. Additionally, studies of straight white men's homosexual activity all too often take these men's own understandings of their homosexual behavior at face value, viewing it as exceptional, circumstantial, or not sexual at all. While I agree that straight men's disidentification with homosexuality is at the heart of the matter, we need not accept that their homosexual encounters are *purely* about humiliation, institutional constraints, or whatever other presumably nonsexual force participants invoke to explain their behavior. To take these exceptionalizing accounts at face value misses an important opportunity to map the multiple and simultaneous meanings of straight white men's homosexual encounters.

The project at hand is an effort to catalogue a broad and diverse range of accounts of straight white men's sex with men. I examine how the homosexual encounters of straight white men are imagined, theorized, represented, and resolved by a broad array of actors—from psychologists to young men in fraternities, from sociologists to military officials, from filmmakers and other cultural producers to people who post personal ads online. Drawing on an eclectic archive of cultural materials and the tools of cultural sociology, this book investigates the stories people tell about why and how straight men might behave homosexually. Its chapters trace not only documented accounts of straight white men's actual homosexual behavior, but also how the homosexual encounters of heterosexual men appear in the realms of fantasy and cultural production. This approach requires a broad theoretical and methodological repertoire, a synthesis of queer studies, cultural studies, sociology, and feminist theory. Together, these approaches illuminate the multiple registers at which an ostensibly "incongruent" sex practice—straight men having sex with men—is simultaneously claimed and denied, and with what cultural and political effects.

Fluid Subjects: The Generation, Gender, and Race of Sexual Fluidity

"Shit Happens": The Heteroflexible Youth Generation

Regardless of how often the elephant walk or similar encounters actually occur in fraternities or elsewhere,[4] they are part of
an increasingly familiar narrative about the sexual fluidity of a
new generation of young heterosexuals. Consider, for instance,
the most popular definition of "heteroflexible" that appears on
the now iconic, youth-driven website urbandictionary.com: "I'm
straight, but shit happens." This definition has received over 11,000
votes of approval by users of urbandictionary. While fraternity
members who engage in the elephant walk, for instance, probably
do not identify as "heteroflexible"—this *identity*, as distinct from
the practice, is reportedly more popular with young women—
the term certainly captures the driving logic behind the elephant
walk. The very concept of heteroflexibility, as defined on urbandictionary and elsewhere, communicates three popular notions
about human sexuality, notions that form the theoretical basis
now used to explain a broad range of homosexual encounters
experienced by heterosexuals, including those of recent interest
to the corporate media, such as "the phenomenon of straight girls
kissing":

1. Sexual *behaviors* are often random, accidental, and meaningless ("shit" can and does "happen").
2. But, regardless of a person's sexual *behavior*, it is possible to
   be certain about one's fundamental sexual *constitution* ("I'm
   straight"), which is increasingly believed to be hardwired or
   biologically determined, a fact I will soon address.
3. And, *individuals are not to be blamed* for sexual behaviors
   that are in conflict with their sexual constitution, especially
   when various circumstances demand, or at least encourage, flexibility. (Consider, for instance, the sentence offered

on urbandictionary.com to illustrate how one would use the term "heteroflexible" in speech: "Dude, it's not my fault. I was drunk and it was fun. What can I say? I'm heteroflexible.")

A fourth "fact" about heteroflexibility, according to some sociologists,[5] is that it is a *new* phenomenon. That heterosexuals engage in homosexual sex is nothing new, they argue. But what *is* ostensibly new is the openness with which young people, especially girls who kiss girls, are approaching their sexual fluidity; in fact, they are so open about it that they have given it a name, an identity—heteroflexible—something heretofore unheard of. In fact, the existence of heterosexuals who cross the border into homosexual terrain is consistently viewed as a signal of the arrival of a new and surprising sexual order, one ushered in by young people with their new-fangled ideas about sex. For instance, sociologist Laurie Essig, blogging for Salon.com, describes her irritated reaction after first being introduced to the term "heteroflexible," a reaction she explains primarily through the lens of a generational divide between her students and herself:

> There is nothing like teaching college students to make a person feel hopelessly out-of-date.... What I'm talking about here is "heteroflexibility." If you don't know what that is, it's time to admit that you're as out of it as I am. Heteroflexibility is the newest permutation of sexual identity.... [It] means that the person has or intends to have a primarily heterosexual lifestyle, with a primary sexual and emotional attachment to someone of the opposite sex. But that person remains open to sexual encounters and even relationships with persons of the same sex. It is a rejection of bisexuality since the inevitable question that comes up in bisexuality is one of preference, and the preference of the heteroflexible is quite clear. Heteroflexible, I am told, is a lighthearted attempt to stick with heterosexual identification while still "getting in on the fun of homosexual pleasures." ... My reaction was predictable.... How

could these kids go and invent yet another identity when "we" solved that problem for them in the 1980s and '90s? The word they were looking for was "queer" or even "bisexual," damnit. I was angry that they would throw out the politics and the struggles of naming that had come before them. . . . And then my middle-aged rage mellowed enough to see the true genius behind this new term. Heteroflexibility—not homosexuality or bisexuality—would bring about an end to the hegemony of heterosexuality. . . . The opposite of heteroflexible is heterorigid. Imagine saying to anyone that you're heterorigid. Sounds awful, right?[6]

Essig's characterization of heteroflexibility as "the newest permutation of sexual identity" mirrors most commentary on the topic. *TIME* reporter Jeffrey Kluger describes girl–girl heteroflexibility as a youth-driven trend, one facilitated by alcohol, girls' need for attention, and occasionally "genuine experimentation."[7] Kluger draws heavily on the work of feminist scholars Leila Rupp and Verta Taylor, who offer a more nuanced analysis, yet one still largely focused on youth and the characterization of heteroflexibility as a new behavior. In their view, college-aged women "are engaging in new kinds of sexual behaviors," namely "using the heterosexual hookup culture [of college] to experiment with or engage in same-sex sexual interactions." They explain that "what young women call 'heteroflexibility' allows for behavior outside one's claimed sexual identity, although the lines between lesbian and non-lesbian women, whether heterosexual or bisexual, remain firmly in place."[8]

Conceptualizing sexual fluidity as trendy and isolated to young adults assists in the construction of "mature" sexuality as stable, exclusive, and less vulnerable to social influence. In the next chapter, I will dispute these arguments that heterosexual fluidity is new and experimental by drawing on queer historiography to demonstrate that almost all contemporary indicators of heterofluidity can be traced back as far as the invention of the heterosexual/homosexual binary itself—from transactional encounters between nor-mal men and fairies to the rebellious homosexual stunts of straight boys gone wild; from "not gay" homosexual sex in the immigrant saloons of early twentieth century New York City to the "not gay" homosexual sex common in public bathrooms in the late twen-tieth century and beyond; from clever monikers for heterosexual men engaged in homosexual sex to elaborate theories designed to account for these men's "discordant" homosexual behavior.

The Gender of Sexual Fluidity

Commentary on heteroflexibility suggests that sexual fluidity is not only a youth trend, but a female one as well. Feminist soci-ologists point out that girls and women are given more room to explore gender and sexuality than boys, and are also influenced by a culture that both celebrates the sexual fluidity of female celebri-ties (Madonna, Britney Spears, Lady Gaga) and depicts lesbianism as an effective means of seducing men. Conversely, boys and men suffer greater gender regulation, have fewer models of male sexual fluidity, and are presumably unrewarded by women for any sexual fluidity they may express. As Rupp and Taylor explain, "men do not, at least in contemporary American culture, experience the same kind of fluidity. Although they may identify as straight *and* have sex with other men, they certainly don't make out at parties for the pleasure of women."[9]

Examinations of heteroflexibility also inevitably turn to the re-search findings of psychologists and human development scholars who believe that men's sexual desire is less flexible than women's for a variety of evolutionary reasons. Lisa Diamond, author of *Sex-ual Fluidity: Understanding Women's Love and Desire*, argues that women's sexual desires are more variable than men's, and that sexual variability, in general, is both hormonal and situational. In Diamond's view, female arousal is more easily triggered by situ-ational factors and more linked to romantic love than men's. This, she argues, is an outcome of the fact that women's hormonal cycles produce a relatively limited window of "proceptive" desire—the kind of intense, visceral, reproduction-oriented,[10] and lust-driven desire that emerges without any particular stimuli—as compared to men's presumably near-constant experience of this state. In contrast with men, women spend more time experiencing "receptive arousal," or sexual responsiveness to nonhormonal, social cues (e.g., watching a romantic movie, developing a strong emotional bond with someone, and so on). In this view, women have a biological leg up, so to speak, when it comes to sexual fluidity. If one accepts the premise of this research—women have more fluid sexual desires than men for reasons that are governed by hormonal cycles and generally beyond our control—it stands to reason that to find "heteroflexibility," we should look to (young) women.

Setting aside the feminist objections one might have to this characterization of women's sexuality, one thing is clear: the now common perception that women are more sexually receptive and flexible, and that men by contrast are more sexually rigid, has rendered men's sexual fluidity largely invisible. Straight men *do* make out at parties for the pleasure of women and engage in virtually the same teasing/kissing/sex-for-show behaviors that straight young women do, though research demonstrating this has received relatively little attention. Sociologist Eric Anderson's research on young men and sports is a goldmine of information about straight male college athletes kissing, taking "body shots" off of one another, and "jacking each other off" during threesome's with girls and male teammates.[11] In ways that are virtually indistinguishable from scenarios in which straight girls kiss or have sex for the pleasure of male spectators,[12] the straight college football players interviewed by Anderson describe a host of situations in which they have sexual contact with one another in order to please a female sex partner. One reported:

> "I'm not attracted to them [men]. It's just that there has to be something worth it. Like, this one girl said she'd fuck us if we both

made out. So the ends justified the means. We call it a good cause. There has to be a good cause." [13]

Another explained:

"There has got to be a reward. If I have to kiss another guy in order to fuck a chick, then yeah it's worth it. . . . Well, for the most part it would be about getting it on with her, but like we might do some stuff together too. It depends on what she wants."[14]

In a different study Anderson conducted,[15] this one in the United Kingdom, he found that of the 145 male students he interviewed, 89 percent had kissed another male on the lips, and 37 percent had engaged in extended kissing with another man. In both cases, participants conceptualized kissing men as "a means of expressing platonic affection among heterosexual friends." Here, men explain their same-sex contact in terms nearly identical to the familiar and century-old narrative about "romantic friendships" among women. Taking Anderson's research alongside research on "straight girls kissing," we discover that heterosexuals, both men and women, conceptualize kissing and other forms of sexual contact in a variety of ways, including as an extension of heterosexual friendship or as a means of heterosexual seduction.

Some accounts of straight men's sex with men suggest that terms like "heteroflexible" might already be outdated, especially to the extent that being heteroflexible has been misinterpreted as a euphemism for bisexuality. In a 2010 article for the *Good Men Project*, developmental psychologist Ritch Savin-Williams describes his interviews with "securely" heterosexual young men who report that they occasionally experience attraction to other men. Savin-Williams explains that many of these men, such as a research participant named Dillon, are uncertain about how to characterize their "potential" for attraction to men:

Though [Dillon] wants to "fuck lots of girls" before graduation, he's not entirely heterosexual. "I'm not sure there's a name for what I am," he says. . . . By his own admission, Dillon says he resides in the "Sexual Netherlands" (his words), a place that exists between heterosexuality and bisexuality. In previous generations, such individuals might have been described as "straight but not narrow," "bending a little," and "heteroflexible." Dillon is part of a growing trend of young men who are secure in their heterosexuality and yet remain aware of their potential to experience far more—sexual attractions, sexual interactions, crushes, and, occasionally romantic relationships with other guys.[16]

Savin-Williams reports that 3 to 4 percent of male teenagers in the United States and Canada describe themselves as "mostly heterosexual" or "predominantly heterosexual," even when given the choice to select the terms "heterosexual" or "bisexual." These percentages increase among college-aged men, which, as Savin-Williams points out, suggests there are more young men who feel they are "mostly straight" than who say they are bisexual or gay. Other studies have yielded similar findings,[17] demonstrating that a good number of straight-identified men feel at least somewhat open to the possibility of a sexual interaction with another man and do not view this possibility as a challenge to their heterosexuality. While such reports are often imagined to be surprising, the same accounts of young straight women's occasional desire for sex with women rarely produce the same puzzlement. As noted in the chapters to follow, constructions of female sexuality allow for "girl-on-girl" encounters to be fleeting, consistent with heterosexual identity, and even taken up for heterosexual ends. Research by Anderson, Savin-Williams, and others points to the need for a similar view of male heterosexuality, one that can more fully capture the ways that homosexual contact takes straight male forms.

Though homosexual contact is a feature of straight men's private lives and friendships, it also takes ritualized forms in the institutional environments in which straight men come into contact with one another's bodies. Avowedly heterosexual institutions, like the United States military, are sites in which sexual encounters between heterosexual men are integrated into the culture and practice of the institution. In his book *Sailors and Sexual Identity*, based on interviews with U.S. sailors and marines, Steven Zeeland explains that the boundaries between homosexual and heterosexual, sexual and nonsexual, are kept intentionally blurry in the military. Zeeland describes a range of intimate and sexual behaviors that are part of standard military practice and "known to the Joint Chiefs of Staff to be a natural part of military life." These are conveniently ambiguous in their meaning:

> Navy initiation rituals involving cross-dressing, spanking, simulated oral and anal sex, simulated ejaculation, nipple piercing, and anal penetration with objects and fingers might be [perceived as] homosexual. An officer's love for his men might be homosexual. The intimate buddy relationships that form in barracks, aboard ship, and most especially in combat—often described as being a love greater than between a man and a woman—might be homosexual—whether or not penetration and ejaculation ever occur. The U.S. military does not want these things called homosexual. To maintain the illusion that these aspects of military life are heterosexually pure it is necessary to maintain the illusion that there is no homosexuality in the military.[18]

Zeeland points not only to the ubiquity and normalization of homosexual contact in the U.S. military, but also to the military's investment in conceptualizing homosexual contact as "heterosexually pure" in its meaning and motivation.

In this book, I take the position that indeed we *should* view straight men's homosexual contact as primarily heterosexual in meaning. The problem, however, is that this perspective has been used as a way to elide the complexity of straight-identified men's sexuality. All too often a "boys will be boys" analysis of straight men's homosexual activity functions more to obscure rather than to illuminate the implications of these behaviors for our thinking about heterosexuality, and the sexual binary more broadly. We can and should be giving far greater attention to the ways that the construction of heterosexuality so thoroughly allows for, and in fact, requires, a remarkable amount of homosexual contact. As I explore in chapter 5, the U.S. military does not simply "look the other way" when it comes to the homosexual behavior of military men; instead, it imagines that intimate homosexual bonding, physical closeness, and tests of heterosexual resilience (which, ironically, take homosexual forms) are *necessary* to build strong men, to win wars, and to preserve national security.

Findings such as Anderson's, Savin-William's, and Zeeland's are hard to accept as they run so deeply counter to conventional wisdom about the rigidity of men's sexuality. Surely these are just exceptional cases, or only the behavior of men who are actually gay or bisexual, or who find themselves in the most extreme of circumstances? To break through this tendency to exceptionalize male sexuality, we need only look to research on *female* sexual fluidity as our guide. For instance, Lisa Diamond opens her aforementioned book *Sexual Fluidity* with the examples of actresses Anne Heche, Julie Cypher, and Cynthia Nixon, all of whom left their heterosexual lives and began lesbian relationships and, in Heche and Cypher's case, later returned to heterosexual relationships. Diamond argues that these women are not "confused"; instead, their cases illuminate the fact that fluidity is a core feature of female sexual orientation:

> The reason such cases are so perplexing is that they flatly contradict prevailing assumptions about sexual orientation. These assumptions hold that an individual's sexual predisposition for

the same sex or other sex is an early-developing and stable trait that has a consistent effect on that person's attractions, fantasies, and romantic feelings over the lifespan. . . . Although this model of sexual orientation describes men fairly accurately, it does not apply so well to women. Historically, women who deviated from this model . . . were presumed few in number and exceptional in nature. In other words, they were just inconvenient noise cluttering up the real data on sexual orientation. Yet as research on female sexuality has increased over the years, these "exceptional" cases now appear to be more common than previously thought.[19]

Though Diamond's analysis reproduces the very error it describes by so easily discounting male sexual fluidity,[20] it offers a useful blueprint for thinking about the ways that men's fluidity, like women's, has been presumed rare, exceptional, or "just inconvenient noise."

There is no doubt that straight men's sexuality is structured differently from straight women's, but not with regard to their capacity for homosexual sex, desire, and even relationships. While attractive white heterosexual women like Nixon, Cypher, and Heche are forgiven, if not celebrated, for their forays into same-sex coupling, men are offered a different, far more limited set of possibilities. Perhaps Nixon's, Cypher's, and Heche's male counterparts are men like evangelical megachurch leader Ted Haggard, former Senator Larry Craig, and former Representative Bob Allen. Ted Haggard, a white male in his early sixties, had a three-year sexual relationship with a male massage therapist; he also identifies as heterosexual and has long been married to a woman. Haggard now reports that his homosexual desires have completely disappeared as a result of effective Christian counseling. Larry Craig and Bob Allen are also both heterosexual-identified, white married men. Both were also arrested in 2007 for homosexual prostitution in public restrooms. Both remain married to their wives.

What are the differences between the women whom Diamond offers up as examples of female sexual fluidity and men like Haggard, Craig, and Allen? For one, these women pursued long-term, romantic, loving, presumably monogamous, public relationships with other women, while the men's sexual relationships with men involved sex for money and were kept hidden from wives and the public. Nixon, Cypher, and Heche are all proponents of gay rights and have expressed no shame about or disidentification from their same-sex relationships. Haggard, Craig, and Allen are committed to their heterosexual marriages, are vocal opponents of gay rights, and wish for the public to view their homosexual behaviors as temporary and unfortunate symptoms of stress, addiction, trauma, and/or loss of faith. Surely, in light of these differences, we would be more inclined to view women like Nixon, Cypher, and Heche as the *real* bi- or homosexuals, while men like Haggard, Craig, and Allen are simply acting from a place of situational need or occasional curiosity. But this is the opposite of the way that commentators have interpreted such cases. Cypher and Heche have received a warm reception upon their return to heterosexual partnerships, their relationships with women imagined as an unusual but ultimately harmless detour in their otherwise heterosexual lives (Heche has since been cast in heterosexual roles, for instance). On the other hand, gays and straights alike have proclaimed Haggard, Craig, and Allen to be closeted gay men, religious or political hypocrites, and cowards who have duped their pitiable wives and children. Commentators seem unconcerned with how these men actually want to live their lives—in heterosexual marriages, in heterosexual communities, and invested in heteronormativity. Haggard, in particular, was thoroughly ridiculed by the American public for sexual hypocrisy, even as his explanation for his behavior was thoroughly consistent with the Christian logic that he, like all of us, is vulnerable to occasional sins of the flesh (a logic that allowed his followers back in Colorado Springs to forgive him).

This is all to say that when straight-identified women have sex with women, the broader culture waits in anticipation for them to return to what is likely their natural, heterosexual state; when straight-identified men have sex with men, the culture waits in anticipation for them to admit that they are gay. Though it may at first appear that women are offered a more nuanced, complex sexuality, it is perhaps more accurate to suggest that women are granted a longer suspension of judgment before their same-sex encounters and even their same-sex relationships are presumed to signal true lesbian subjectivity (and not a hetero-erotic "bi-curiosity"). Men, conversely, must manage their sexual fluidity within the context of a culture that they know will immediately equate male homosexual behavior with gay subjectivity. It should come as little surprise to us, then, that for the most part, straight men's homosexual behaviors are marked by shame, secrecy, homophobia, and disavowal of queerness. In other words, the fact that the homosexual behaviors of heterosexual men and women take very different cultural forms is important and needs investigation, but it is hardly evidence that male sexuality is less fluid or receptive to cultural stimuli than women's.[21]

The evidence of men's sexual flexibility (and *all* people's sexual flexibility) surrounds us, so this raises the question: Why this investment in telling a different story about women's sexuality than we do about men's? The main purpose of this book is not to dispute the notion that women are more sexually fluid than men, so I won't belabor this point. However, the persistent refusal to recognize male sexual fluidity is important here to the extent that it is the primary reason I have chosen to focus my analysis on men. Over the past few years, students and some colleagues have reacted to early iterations of this book with outright denial. Many state that they simply cannot believe that straight men behave in such ways. Others can only assume that, whether I am aware of it or not, what I am truly studying is the experience of being in the closet. Heterosexual women, I have come to find out, are among the most fervent deniers of male sexual fluidity. Many are only able to conclude that men who have had homosexual sex, even if only once, must be gay and closeted. And yet, they do not come to this same conclusion about straight women, for whom they imagine that circumstances mean everything, and "playing around" with other women ultimately means little. It is not a stretch to imagine that this view of women is the enduring legacy of the Victorian belief that what women do together sexually is simply not real sex, but a precursor to, or substitute for, heterosexual intercourse.[22] In light of these notions about the inherent fluidity and rigidity of female and male sexuality respectively, my goal in focusing on men is not to highlight male sexuality per se, but to add men and masculinity to our understanding of the permeability of heterosexuality.

The Race of Sexual Fluidity

This book is also limited to an analysis of *white* men. While some might wonder why straight white men would deserve any more attention than they already receive, my hope is to make a compelling case that investigating white male heterosexuality deepens our understanding of the racial construction of sexuality, particularly the ways that whiteness continues to function—even in an allegedly "post-racial" era—as a stand-in for normal sexuality. Straight white men, as I will show, can draw on the resources of white privilege—an "invisible package of unearned assets"[23]—to circumvent homophobic stigma and assign heterosexual meaning to homosexual activity. Among the many privileges of whiteness, the power to both normalize and exceptionalize one's behavior, including one's "discordant" sex practices, is central.[24] But as white supremacy and privilege "smooth over" any imagined inconsistencies in the sexual behavior of whites, especially white men, the sexual fluidity of men of color quickly falls subject to heightened surveillance and misrepresentation. Illustrating this, the last two decades have been marked by a media-fueled panic about the sexual fluidity of men of color, particularly black men.

Indeed, to the extent that the media has acknowledged that straight-identified men have sex with men, it has focused disproportionately on men of color "on the down low." Like heteroflexible college women who have been the subject of media fascination—and who, significantly, are almost always white in these accounts—black and Latino men on the down low (DL) are reported to "live heterosexual lives": we are often told that they have wives or girlfriends; that they are invested in heterosexual culture and appearances; and that they don't identify as gay or bisexual. Though there are some parallels between this construction and the story of (white) girls "hooking up" with girls, men of color on the DL are not granted the sexual fluidity and complexity attributed to young white women. Instead, as C. Riley Snorton illuminates in the incisive book *Nobody Is Supposed to Know*, "the 'down low' has been one in myriad discursive practices that link black sexuality to duplicity," thereby airing white "anxieties about the possibilities of refusing to comply with sexual identifications, of resisting being gay."[25] In media coverage of the down low, black men have been repeatedly depicted as closeted and as fundamentally dishonest about their real lives and desires. Black men on the down low and Latino "men-who-have-sex-with-men" (an epidemiological category, typically abbreviated as MSMs) have been central figures in both scholarly and popular discussions regarding internalized homophobia, sexual repression, extreme religiosity, HIV/AIDS, the betrayal of unsuspecting wives and girlfriends, and the failure to come out of the closet.[26] To make sense of their sexual practices, analyses of men of color who have sex with men have drawn heavily on theories of the closet and its racialized underpinnings.[27] Black men on the DL, in particular, have been described as "a new subculture of gay men" for whom "masculinity . . . is so intertwined with hyper-heterosexuality [that it] renders an openly gay identity impossible."[28] Similarly, Latino MSMs are implicitly characterized as closeted gay or bisexual men for whom cultural barriers, rigid cultural ideas about gender, and strong ties to family and religion prevent public identification as gay or bisexual.[29]

In contrast with the media's sensationalized and panic-inducing representation of a dangerous black male sexual under-world, scholars working in black queer studies have described the discursive construction of the DL as the latest example of the hyper-surveillance of black men's sex practices. According to Jeffrey McCune, whites have long viewed black male sexuality as a spectacle, leaving black men with no closet to hide in, and hence nowhere from which to "come out." In contrast with the dominant white view of the DL as a tragic and dangerous consequence of black homophobia, McCune views the DL as a subversive practice of black sexual world-making, one that both adheres to the black politics of sexual discretion while also refusing to conform to the mainstream/white lesbian and gay movement's emphasis on sexual labeling and "coming out." The embrace of heteronormative hip-hop, masculine cool, sexual discretion, and other features of black heterosexual culture is not so much a denial of queer de-sire, argues McCune, but a mode of connecting with a broader black culture. He explains that when men on the DL go to black queer clubs, "they have arrived in a queer space that welcomes them, but does not require them to become official members. . . . The discursive demand that one must be 'out' to participate in gay activities ignores that all gay activity does not take place in ac-tual public domain; neither does individual participation always guarantee membership."[30] C. Riley Snorton concurs that while the down low is ostensibly a secret practice, the media's fascination with it serves to expose the racist conditions of hyper-visibility in which black sexuality takes form.[31] Drawing on Eve Sedgwick's conceptualization of the "glass closet," a form of visible conceal-ment maintained through silence, Snorton points to volumes of troubling media commentary on the down low, reading these texts not as accurate accounts of a hidden sex practice, but as examples of the regulation and exposure of black sexuality more generally.

These critiques of the media's framing of the DL illuminate the racialized and gendered conditions of visibility and invisibility that shape how we understand the sexual fluidity of people of color and whites, women and men. Bringing together these critical analyses of DL discourse with feminist critiques of the objectification of women's bodies, we can begin to see why and how straight white men's sexual practices are those that are truly invisible and unmarked, while men of color and women are subject to narratives that reinforce their already subordinate position within hierarchies of normal sexuality. For women, the hetero-patriarchal view that female sexuality is naturally receptive and flexible, more subdued or controllable than men's hydraulic sexuality, and a commodity to be exchanged among men is a perfect set-up to interpret "straight girls kissing girls" as a titillating spectacle of special interest to straight men and a nonthreatening extension of women's innate sensuality. For black men, the long-standing construction of black male sexuality as predatory and violent and of black culture as beholden to traditional gender and sexual formations is the context in which the homosexual contact of not-gay black men is offered up as a matter of considerable risk and urgency, a black secret—and in many accounts, a black *lie*—in need of exposure and management.[32] Women of color arguably sit at the intersection of these forces, often scrutinized, patholo-gized, and criminalized for any sexual practice that extends be-yond dominant constructions of normative female sexuality.

The story is different for straight white men. When straight white men have sex with men, they are either presumed gay or their behavior is dismissed as inconsequential and nonsexual. Rarely, if ever, are their sexual practices racialized, or attributed to particular ethnoracial sexual norms within white culture. Blacks, Latinos, Muslims, and other non-white and non-Christian "cultures" become the repository for cultural difference, sexual repression, homophobia, and hyper-religiosity, thereby masking the normative white Christian secularism that fuels white male homophobia and undergirds dominant U.S. discourse about the relationship between sexuality and subjectivity.[33] In contrast with this narrative about the rationality of whiteness (and maleness), I will show that white male privilege, rituals, anxieties, and delusions are central to the operation of homosexuality within straight white men's lives. While straight white men not only draw on many of the same logics used by women to account for their homosexual experiences (such as the football players in Anderson's study who engage in sex acts with men in order to seduce women), they also leverage white masculinity to assist in the preservation or recuperation of heterosexuality in the context of sex with men. This set of uniquely white hetero-masculine logics—namely, that sex with men is often necessary, patriotic, character-building, masculinity-enhancing, and paradoxically, a means of inoculating oneself against authentic gayness—forms the subjects of the chapters to follow.

The late sociologist Ruth Frankenberg explained that one of the truisms about whiteness is that it is an invisible or unmarked category, an empty container that white people themselves cannot describe. And yet, Frankenberg also asserted, the notion that whiteness is unmarked is also a white delusion, as whiteness has a clear history and set of forms, both past and present, and is certainly not unmarked in the eyes of people of color. "Whiteness" first emerged as a Western European colonial project, a self-made category used to justify the colonization of "Others"—people of African, Native American, Latin American, and Asian descent. Colonization was not only a process of violent occupation and theft of culture, land, and resources, but also a process whereby self-proclaimed white colonizers named themselves, named the Other, and then became "apparently invisible."[34] For Frankenberg, whiteness in the contemporary United States is "a place of advantage and privilege intersected by other social categories (gender, class, sexuality, & ability); a position, an attitude or outlook from which to see 'selves' and others; a complex spectrum of cultural practices that are either seen as 'normative' or rational and not racial; and a culture whose character and identity have been shaped by history (e.g., colonialism)."[35] Drawing on Frankenberg's definition of whiteness, this book attends to the ways that whiteness intersects with masculinity and sexuality, shaping the relationship between men's homosexual sex and their sense of "self," their status as "normal," and their position within structural hierarchies. In making whiteness a central unit of analysis, along with masculinity and heteronormativity, my aim is to build on a growing body of work that racializes whiteness and unmasks its delusions.

In sum, the pairing of homosexual sex with heterosexual life is not a new phenomenon; nor is it limited to young people, women, or Black, Latino, or other men of color. And yet, despite a good amount of evidence suggesting that homosexual contact is part of the basic fabric of human sexuality, and central even to the social organization of heterosexuality, it is of course difficult to chart homosexuality's presence within cultural formations—like that of straight white American masculinity—that have defined themselves, in large part, by homosexuality's absence. Hence, we must attend to the apparent paradox that homosexual encounters are both everywhere and nowhere within the lives and culture of straight white men. Doing so requires some attention to the cultural construction of the heterosexual/homosexual binary itself, the subject to which I now turn.

What Is Heterosexuality?

When I think about the mood and flavor of straight men's sex with men, I am reminded of the kind of sexual games my friends and I played as young girls (starting around seven or eight years old), before any of us knew what sex would later be. In the absence of a coherent and normative conceptualization of sex, we cobbled together the gendered and sexual tropes familiar to us as kids.

We crafted highly detailed narratives about ourselves (we were beautiful fairies, rebellious teenagers, wealthy movie stars, doctors and patients), and our circumstances (the various events that presumably resulted in the *need*—whether we liked it or not—to reveal/touch/kiss certain body parts). We knew we were playing. We invented scenes. They had to be negotiated. There were rules. People were bossy. Body parts were gross. But we touched each other anyway.

Homosexual encounters between adult heterosexuals constitute a unique erotic domain that is characterized by many of the features of childhood sexuality. This is not because it is a "childish" act for adult heterosexuals to have sex with one another, or because straight men in fraternities (or military barracks, prisons, and so forth) are less evolved or self-aware than men in other contexts, or for any other reasons that might stem from such a simplistic and moralizing reading of sexuality. Instead, it is because homosexual sex enacted by heterosexuals—like sex between children—occupies a liminal space within sexual relations, one that sits outside of the heterosexual/homosexual binary and is sometimes barely perceptible as sex. Like childhood sex, it goes by many other names: "experimentation," "accident," "friendship," "joke," "game," and so on. Participants must painstakingly avoid being mistaken as sincere homosexuals by demonstrating that the sexual encounter is something other than sex, and in many cases, they do this by agreeing that the encounter was *compelled* by others (such as older fraternity brothers) or by circumstances that left them little choice (such as the apparently quite dire need to obtain access to a particular fraternity).

In the United States, where homosexual accidents make for great comedy, the identitarian context in which homosexuality takes place is of the utmost consequence. Two decades ago, in the mid-1990s, this was exemplified by the positive publicity given to sitcoms like *The Drew Carey Show* in which two heterosexual male characters were shown jokingly kissing, while a "sincere" kiss between gay or lesbian characters (such as appeared on the sitcom *Ellen*) could be shown only following a somber disclaimer about "adult content." The actors on both shows performed virtually the same homosexual kiss, but the networks knew that these two same-sex kisses had fundamentally different meanings and cultural implications. Today, thankfully, two men accidentally kissing is no longer as funny, and though much of the commentary on heteroflexibility misses the mark, we have at least become more transparent about the fact that some television forms of homosexual contact—especially that which occurs between two young straight (or straight-appearing) women—are about ratings and not social progress, normalcy and not difference, heterosexual and not queer "ways of life."

Part of what is said to distinguish heteroflexibility from gayness is that it involves engaging in same-sex sexuality while distancing oneself from the lesbian and gay movement, or, in Essig's words, "throw[ing] out the politics and the struggles" associated with same-sex desire. But this characterization could use a bit more nuance, as many sexually fluid straight people *do* identify as allies to the LGBT movement, or even loosely as "queer." This is not to mention that many self-identified gay men and lesbians couldn't be less political about their sexuality, or more invested in assimilation and respectability. While some degree of insistence that one is "not gay" is generally part and parcel of heteroflexibility, a more significant distinction is that people who identify as heterosexual, unlike gay men and lesbians, are generally content with *straight culture*, or heteronormativity; they enjoy heterosexual sex, but more importantly for the purposes of this book, they enjoy heterosexual culture. Simply put, being sexually "normal" suits them. It feels good; it feels like home.

Unfortunately, the domain of culture is generally lost in popular discourses about sexual desire, which focus largely on whether homosexual activity is either "chosen" or "biological." This entire framing is far too simplistic. People certainly have tendencies toward particular objects of desire, including bodies defined in their time and place as "the same" or "the opposite" from their own. And yet, for the vast majority of us, these tendencies—whatever they may be—are shaped and experienced under the constraints of heteronormativity, or within cultures strongly invested in opposite-sex coupling. The amount of psychic and cultural labor expended to produce and enforce heterosexual identification and procreative sexuality suggests that heterosexuality, as we now know it, is hardly an automatic human effect. It is for this reason that scholars of heterosexuality have described it as a psychic and social accomplishment, an institution, and a cultural formation.[36]

Of course the traditional view of sexuality is that heterosexuality is nature's design, the driving force behind human reproduction and the gendered division of labor that keeps societies running (i.e., the unpaid care work done by women to sustain children and male laborers). In the last several decades, this view has been slightly revised to account for the existence of the homosexual, who is now typically understood to result from a harmless hormonal or genetic aberration in nature's plan.

But from a queer perspective, sexual desire is not determined by bio-evolutionary processes, but is instead fluid and culturally contingent. As first elaborated by Freud in *Three Essays on the Theory of Sexuality*, nature may provide human infants with sexual desire, but this desire takes form as a polymorphous capacity to experience pleasure in response to a broad range of stimuli, including an array of one's own bodily functions as well as various modes of contact with objects, animals, and humans of all types. It is only through disciplined conformity to societal norms, typically directed by parents, that young children's sexual impulses are re-directed toward a sanctioned, and most often singular, object of desire (most often, a person of the "opposite" sex). Hence, from both psychoanalytic and social constructionist perspectives, the hetero/homo binary is not the essential order of things, but the product of cultural norms and political-economic imperatives.

And yet, sexual binaries often *feel* natural because they are internalized in early childhood, resulting in strong sexual (and gender) identifications. But central to the larger project at hand is the question of what happens to all of those polymorphous desires once they are repressed in the service of conformity to prevailing sexual norms. For Freud, the process of sublimating these desires in order to achieve heterosexuality and normative gender is not an easy one; instead it is tenuous, labored, and requires the disavowal and loss of original homosexual attachments. Moreover, this loss cannot be recognized or grieved, as doing so would expose the fragility and constructedness of heterosexuality. As the philosopher Judith Butler has argued, this bind produces a unique form of melancholy, a kind of repressed sadness that is generated as heteromasculinity comes into being through the disavowed and unmourned loss of homosexual possibilities.[37]

Psychoanalytic accounts of sexuality provide us with some language for thinking about the psychic life of these repressed homosexual attachments, which take form in the fantasies and fetishes of heterosexuals. In Freud's original use, the fetish is an object or practice that substitutes for the phallus—specifically, the castrated phallus a child imagines has been taken from his mother. In the chapters to follow, I occasionally use the term "fetish," which I deploy to more broadly describe the ways that heteronormativity (or the investment in sexual normalcy) and hetero-masculine scripts (adventure, male bonding, hazing, humiliation, national security, etc.) function to displace or mask homosexual attachments—even in the context of homosexual sex! In other words, as I argue in chapter 5, scenes and scripts that constitute "hazing" are not purely about initiation into male groups; homosexual contact is such a common feature of male hazing scenarios that we might question whether hazing itself is a hetero-masculine festish, one that allows men access to homosexual activity without the stigma of gay identity. Hence, we might conceptualize straight men's not-gay homosexual activity as a surfacing of polymorphous desires generally confined to the unconscious, the unacknowledged repository for all "unacceptable" thoughts and feelings. The conscious male subject disidentifies[38] with these desires, drawing on the power of heteronormative scripts in an effort to sustain the performance of his utterly normal sexuality—even and especially as his fingers, tongue, and/or penis find themselves in contact with other men.

Cultural theorist Sara Ahmed offers us yet another way to think about the reproduction of heterosexuality.[39] Ahmed emphasizes heterosexuality's inherited quality, its offering as both obligation and "gift" by parents to their children. Required to follow the family line, the child's entire social world is oriented toward heterosexuality while other object orientations are cleared away. Heterosexuality, as the intimately close, familiar, normalized, and celebrated couple formation, is the space in which the child lives and becomes the space in which the child feels "at home." The child's body itself, like bodies desiring familiar foods, gets shaped by its cultural context and begins to tend toward the familiar. The child learns to repeat the sensations, gestures, and practices that orient him or her toward heterosexuality—e.g., ways of relating and communicating that are premised on a gender binary in which "opposites attract." This ongoing repetition is the very process that sustains heterosexual selfhood.

This way of understanding the formation of sexuality helps to explain the apparent paradox that homosexuality is a constitutive feature of hetero-masculinity. Because homosexual attachments are always present within the psychic structure of heterosexuality, boys and men, rather than mourning "the homosexuality that could not be," arguably work out this loss via ongoing acts of homophobic repudiation, wherein they locate "the homosexual" outside of themselves and go to great and performative lengths to reject people and things associated with it. As I will soon make clear, this rejection of homosexual subjectivity sometimes occurs within and alongside straight men's sexual activity with men. As long as these activities are recast as nonsexual and the dividing line between gay and straight subjectivity is secured, homosexual contact can function as a powerful means of asserting heterosexual authenticity, or a "not gay" constitution.

Viewing sexuality as Freud, Butler, and Ahmed do allows us to see that, indeed, people often feel in their bodies the pull toward particular sex acts. But the way these urges get "oriented" both internally and in social space is a psychic and cultural process, not a genetic or hormonal one. It should come as little surprise that heterosexual orientation, in particular, is often experienced as fixed and innate, as a bodily orientation largely outside one's control. This is because our bodies have, in fact, been oriented toward straightness. Most of us have been required to inhabit heterosexuality from early childhood, even if we've never engaged in heterosexual sex.

But how then, do we make sense of homosexual desire, a force presumably so strong as to overcome what the late lesbian feminist poet and theorist Adrienne Rich so aptly called "compulsory heterosexuality"? Ahmed's account is again useful here, as she argues that an initial pull or tendency toward bodies of the same sex does not in itself constitute being or becoming lesbian or gay. Indeed, as I argue in this book, an urge toward homosexual activity may well be one of the more common features of human sexuality, one flexible enough to be oriented toward the very category that presumably excludes it (heterosexuality). This is possible in part because, under the conditions of heteronormativity, to actually *become a gay or lesbian person*, one must also do a good amount of work to reorient oneself away from heteronormativity. For instance, Ahmed explains:

> Even lesbians who feel they were "always that way," still have to "become lesbians," which means *gathering such tendencies into specific social and sexual forms*. Such a gathering requires a habit-change, to borrow a term from Teresa de Lauretis . . . : it requires

a reorientation of one's body such that other objects, those that are not reachable on the vertical and horizontal lines of straight culture, can be reached.[40]

Crucial to Ahmed's analysis is that straightness and queerness are not simply matters of sexual object choice; they also carry a vast array of cultural requirements and implications that, in turn, shape how people orient their bodies and move through space. Because heterosexuality is the default sexual orientation, reorienting oneself in the direction of public queer legibility takes some significant effort. As queer theorist David Halperin puts it, being gay is a resistant cultural practice that gays must learn from one another.[41]

I read Ahmed's argument to suggest that straightness and queerness are differentiated not by early tendencies toward same- or opposite-sex desire, but by the way these tendencies are "gathered into specific social and sexual forms." In this vein, my analysis moves away from the question of who has homosexual impulses and why, presuming instead that most people do, even as most people are, for the reasons outlined above, "at home" within the culture and structures of heterosexuality. The question at the center of my analysis is, then: How do straight white men gather homosexual tendencies into heterosexual forms? What kinds of "work" are required to engage in homosexual sex while staying oriented toward heterosexuality?

Many social scientists have attempted to elaborate the difference between sexual orientation (most often defined as the quantity and duration of one's same-sex or other-sex desires, often believed to be hardwired), sexual identity (how one identifies oneself—as straight, lesbian, gay, bisexual, etc.), and actual sexual behavior. In this book, I take the less popular position that the question of "sexual orientation"—as it is conventionally understood—is not a very interesting one. I am not concerned with whether the men I describe in this book are "really" straight or gay, and I am not arguing that they (or that all men) are really homosexual or bisexual in their orientation. Instead, what I am arguing is that homosexual sex plays a remarkably central role in the institutions and rituals that produce heterosexual subjectivity, as well as in the broader culture's imagination of what it means for "boys to be boys." To my mind, the nearly obsessive focus on whether individual people are born gay or straight functions as a bizarre distraction from the greater cultural significance of homosexuality, both historically and at present.

In this book I conceptualize straightness and queerness primarily as cultural domains. I recognize that people have real bodies and real sexual responses to other bodies, but I also contend that bodies do not respond only to the "raw facts" of other people's genitals or other sexed body parts. Instead, our bodies desire other bodies and particular sex acts *in their social context*; we desire what those body parts *represent*. We desire particular bodies and particular sex acts and particular erotic scenes and cultural spheres in large part because they have significant cultural and erotically charged meanings. As Judith Butler's work has made clear, sexual desire itself operates under the conditions of a heterosexual matrix, in which sex (femaleness and maleness), gender (femininity and masculinity), and heterosexual desire are imagined and required to follow logically from one another. Bodies that fall outside this matrix are rendered abject and unintelligible. That our desires are subject to these enduring cultural prescriptions does not make them any less embodied, but it does indicate that our bodies respond to a social field already characterized by narrow gender and sexual binaries to which much cultural significance has been assigned. In other words, to call oneself "gay" or "straight" is to take on the cultural baggage associated with these categories, and whether or not this baggage is appealing is a separate matter altogether from the appeal of homosexual or heterosexual sex.

As I will show, whether a man thinks of himself and his homosexual behavior as "gay" or "straight" makes all the difference with regard to how he will make sexual contact with men: how he will set the scene, the narratives he will use to describe what it is happening and why, the time and place the sex occurs, and whether it will be possible to imagine that the sex was never actually "sexual" at all. Let me be more concrete. Some men like to have sex with men in backrooms of gay bars after dancing to techno music; others like to have sex with men while watching straight porn and talking about "banging bitches" (see chapter 4). Some women like to have sex with women in the woods at feminist music festivals or while cohabitating in the suburbs; others, as sociologist Laura Hamilton's research explores, like to "hook up" with women on couches at fraternity parties in front of cheering male spectators.[42] These temporal, spatial, and cultural factors are not inconsequential; they are precisely what make sex "hot" for participants, *and* they are the details that people take as evidence of their heterosexual and homosexual orientations. It is for this reason that I conceptualize heterosexual subjectivity as constituted not by a lack of homosexual sex or desire, but by an enduring investment in heteronormativity, or in the forces that construct heterosexuality as natural, normal, and right and that disavow association with abnormal, or queer, sexual expressions. This investment in heteronormativity is itself a *bodily desire*; in fact, I believe it is *the* embodied heterosexual desire, more powerful than, say, a woman's yearning for male torsos or penises or a man's longing for vaginas or breasts. It is the desire to be sexually unmarked and normatively gendered. It is the desire not simply for heterosexual sex and partnership, but for all of its concomitant cultural rewards. It is a desire that people may well feel within their genitals. In sum, this book works from the premise that heterosexuality is, in part, a fetishization of the normal.[43]

There is no doubt that many, and perhaps most, gay and lesbian people also want to be "normal." But even those who might wish for complete homonormative[44] assimilation (with regard to their political, employment, or economic standing) often find themselves unable or unwilling to achieve gender normativity or to conform to heteronormative dictates for appropriate sexuality. In other words, they find themselves generally not "at home" within, and sometimes repelled by, heterosexual ways of life. Conversely, the straight men who are the subjects of this book find heteronormativity attractive and compelling. They desire it; they are aroused by it. It calls to them; it feels like home. In this way, I do not discount the possibility of a mind/body connection or of the interplay between nature and nurture in shaping our desire. Instead I want to suggest that what we are desiring may not be body parts or people who fall within particular sex and gender categories, but the far broader experiences of sexual and gender normalcy and difference. Some of us, for understandable reasons, are very invested in sexual and gender normalcy; others, for less well-known reasons (which need hardly be innate), desire rebellion, difference, or outsiderness—a desire that may have been present for as long as we can remember. Some of us—who typically go by the names "gay," "lesbian," "bisexual," or "queer"—want our same-sex desires to be taken seriously, viewed as meaningful and sometimes political features of our lives. Others—who typically go by the names "heterosexual" or "straight"—want our same-sex attractions and encounters to be viewed in opposite terms, as accidental, temporary, meaningless, and decidedly apolitical.

Sara Ahmed describes the cultural material of sexuality as that which "sticks" to us when we become oriented one way or the other. We know, because we have learned, that our sex practices mean something not only about who we are (straight or gay), but also about who our friends will be, where we will live and be employed, how we will dress and what we will buy, which institutions will grant or deny us access, and all the other cultural and structural factors that have solidified around straight and gay identities. While the triad of orientation/identity/behavior is the dominant model within most research on human sexuality, it is one that has largely overlooked that we do not simply desire bodies and sex acts; we desire everything that those bodies represent.

A Note on Key Terms

In this book I use the term "homosexual" as a technical description of same-sex sexual behavior and desire, but not to describe *people* who identify as gay or queer, nor to describe gay or queer culture. You will notice that I use the term "heterosexual" more broadly, to describe other-sex sexual behaviors and desires *and* to describe people who identify as heterosexual. The reason for this inconsistency is that the term "heterosexual" carries no cultural stigma and is commonly used by straight people to describe themselves, while the term "homosexual" has a long association with medical pathology, and consequently, it is a term rarely used by gay men or lesbians. I often use the terms "heterosexual," "hetero-erotic," "hetero-cultural," "hetero-masculine," and "heteronormative" to describe sex between straight men, which I do as a way of signaling the *culture of heterosexuality* shaping these homosexual encounters. I use the term "gay" to describe men who self-identify with that term or to describe mainstream gay culture and politics. In some cases, I have used the terms "gay" and "queer" interchangeably, though I have tried to reserve my use of the term "queer" for instances in which I am describing what some might call "the gay left," or the movement to resist gay assimilation and celebrate sexual and gender non-normativity.

I want to acknowledge that in some cases I have used the term "sex" to describe behaviors that participants themselves understand as something else, something nonsexual. For straight men, calling homosexual sex by many other names—an "experiment," "male bonding," a "game," a "joke," a "performance," an "accident," a "hazing ritual," "dominance," "aggression," "boys will be boys," "desperation," "deprivation," "toughening each other up," and so on—is the very way that homosexual sex becomes possible, by which I mean, that it *becomes heterosexual.* If I were to trust straight men to point me in the direction of homosexual sex, I would perhaps be sitting in a gay bar all day, missing an entire universe of hetero-erotic homosexuality.

With this in mind, I have used gay/queer definitions of what "counts" as sex as my guide. I asked myself, "Would a queer couple, perhaps on a first date, be likely to define this behavior as 'sex' or 'sexual' if they participated in it?" and if the answer was yes, I referred to the behavior as "sex" or "sexual." In this vein, I include all forms of anal penetration, hand jobs, blowjobs, and mutual masturbation. For instance, I believe it is likely that if a gay male couple were on a date that at some point included one man penetrating the other man's anus with his fingers, they would likely perceive that they had been sexual with one another. In contrast, the straight men, and perhaps to a lesser degree the gay men, who engage in this same form of digital anal penetration as part of fraternity or military initiation rituals may perceive that the act is not strictly sexual or even sexual at all.

Of course I understand that context is everything, and therefore I have been especially attentive to questions of *intent.* I do not, for instance, believe that prostate exams are intended to be sexual experiences (even if some men are aroused by them), and therefore I would not classify them as sexual. Hazing rituals involving anal penetration or analingus, on the other hand, are extreme, exciting, humiliating, and effective at building cohesion and establishing hierarchy among men precisely *because* the participants know that these acts have sexual meaning. They are designed to occupy or evoke the fine line between sex and humiliation or submission. During the prostate exam, no one is assessing whether you are a fag (or having a fag's response), but this possibility is always looming in the contexts in which straight men make sexual contact with men.

The Birth of the Congenital Heterosexual

Another key piece of the story this book tells about heterosexuality is that straightness always takes form in relation to its Other—or to queerness—with the latter serving as the former's mirror and foil. To the extent that straight people think about what it means to be heterosexual, and to be part of a heterosexual culture with particular norms and practices, they often do so by imagining themselves through the eyes of queers. As Jonathan Ned Katz explains in *The Invention of Heterosexuality*, the budding visibility of gay culture in the 1960s produced what we might call a "heterosexual looking-glass self," in which the more visible gay men and lesbians became, the more possible it became for heterosexuals to compare themselves to their "homosexual" counterparts. Katz cites, for example, a 1963 *New York Times* article in which a heterosexual reporter attempts to describe gay subculture for the paper's presumably heterosexual readership, and in so doing, speculates that homosexuals "probably derive secret amusement" from coopting innocent heterosexual words (like the word "gay" itself). According to Katz, "the image of two gay people laughing together secretly over the unknowing language of straights marks the emergence in *The New York Times* of heterosexuals as a majority newly nervous about the critical gaze of The Homo-Other."[45]

Today, over fifty years after the publication of this article, the relationship between straight culture and gay culture is more interconnected than ever, especially as the latter—in the form of queer style, queer music, queer imagery, queer political discourse—has demonstrated its appeal and profitability within mainstream culture. The influence of mediated, mainstream gay culture on straight people's lives has consequences not only for how straight people consume or fashion themselves, but also for how they have sex. Many commentators believe that the increasing visibility and acceptance of gay and lesbian people has given heterosexuals permission to explore same-sex desire without fear of devastating stigma. And yet, if heterosexuals' erotic possibilities are broadened by a gay rights movement that celebrates the fluidity of sexual *behavior*, what about the effect of the movement's stance on the immutability of sexual *orientation*? The percentage of Americans who believe in the biological foundations of sexual orientation has steadily increased over the last four decades, from 13 percent in 1977, to 31 percent in 1998, to 52 percent in 2010.[46] Many gay-friendly heterosexuals have been taught, primarily by proponents of gay rights, that gay people—and, by extension, straight people—have a fundamental sexual constitution, one already determined by nature. If sexual orientation cannot be changed, acceptance of gay people becomes the compassionate heterosexual's best option.

Scientific efforts to prove that sexual orientation is innate are not new; they are rooted in nineteenth- and early twentieth-century sexology. In fact, research aimed at identifying body parts that might hold the tell-tale signs of homosexuality—from bad blood, beady eyes, and angular facial features, to finger length and brain structure—have persisted since the very advent of heterosexual and homosexual categories in the nineteenth century.[47] Nonetheless, it is only in the last two decades that the notion that homosexuals are "born this way" has gained widespread public acceptance in the United States, including (and especially) among lesbians and gay men. Though numerous feminist and queer scholars have been critical of biological determinism and the concomitant depoliticization of queer difference, little attention has been paid to the effects of the "biological turn" on *heterosexuality*. How has over forty years of a visible lesbian and gay identity movement—increasingly articulated in sociobiological terms[48]—influenced the way that heterosexuals understand *their* sexuality?

According to Lisa Diamond, proponents of the argument that sexual orientation is hardwired have steered clear of the subject of sexual fluidity, fearing that fluidity might appear to suggest that sexual orientation can be chosen or learned. In response to the question "does fluidity mean that sexual orientation is a matter of choice?," Diamond offers some apparently reassuring words: "No. Even when women undergo significant shifts in their patterns of erotic response, they typically report that such changes are unexpected and beyond their control. In some cases, they actively resist these changes, to no avail."[49] Diamond's defense of sexual fluidity as consistent with immutability represents what is soon likely to become the prevailing sexual logic of our time. Diamond, like other sexologists and psychologists I discuss at length in chapter 3, believes that people are born with a core sexual orientation that remains the same regardless of periodic and/or situational attractions and desires that fall outside of its boundaries. Sexual fluidity is not a challenge to the fixity of sexual orientation; in many ways, the opposite is true. When we know we are born straight or gay, this knowledge enables us to experiment, to stray, to act out, and to let "shit happen" without fear that we have somehow hidden or misrecognized or damaged our true sexual constitution. More importantly, knowing that our sexual orientation was present at birth allows us to make sense of our discordant behaviors as exceptional, not bound to the same identitarian consequences experienced by true homosexuals (or heterosexuals).

Returning, then, to the question about the consequences of the biological turn for heterosexuals, we see that like the homosexual-at-birth, the heterosexual-at-birth can do nothing to change his or her innate sexual constitution. Compassionate heterosexuals accept this biological imperative as it reportedly determines the sexual subjectivities of their gay friends, and now, too, they accept the way it determines their own. No amount of homosexual sex or desire can change nature's heterosexual design. If one knows one is not born gay, then one's homosexual desires and behaviors simply cannot be gay, regardless of their content or frequency. So accepted now is the idea of sexual hardwiring—and so central now is this idea to most thinking about "heteroflexibility," "situational homosexuality," and all other homosexual behaviors of heterosexuals—that it is no longer possible to investigate straight men's sex with men (or straight women's sex with women) without starting from this foundation.

To be very clear, I agree with the contention that when straight-identified people participate in homosexual behavior, they are still best understood as straight. In fact, as I hope is clear at this point, this is a basic premise of this book. What I take issue with here, however, is the need to explain the sexual desires we experience and the sexual cultures we inhabit as forces purely outside of our control and buried within our bodies. This explanation leaves little room to consider the ways that sexual desires are culturally embedded and performative, or the ways our desires direct us not simply towards bodies with particular "parts," but towards the complete cultural experience that those bodies represent and make possible. The biological hypothesis treats heteronormativity, for instance, as an unfortunate byproduct of a neutral, clinically descriptive sexual orientation called "heterosexuality." In contrast, from a more critical and queer perspective, attraction to the culture and privileges of heteronormativity is inseparable from the sensation of "straightness." It is in this way that the original construction of heterosexuality, or its historical *invention* to use Jonathan Ned Katz's term, provides a crucial backdrop for this project, and an essential counterpoint to the now nearly hegemonic narrative about the congenital nature of sexual orientation. The next chapter provides precisely this backdrop, tracing the persistent present-absence of homosexuality (and the homosexual) within the project of building heterosexual men.

Heteronormative Violence and the Demand for Sincere Queers

I find sexual practices interesting in their own right, but I come to this book not simply out of interest in the details of the sex that straight people are having. In this project, as elsewhere, my investment is in the work of resisting heteronormativity, particularly the violent ways that state and cultural institutions punish gender and sexual non-normativity. On its surface, the sexual fluidity of heterosexuals—especially when represented by young women playfully kissing one another at parties—appears to have little to do with heteronormative violence. If anything, it appears to be a progressive development, one marked by the expansion of acceptable ways to be heterosexual men and women.

And yet, when straight men have sex with men, it is frequently—though certainly not always—bound up with violence. The line between straight men having sex with men and "actual" homosexuality is under constant scrutiny, and for straight men, violence is a key element that imbues homosexuality with heterosexual meaning, or untangles hetero-erotic forms of homosexuality from the affective, political, and romantic associations with gay and lesbian life. Sometimes this violence takes the form of humiliation or physical force enacted by one straight man as he makes sexual contact with another; in other cases, it may take the form of two men fantasizing about sexual violence against women. In many cases, violence is a central part of the work of reframing homosexual sex as an act that men do to build one another's strength, or to build what I call "anal resilience," thereby inoculating one another against what they imagine are the sincere expressions of gay selfhood.

Following the lead of feminists who argue that "rape is about violence, not about sex," some have argued that the sexual hazing men experience in fraternities and the military is better understood as violence than as sex.[50] But here I take a different position—namely, that this kind of sex is fairly normal by straight male standards *and* that it is violent. Within the circuits of hetero-masculinity in the United States, violence and sex are mutually constituted, a fact most evident among adolescent boys, who hardly know how to think or talk about sex with girls without drawing on themes of abjection and violence.[51] The language of heterosexual sex—banging, nailing, "hitting that," and so forth—is the language of violence. Characterizing an activity like the Navy's "crossing the line ceremony," in which seasoned sailors anally penetrate newer sailors (typically with hands and objects), as a purely traumatic and nonconsensual act of sexual violence ultimately diminishes its erotic and self-perpetuating quality. More, it fails to account for the reasons that these sorts of boy-on-boy games and rituals appear in both straight and gay pornography noncoercively consumed by straight and gay men (see chapter 5), as well as in personal ads posted online by people who wish to voluntarily enact similar scenes (see chapter 4).

I support people's right to integrate consensual violence into their sex practices. The problem I see here is the way that heteronormative violence gets ramped up, not only for purposes of pleasure, but for the purpose of recuperating heterosexuality (though the latter arguably constitutes its own pleasure). As I discuss in the chapters to follow, the use of violence to police the borders of hetero-erotic homosexuality, on the one hand, and of perverse/sincere queerness, on the other, can be traced through multiple sites ranging from white men's living rooms to fraternity houses to military institutions. Policing this border not only involves homophobic disidentification with gay men and misogynistic narratives about women, but also avoidance of cross-racial desire and the potentially queering presence of men of color, particularly black men, in the spaces of "white male bonding."

Much of this book admittedly focuses on what might be interpreted as extreme or unusual examples of homosexual contact between straight white men, such as the kind that occurs in biker gangs, or rest-stop bathrooms, or within military hazing. These realms are clearly not environments in which all white men circulate. And yet, attention to the psychic and cultural accomplishment of heterosexuality sheds light on the way that all straight men—including average straight guys who have never experienced a sexualized humiliation ritual or sought out a hand job from another dude—inhabit a heterosexuality that is constituted, at least in part, through a disavowal of homosexuality, or through the ongoing accomplishment of being "not gay." As I demonstrate in chapter 3, the rigid constraints of masculinity and the often violent policing of intimacy between men, especially white men in United States who are trained at early ages to fear the ever-looming specter of the fag, means that many of the same hetero-authenticating narratives deployed in prisons and military barracks also surface in men's everyday friendships, in bromance films, and other contexts where intimacy and tenderness between men is carefully monitored. In other words, investigations into the way that straight men "keep it straight" have implications for all men, including those who have never engaged in homosexual sex (however they might define this term).

In addition to investigating the racist, misogynistic, and homophobic effects of the production of heteronormative homosexualities, this project is concerned with the homonormative effects of "sexual fluidity" discourses on queer politics. At issue here is the mainstreaming and containment of queer life, accomplished primarily by the gay and lesbian movement's push to normalize itself by promoting images of happily married lesbians, patriotic gay male soldiers, and the like. These widely circulated images of normal—and presumably homosexual at birth—gay and lesbian Americans are fast becoming the standard against which "heteroflexibles" can be measured and contrasted. If *real* gays have sex for love, if they aspire to monogamous marriage with people of the same sex, and if they have always known that they were gay, then certainly frat boys seeking only to climb atop a pile of other naked boys are not gay. While I do not dispute this conclusion (indeed, most in that pile of boys will go on to live straight lives), I am concerned with the way this comparison works to elide the casual, performative, and antidomestic forms that queer sex takes. As I discuss at length in chapter 6, this demand for the sincere gay subject—the real gays and lesbians against whom straights can be contrasted—does not come without costs for queer history, politics, and subculture.

In attending to the mutual construction of heterosexuality and queerness, my analysis pushes back against the notion of an essential sexual binary in which heterosexuality and homosexuality are oppositional sexual orientations determined by nature. And yet, my arguments also rest on the premise that straightness and queerness are distinct cultural domains that differently conceptualize homosexual encounters—a premise that may appear to reinforce a hetero/homo binary. To argue, as I do, that straightness relates to homosexual sex in unique ways raises the question: "Unique from what?" The answer is complex because the subject positions and sexual and political orientations that fall under the banner of "straightness" and "gayness" are themselves complex and multiple. Many queer scholars have noted that the radical queer relationship to homosexual sex departs from the mainstream gay relationship to homosexual sex, with the former ironically sharing in common some of the insincerity and "meaninglessness" I have attributed to most straight engagements with homosexual sex, and the latter sharing in common with straightness the claim to "being normal." Heterosexuals who have disinvested in sexual normalcy—through engagement with kink, non-monogamy, and other marginalized sex practices—are queered via these practices, and hence, differently arranged vis-à-vis homosexuality. In sum, and as I explore in the concluding chapter, the relation between straightness and queerness is more a complex network than a linear dualism.

Organization of the Book

This chapter has laid out the intellectual stakes of rethinking the way we understand the homosexual activity of straight white men. The next chapter moves back in time, exploring the evolving ways that straight white men have engaged in homosexual behavior since the late nineteenth century, and concomitantly, the ways that Americans have understood these sexual practices and their local and contextual meanings. Here I draw on historical evidence of the homosexual encounters of "normal" white men dating back to the early twentieth century, with focus on the sociocultural and institutional sites in which white men have had sex with men. From saloons and tenement houses, to military barracks and fraternal clubs, and to truck stops and bathrooms, "normal" (heterosexual) white men have long found ways to have hetero-masculine sex with one another. To elucidate the forces that gave rise to the contemporary "white dude" and his "meaningless" homosexual sex, chapter 2 examines the mutually constitutive production of modern masculinity, heterosexuality, and whiteness, alongside the concurrent evolution of the sociobiology of gender, sexuality, and race.

Moving into the contemporary period, chapter 3 examines the ways that various experts—psychologists, sociologists, sexologists—are making sense of straight white men who have sex with men and attempting to educate the public about a new menu of heterosexual options. Gay? Straight? Hetero-flexible? Fauxmosexual? Metrosexual? Telling the truth or lying? How are wives, parents and other inquiring stakeholders to know the difference? Chapter 3 examines the rapidly multiplying and often bizarre techniques used by contemporary experts to distinguish the "truly gay" from the "merely heteroflexible." The chapter centers on the three primary explanatory discourses offered by popular experts: (1) Homosexuality is sometimes circumstantially *necessary*; (2) homosexuality is sometimes a feature of *homosociality*, or an extension of (white) male bonds; and (3) homosexuality is sometimes *accidental*, unexpected, and out of one's control. White fear of men of color, paired with the imagined necessity of white male bonds and the strong desire for access to white male space, runs through each of these narratives, imbuing them with additional normative power. These explanations function to simultaneously exceptionalize and normalize the homosexuality of straight white men, treating as surprising and meaningless what seems to be a fairly predictable and significant feature of white heterosexual men's lives. I conclude the chapter by suggesting that, in attempting to elaborate the reasons that people don't always behave in accordance with their "true nature," such approaches lend support to the notion of fixed sexual personage, a concept at odds with queer resistance.

Chapter 4 proceeds with a deeper investigation of the relationship between heteromasculinity and whiteness. Here I consider examples from contemporary popular culture that link homosexual sex with straight white male rebellion and adventure-seeking. The chapter takes a particularly close look the 2009 independent film *Humpday*, in which two straight white dudes decide to have sex with one another for the sake of "radical art." In *Humpday*, white male hipsterism and its celebration of edgy, exotic, and memorable experiences are what propel the narrative forward as the protagonists dare themselves to be cool enough to "bone" each other. I then move to a close reading of personal ads posted on craigslist.com by posters claiming to be "white straight dudes" seeking one another for "not gay" sex. Reading the ads alongside themes in *Humpday* and other examples from popular culture, I examine how the ads draw on whiteness as a rhetorical resource for establishing hetero-masculine realness. Both *Humpday* and the craigslist ads represent texts in which fantasies about straight white male sexual fluidity are exchanged, and in which both white and heterosexual "authentification" takes center stage.

Chapter 5 examines the cultural function and effects of homosexuality in the hazing rituals of the United States military. The chapter analyzes these military hazing practices alongside the representation of homosexual hazing in the widely popular series of "reality" internet porn, HazeHim.com. Drawing on sociological and media accounts of high-profile military hazing events, I consider how male-male anal penetration is framed by the military as a practice of hetero-masculine resilience, one to be suffered with repulsion and endurance. While the spectacle of homophobic repulsion is often offered as evidence of the nonsexual nature of the hazing experience, a reading of gay hazing porn—wherein flaccid penises, expressions of disgust and repulsion, and homophobic outbursts take on erotic currency as signals of authentic heterosexuality—illuminates a more harmonious relationship between hetero-masculine repulsion and homosexual desire. In both examples, the hazing undertaken by the U.S. military and the hazing eroticized in gay porn, the whiteness of participants is central to the homosocial narrative, wherein average white boys—utterly normal and undoubtedly American—are offered the opportunity to inoculate themselves against sincere homosexuality and enemy perversion and to demonstrate their allegiance to a white brotherhood.

Chapter 6 concludes the book by examining the implications of "sexual fluidity" for queer politics. Here I argue that queer scholars may wish to pay close attention to how narratives about fluidity rely on the existence of romantic gay love and sincere gay subjects, both of which are increasingly compelled into being as congenital heterosexuals distinguish their frivolous and politically inconsequential homosexual experiments and accidents from the romantic, affected, and homonormative conditions of an essentialized gay life. The book concludes by showing that the discourse surrounding heterosexual fluidity feeds into the production of the homonormative homosexual, who in contrast with lascivious butch dykes, sadistic leather daddies, and other fear-invoking queer figures, is motivated by a complex of sincere gay feelings—namely, the desire to fall in gay love, to have a gay family, to be out and proud. In an unexpected turn, "heteroflexibles" co-opt much of what is "naughty" about homosexual sex, casting heterosexuality as the domain of the masculine, the virile, the erotic, the unfettered, and even the forbidden, while homonormativity and genetics converge to redefine "gay" in affective, domestic, and sexless terms. But we need not be complicit. Chapter

6 ends with some considerations of how queers might resist this co-optation.

This book aims to illuminate the cultural underpinnings of straightness and its relationship to queerness. I offer this close examination of the cultural contours of the sexual binary not simply to expand awareness of the sex practices that fall under the banner of white male heterosexuality, but more importantly, to redirect our attention away from soothing tales of sociobiology and toward the more complex, intersectional, and culturally embedded human strivings for straight and queer ways of life.

2

Bars, Bikers, and Bathrooms

A Century of Not-Gay Sex

HETEROSEXUAL fluidity is often described as a new
trend, but it is far more accurate to say that straight-
identified people, including straight white men, have engaged in
homosexual activity since the modern invention of heterosexual
identity itself. In many senses, the heterosexual/homosexual
binary has always been a flawed schema, one that has suffered not
only from considerable disagreement about the nature of sexual
orientation (an identity? a set of behaviors? hardwired or constructed?), but also from its inability to capture or predict erotic
complexities and gender and sexual fluidity.[1] And yet, in another
sense, because the hetero/homo binary is the fundamental framework through which sexuality is understood in late modernity and
around which social life is now organized, it is also a self-fulfilling
prophecy, producing a good amount of its own accuracy. Most
people do identify as either heterosexual/straight or homosexual/
gay (or, still somewhat dualistically, as bisexual[2]). Most of us collectively ignore the fluid, multifaceted, and transitory desires that
would complicate such a simplistic schema. But we can hardly be
blamed. These are the categories we are provided with and compelled to locate ourselves within, to be socially legible or to secure
our survival, so it is no wonder that most of us do.

Of especially little surprise is the fact that large majorities of
people identify with, and are deeply invested in, heterosexuality—

regardless of whether they sometimes or often engage in homosexual sex. For much of its relatively short history, the hetero/homo binary has been premised on the view that to be heterosexual is to possess a normal, natural, and ethical sexual orientation, and that to be homosexual is to be deviant, pathological, and depraved. Of course no one wants to suffer the heinous forms of violence that have been committed against people identified as sexual deviants. But more to the point at hand, some people—people we now aptly call "straight"—have also bristled at the subcultural associations with queer life, wanting nothing to do with the circuits of sexual and gender rebellion and outsiderness that would later be embraced under the banner of queerness. For straights, the invention of ways to engage in homosexual sex while being unquestionably anchored in normalcy has arguably been a vital part of the heterosexual experience.

The point here is that as a sexological tool that presumes a predictable link between sex practices and subjectivity, the hetero/homo binary lacks the capacity to help us account, for instance, for the frequency with which straight-identified people engage in homosexual sex. But as a moral imperative, it reveals a great deal about why straight-identified people—regardless of their homosexual sex practices—would remain invested in being straight. Holding this tension in view, this chapter offers a brief historical overview of straight, or "normal," white men's homosexual activity since the early twentieth century. I illustrate that to the extent that the sexual binary has purported to describe two distinct types of men—heterosexuals or homosexuals who are engaged in wholly different sex practices—it has always been something of a fiction. And yet, the widespread circulation of this fiction has produced truly divergent cultural formations, erotic desires, and political investments that, still today, can be productively understood as normative on the one hand and queer on the other.

Keeping these considerations in the foreground, this chapter surveys the homosexual activity of "normal" white American men.

I begin with a very brief account of the emergence of "straight white male" subjectivity and its status as the original exemplar of normal sexuality, and then move into a chronology of the not-gay sexual encounters enacted by white men throughout the twentieth century. Touring through the immigrant saloons of early twentieth-century New York, the California highways traversed by the Hell's Angels biker gang in the 1950s, the public bathrooms at the center of "gay sex scandals" in the 1980s, and beyond, we will examine the evolution of the sexual binary across the twentieth century and its effect on Americans' thinking about the meaning of homosexual sex among normal—masculine, heterosexual, and white—men.

The Invention of the Straight White Man

Much of the homosexual activity of contemporary "straight white dudes" has flown under the radar of the stigmatizing forces that take aim at men of color on the down low and at queers of all stripes. As we will explore in the chapters to follow, this is because straight white men have some powerful cultural tools available to them that other groups do not—namely, a set of rhetorical narratives that recast white men's intimate contact with one another's bodies as the necessary and nonsexual material of white male brotherhood, white male risk-taking, and initiation into white male groups. But to understand how and why straight white men became the beneficiaries of these narratives requires that we do some historical backtracking, or that we trace notions about the fluidity or rigidity of straight white male sexuality back to the birth of the straight white guy himself.

Such is the aim of this chapter, and one that upon first blush, sounds as though it would require countless volumes to address. And yet, while the history of straight white manhood is a dense and significant one—one that serves as a powerful example of the intersectional construction of sexual, gender, and racial categories—it is also surprisingly short. This is because, as has now been well established by historians of sexuality, heterosexual and homosexual categories are themselves relatively new, emerging in medical journals in the late nineteenth century but not popularized, or accepted among the general American public, until well into the twentieth century. While whiteness and maleness were well-established structures in the nineteenth century, heterosexual identity as we know it today had no nineteenth-century counterpart. There were "normal men," and there were those men whose gender expression marked them as queer or strange in some way, but as I will soon discuss, these were nuanced categories that had far less to do with homosexual activity (or lack thereof) than we would imagine today. People have long engaged in opposite-sex and same-sex sexual activity, of course, but the sense that these sexual behaviors constitute an identity or personage is a quite modern idea, one that emerged in complex relation to twentieth-century race, gender, and class formations in the United States.[3]

According to historian Jonathan Ned Katz, in his now classic book *The Invention of Heterosexuality*, the term "heterosexuality" first appeared in medical literature in the late 1800s, not as a description of nature's default, but as a sexual perversion characterized by men and women's desire for nonprocreative sex with one another. For many centuries prior to the Victorian era, sex was imagined to follow directly and exclusively from a procreative instinct, and it was in this context that the term "heterosexual" came into American medical usage to describe a deviant desire for opposite-sex sexual activity not linked to procreation. Describing the treatment for heterosexuality recommended by prominent physicians of the late 1800s, Katz explains:

> As treatment for his abnormal heteros and homos Dr. Hughes (an American physician) suggested heroic measures—hypnosis and sometimes surgery. For Hughes, as for Dr. Kiernan in 1892, the heterosexual, as a person of mixed procreative and nonprocreative

disposition, still stood with the nonprocreative homo in the pantheon of sexual perverts.[4]

In its first sexological iteration, heterosexuality was hardly safe from scrutiny, but was one of a number of sexualities that could potentially involve the perverse waste of semen, quite on par with masturbation and homosexuality. Some evidence of this view can be found well into the twentieth century, in documents depicting heterosexuality as a perversion expressed not only in the form of opposite-sex passion, but also as an impulse toward masturbation, bestiality, or sexual violence. Among the most succinct and telling examples of heterosexuality's meaning during this period comes from the 1923 edition of the Merriam-Webster Dictionary, which offered the following definition of heterosexuality: "a morbid sexual passion for one of the opposite sex."[5]

But in a simultaneous and competing vein, one that would ultimately win out, a handful of influential European and American physicians had also begun the work of normalizing the heterosexual. In 1893, the Viennese doctor Richard Von Krafft-Ebing revised the concept of heterosexuality in a way that would later send rippling effects across the globe and into the next two centuries. Krafft-Ebing argued that when men and women have sex with each other, they may not be *consciously* thinking about procreation, and they may in fact be engaged in all manner of less-than-desirable nonreproductive activities, but they are always nonetheless motivated by an innate and deep-seated procreative impulse. Though still largely confined to medical journals, this view newly conceptualized the heterosexual as a fundamentally noble and normal subject, always oriented toward the opposite sex for virtuous reproductive purposes. Helping to solidify this association, Krafft-Ebing used the term "normal-sexual" synonymously with the term "heterosexual," positing the homosexual as its pathological opposite.[6]

With elaboration from other like-minded American and European sexologists, this conflation of heterosexuality with normality gained quick and widespread popularity among physicians, lawmakers, religious institutions, and state authorities in Europe and the United States.[7] By 1934, just eleven years after being defined as a morbid passion, heterosexuality appeared in Webster's Dictionary as a nearly opposite animal: "a manifestation of sexual passion for one of the opposite sex; *normal sexuality*." According to historian Hanne Blank, the general public's fear of being labeled deviant or degenerate, and their demand for ways to know with certainty that they were neither of these, can account for the enthusiasm with which many people learned to "experience heterosexuality—to think about themselves as 'being' and 'feeling' heterosexual, [and] to believe that there is a difference between 'being heterosexual' and 'being homosexual.'"[8]

But who, exactly, was this new healthy heterosexual? And in what form was heterosexuality most purely expressed? As sexology developed in the late nineteenth century, with its focus on sexual categorization, the field's leaders turned to yet another scientific discipline already engaged in the work of cataloguing abnormal bodies and unnatural desires: the white supremacist "sciences" of eugenics and craniometry. Early sexologists drew heavily from eugenicist theories about the anatomical differences between black and white bodies and the dangerous perversion of racial "mixing."[9] Sexologists described what they imagined were the oversexed natures and gender-ambiguous bodies of homosexuals in terms that were remarkably similar to those being used by eugenicists in their mythology of the hypersexuality and gender-ambiguity of people of African descent. Sexologists drew a line in the sand between the healthy heterosexual and the perverse and dangerous homosexual (the latter in need of institutionalization), a line that, according to Siobhan Somerville in her groundbreaking book *Queering the Color Line*, was intentionally modeled after the system of racial segregation in place in the United States. Significantly, the more that sexologists borrowed from the logics of racial difference, the more they positioned heterosexuality as analogous to whiteness and homosexuality as analogous to blackness.

Ideas about the differences between black and white sexuality, and female and male sexuality, were also used by whites to justify white supremacy in the United States, with one consequence of this strategy being that white men were posited as the paragons of proper heterosexual agency. Whites defended racial segregation as a means of protecting passive and vulnerable white women from sexually violent black men, and, less commonly, from the corrupting influence of hypersexual black women. In this formulation, white male sexuality was left unmarked and unproblematized, visible only as that which was properly positioned vis-à-vis women. While whites (both men and women) embodied the most visible early cases of homosexuality,[10] the figure of agentic *heterosexuality* was also not only white, but always male.

According to race and gender ideologies of the early twentieth century, white women's sexuality was too repressed and vulnerable to serve as the model of heterosexual passion, while people of African descent were too subject to brute impulses to reliably direct their desires toward proper objects.[11] Under the logic of white supremacy, men of color and Jewish, Italian, and Irish immigrants not yet considered white were insufficiently hetero-patriarchal, possessing an immature, polymorphously perverse, and more fluid or passive sexuality than allowable under the newly concretized sexual binary.[12] Women of color and poor immigrant white women were, for all intents and purposes, excluded from the modern construction of womanhood itself, which linked femininity with white middle-class domesticity, seclusion in the private sphere, and the privilege of being protected, by men, from the sexual aggression of other men.[13] Wealthy white women, with their presumed capacity for hysteria or frigidity, and their vulnerability to sexual violation and defilement, also troubled the category of normal sexuality.[14]

While women have, of course, been among the ranks of heterosexuals since the concept's inception, their place within the sexual binary has been, and continues to be, particularly fraught with suspicion (and titillation) about the complex and unpredictable nature of female sexuality. When the hetero/homo binary made its nineteenth-century debut, sex itself was still the purview of men, something that happed *to* women, synonymous with the presence of the penis. The notion that women cannot be full sexual agents, either heterosexual or lesbian, clearly persists today, expressed through characterizations of women's sexuality as fundamentally docile, receptive, or motivated by emotions over lust, or in the form of confusion about how two women can possibly have sex with one another. In the late twentieth century, the belief that women were innately more sexually fluid than men also emerged, along with the notion that they were susceptible to a much broader array of sexual stimuli. This view gained momentum alongside a shift from the mid-century perception of women as frigid or sexually repressed to the late-century view of women as enthusiastic, although often vain and manipulative, seekers of sexual attention.

The early twentieth-century heterosexual ideal was not only white and male, but Protestant as well. As waves of Jewish men and Irish and Italian Catholics immigrated to the United States, their whiteness, masculinity, and heterosexuality were subject to considerable scrutiny, and measured against the stoicism and patriarchal "leadership" associated with white Protestant masculinity. While these groups achieved whiteness largely through cultural and linguistic assimilation and alignment with anti-black racism, their path to "normal sexuality" was dependent on conformity to binary gender roles, displays of working-class physical strength, and male sexual aggressiveness. In *Unheroic Conduct:*

The Rise of Heterosexuality and the Invention of the Jewish Man, Daniel Boyarin argues that Jewish men, in particular, have long been suspect—perceived as both feminine and queer—for failing to conform to Christian gender norms. In contrast with those who suggest that the feminization of Jewish men is simply an anti-Semitic projection, Boyarin advocates for a recovery and embrace of "the Jewish ideal of the gentle, receptive male."[15] Attention, such as Boyarin's, to the nexus of religion and normative gender and sexuality suggests that whiteness, maleness, and heterosexuality are, in and of themselves, insufficient to constitute normal sexuality. In the United States, normative sexual subjects are also Christian.

In sum, white Christian men were the exemplars of heterosexuality, or normal sexuality, from the inception of the category. This was possible in large part because heterosexuality, for most of the twentieth century, referred not simply to opposite-sex attraction, but to a medical, legal, cultural, and religious ideal—to an aspiration for procreation-focused, male-initiated, male-centered, male-controlled, nonadulterous (at least on women's part), private, and static sexuality. White Christian European and American male physicians, sexologists, and psychologists shaped heterosexuality in their own image, constructing a sexual ideal in which indigenous people, people of African descent, Jews, and women were already problematic figures. As queer historian Julian Carter has argued, it was precisely this fusing of discourses of whiteness, masculinity, and heterosexuality in the twentieth century that formed the concept of the "normal" American, a subjectivity most readily embodied by white men.

I offer this brief overview of the race and gender construction of heterosexuality because it forms the context in which the homosexual sex of heterosexual white men has been elided or exceptionalized within accounts of human sexuality. Already paradigmatic figures of normalcy, white boys and men arguably enter the terrain of sexuality burdened by less suspicion, bolstered by more erotic agency, and attributed greater benefit of the doubt that their sexual constitution is normal.

It goes without saying that white men are also gay-identified men, and that, particularly in the European context, white men have suffered incredibly violent persecution—in concentration camps, in mental institutions, at sodomy trials—as punishment for their homosexual activity. The severity of this persecution cannot be overstated. And yet it is also true that the intersections of racism and patriarchy have played a significant and seemingly paradoxical role in determining what counts as punishable, worrisome, or meaningful homosexual contact. In some respects, patriarchal ideology has resulted in less scrutiny for women's same-sex sexual behavior than men's, as the former has been conceptualized as only quasi-sexual and therefore nonthreatening, and the latter as a deeply troubling abdication of male power and control of women.

And yet, white men invested in heteronormativity—white men invested in living normal, heterosexual lives, even as they engage in homosexual sex—have also had access to a series of loopholes and justifying logics whose effectiveness are bolstered by the already strong cultural association of white masculinity with normality. As we will soon see, normative masculinity alone—the absence of any hint at womanliness or effeminacy— has often been sufficient to signal that "there's nothing queer here" when white men have engaged in sexual contact with other white men. Moreover, whiteness—and its conflation with propriety, especially in the postwar, desegregation era of U.S. history—has occasioned a "looking the other way" among the ranks of straight white men invested in preserving the normative status of their group. Let us now turn to our tour of straight white men's sex with men in the American twentieth century, with particular attention to these "loopholes" and their continuity and disruption.

The Homosexual Sex of Normal Men: A Chronology

Trade: Heteroflexibility in the Prewar American City

Although the terms "gay" and "straight," "heterosexual" and "homosexual," did not come into their current meaning as sexual orientations and self-identifications until around the mid-twentieth century, subcultures organized around same-sex practices existed in the United States and elsewhere long before this period. Resisting claims that social scenes organized around homosexuality were invisible or isolated prior to the Stonewall Rebellion in 1969, historian George Chauncey's exhaustive study of gay life in New York from 1890 to 1940 offers a wealth of information about a burgeoning, vibrant, integrated, self-affirming, and working-class subculture that would later come to be known as "gay." This early, urban, queer world was centered in Irish and Italian immigrant communities,[16] and organized not around homosexual identity but around male effeminacy, drag, theatricality, and homosexual sex. Though Chauncey's study is centered on men who were connected by these queer ways of life, it also offers an invaluable window into the lives of men who engaged in homosexual sex but rejected or only occasionally passed through this queer subculture, remaining for the most part anchored in mainstream, heteronormative, middle-class society. At a time when men's queerness was marked largely by their effeminacy or womanliness, these "real men" escaped the stigma of queerness and remained normal, irrespective of their homosexual encounters, by having a conventionally masculine gender presentation.

In many parts of the United States prior to the 1950s, the homo/hetero binary marked a distinction between effeminate men, or fairies, and masculine men, or real men, and not between men who did or did not engage in homosexual sex. As late as the 1940s, working-class white men in New York understood themselves to be queer based on their cross-gender presentation and not based on their homosexual behavior, a system illustrated by the common use of gendered terms—"fairy," "queen," "sissy," "nance," and "pansy"—to describe men whom we would now call "gay" (the term "gay" did not begin to gain prominence until the 1940s).[17] Conversely, while the broader culture had no distinct term for straight men who engaged in homosexual sex, such men were referred to as "trade" within gay subculture. Trade were real men: sailors, soldiers, and other embodiments of idealized masculinity. They were normal men who would have sex with men for money or who would agree to have sex with men as long as they remained in the dominant, masculine role.

Reflecting the centrality of gender presentation to the pre–World War II hierarchy of normal and abnormal sexuality, especially in working-class communities, these conventionally masculine straight men could engage in sex with men, often quite frequently, without threat to their normalcy, or straightness. As Chauncey highlights, the fact that this system prevailed in the daily life of urban, white working-class neighborhoods reveals the disjuncture between elite, medical accounts of the sexual binary (which emphasized homosexual behavior over effeminacy) and the way that working- class men themselves conceptualized the line between normal and abnormal. Definitions of normalcy and queerness were so significantly crosscut by socioeconomic class, Chauncey explains, that "the homosexual displaced the fairy in middle-class culture *several generations earlier* than in working class culture."[18] Through much of the first half of the twentieth century, normal working-class men mixed with fairies in saloons that were central to working men's lives, as places to exchange information about employment and to access basic amenities (cheap meals, water, toilets). With sex segregation being the general rule for single men and women in the early twentieth century, the private back rooms of saloons were also sites of sexual activity between normal men and fairies, with the latter perceived as a kind of intermediate sex, a reasonable alternative to female prostitutes.[19] Public parks and restrooms were also common sites for sexual interaction between straight men and fairies.

In such encounters, the fairy served as the sole embodiment of queerness, the figure with whom normal men could have sex, just as they might with female sex workers, without any sense that they themselves were queer. Fairies affirmed straight men's hetero-masculinity by embodying its opposite. Mirroring some of the working-class and hyper-masculine discourses explored later in this book, this sexual system dominated in working-class space, "in the highly aggressive and quintessentially 'masculine' subculture of young and usually unmarried sailors, common laborers, hoboes, and other transient workers, who were a ubiquitous presence in early twentieth-century American cities."[20]

Though Chauncey also looks closely at black gay life during this period, much of his research is focused on white immigrant men, namely Italian and Irish immigrants, who would be considered white today, even if not during their own era. New York was home to especially large numbers of Italian and Irish immigrant men who were either single or had left their families back home, while Jewish men were more likely to immigrate with their families. The concentration of these men, often living together in all-male boarding houses, gave rise to a "bachelor subculture" that was arguably a precursor to the straight white male culture of today. Central to this working-class and all-male bachelor subculture was a rejection of the domesticity and morality associated with women. Foreshadowing an ethic that would later be described as "bros before hoes," bachelors celebrated the value of rough-and-tumble, work-hard-and-play-hard manliness, forging a common brotherhood centered on independence from women. The presence of fairies in this subculture, rather than threatening the bachelor's masculinity, confirmed the normalcy and superiority of straight men by occupying the degraded position of the feminine.

As Chauncey points out, the prevalence of the view that normatively masculine men could engage in homosexual behavior without thinking of themselves as queer is confirmed by Alfred Kinsey's infamous publication *Sexual Behavior in the Human Male*, based on research conducted in the 1930s and 1940s (and published in 1948). Thirty seven percent of Kinsey's research subjects reported having sex with another man at least once during their adulthood (while only 4 percent reported being exclusively homosexual). Though now commonly believed to be an inflated figure out of step with current statistics on male homosexual behavior, this figure may suggest that social norms in the 1930s and 1940s facilitated more homosexual contact among men—and less queer stigma—than in later decades. Chauncey points out that Kinsey's own critical commentary also provides a window into the sexual ideology of the era. In discussions of his findings, Kinsey went to great lengths to dispel what he understood as common beliefs of his time, namely that fairies were "she-men" (i.e., the intermediate sex) and that gender presentation (masculine or effeminate) and sexual role (active or passive) determined whether one was truly heterosexual or homosexual.

Ultimately, by the last third of the twentieth century, the influence of sexology and developments within gay subculture resulted in a widening of the field of queerness, and a concomitant narrowing of who or what could count as straight. At mid-century, gay men pushed for a shift in perception of gay from a *gender* category signaled by male effeminacy to a *sexual* category signaled by homosexual activity. The meaning of "trade" necessarily evolved in relation to these changes, with the emphasis now placed on men's self-identification as straight over their masculine gender presentation (though normative masculinity remained still very much idealized). While in the early twentieth century "trade" had referred primarily to straight masculine men who paid effeminate men for sex, this relationship was reversed by mid-century, with "trade" commonly used as a term describing straight prostitutes who could be paid to have sex with gay men. The meaning of "trade" shifted yet again with the early 1970s emergence of a gay liberation movement focused on the purportedly liberating effects of coming out of the closet. As straight men's participation in homosexual activity became increasingly viewed as a sign of repressed homosexuality, "trade," as a truly straight subjectivity, had all but disappeared.

While this rapid transformation in understandings of straight men's homosexual activity likely produced some dissonance for straight men, so too did it have its effects on gay men who had come out during the prewar era and had benefitted from a looser definition of straightness. As one gay man quoted by Chauncey contends, the gay liberation movement made it "a lot harder to find straight guys to do it with," as its claim that "we are *everywhere*" logically extended to heterosexuality itself, threatening to reveal the real homosexuals among the ranks of straights.[21] As another gay man quoted by Chauncey explains:

> Most of my crowd [in the 1930s and 1940s] wanted to have sex with straight men. There was something very hot about a married man! And a lot of straight boys let us have sex with them. People don't believe it now. People say now that they must have been gay. But they weren't. They were straight. They wouldn't look for [it] or suck a guy's thing, but they'd let you suck theirs. If you want to say they were gay because they had sex with a man, go ahead, but I say only a man who *wants* to have sex with a man is gay.[22]

In sum, a new burden of caution and self-doubt was placed on straight men by a gay movement determined to attach identitarian meaning to all homosexual encounters. This approach helped call attention to the prevalence of homosexuality, and on the surface appeared to be a winning strategy for the gay liberation movement. But it also concretized an exceedingly binary way of thinking about sex practices. Any engagement in homosexual activity now risked association not only with gay identity, but also with a gay political movement and a gay subculture that held little appeal to many people who might otherwise be interested in homosexual sex. The previously wide field of ways to make homosexual contact had significantly narrowed.

Bikers and Bathrooms: Straight Men's Homosexual
Activity in the 1950s and 1960s

Still, the notion that homosexual activity might not be "gay" when undertaken by real men continued into the 1950s and 1960s, when the homosexual contact of straight men began to be reconfigured from relatively mundane behavior to the bold behavior of white male rebels. Significantly more stigmatized during this period, homosexual contact was no longer so easily justifiable. It either had to be situated within an exceptionally hyper-masculine ethic of working-class rebellion or to occur in secrecy, as in isolated public restrooms.

The notorious white American biker gang, the Hells Angels, formed in 1948, provides a rich example of the first possibility, or of the place of homosexual sex in the life of the straight white male outlaw of the 1950s and 1960s.[23] As one documentary film about the group contends, the Hell's Angels were born out of the rebel spirit of young white men who returned from World War II still looking for action, and finding it "on a big bike, with a big engine."[24] By many accounts, early members of the Hell's Angels were violent and highly feared white thugs, known for rape and drunken assaults of both men and women, including an assault that resulted in the murder of Meredith Hunter, an eighteen-year-old African American man, during a Rolling Stones concert in 1969. There are few figures more "macho" than the heavily tattooed and leather-clad Hell's Angel, whose heterosexuality was as much on display as his masculinity. Fighting over women, and exhibiting women on the backs of bikes, was central to the subculture of the gang. Still today, some members of the Hells Angels view themselves within a lineage of white working-class outlaws and vigilantes like Robin Hood and Billy the Kid.[25]

And yet, as the journalist Hunter S. Thompson revealed in his 1966 book, *Hell's Angels: A Strange and Terrible Saga*, the Hell's Angels were also men who had sexual encounters with men. For instance, Thompson quotes a San Francisco Hell's Angel describing his enthusiastic willingness to have sex with men for ten dollars:

> Hell yes, I'll take a blow-job any day for ten bucks. Just the other night in some bar downtown I had a queer come up to me with a big tenner. . . . He laid it on me and said what did I want to drink? I said, "A double of Jack Daniels, baby," so he told the bartender, "Two of those for me and my friend," and then he sat down there on the bar rail and gave me a hell of a blow-job, man, and all I had to do was smile at the bartender and keep cool. . . . Shit, man, the day they can call me queer is when I let one of these faggots suck on me for less than a tenner. . . . Man, I'd go underwater and fuck fish for that kind of money, you just tell me who's payin'.[26]

Thompson's discussion of the meaning of the Hell's Angels' homosexual activity is in and of itself quite revealing. Forcefully affirming the heteromasculinity of the group, Thompson dismisses the question of whether the gang might consist of latent homosexuals as "entirely irrelevant" in light of what he perceives to be the truly authentic nature of their outlaw masculinity. Even if they *were* homosexuals, Thompson claims, their brutality "would not be changed or subdued for a moment."[27] Mirroring the ambivalent response of the American public to the Hell's Angels, Thompson wavers between deep concern about the destructive potential of the gang and admiration for their outlaw spirit and street realness. Noting the apparent stylistic links between biker culture and gay leather scenes, Thompson is emphatic, if not also homophobic, in his claim that the Hell's Angels occupy a "harsh, unique corner of reality," while the gay male leather enthusiast is simply a "passive worshipper, a sloppy emulator of a style that fascinates him because it is so hopelessly remote from the reality he wakes up to every morning."[28]

Thompson's analysis of the Hell's Angels suggests a site in which the early twentieth-century sexual system—whereby "real men" could pay, or be paid, for homosexual encounters without attributing queer meaning to the transaction—is extended into mid-century. But something more was at work for the Hell's Angels of the 1960s, who also viewed their sexual contact with men as a form of hyper-masculine defiance, a crude and macho challenge to social conventions. Alex Gibney's 2007 documentary *Gonzo*, about Hunter S. Thompson's life and writing career, incorporates some of Thompson's own footage of the biker gang, including film recordings of members of the Hell's Angels deeply French kissing one another—with tongues extended out of their mouths in a type of tongue-licking kiss often reserved for girl-on-girl porn. Thompson described the kissing in his book *Hell's Angels* as a kind of publicity stunt: "The Angels are gleefully aware of the reaction it gets. . . . The sight of a photographer invariably whips the Angels into a kissing frenzy, but I have never seen them do it among themselves."[29] Mirroring this view, Gibney (the *Gonzo* filmmaker) explains that French kissing "was something that the Hells Angels loved to do because it really just freaked people out. They used to say they loved that tongue bit. . . . They would say, 'We don't care what you think, this is an expression of our lust and our spirit.'"[30]

And yet, lest the kissing be understood purely as an act of attention-seeking, Thompson elaborated in his ethnographic account of the group that "there is an element of something besides showbiz to it and in serious moments now and then one of the Angels will explain it as 'just one of the ways we let the world know we're brothers.'"[31] Somewhat contradicting his claim that the Angels never kissed "among themselves," Thompson also describes a night when, during a small gathering at a bar, an Angel greeted him with a "hairy kiss" and expected it to be heartily returned. Thompson recounts that his kissing companion was of-

Figure 2.1. Hell's Angels, Kissing Guys (Hunter S. Thompson, 1960s, http://jetingenue. wordpress.com/tag/ hells-angels/).

fended by his awkward and lukewarm response, which turned out to be a social error after which the Angels treated Thompson with "a gentle sort of detachment, as if I were somebody's little brother with an incurable disease."[32] Taken together, these accounts suggest that deep kissing had multiple meanings for the Hell's Angels: It was both a defiant stunt that produced among onlookers the desired degree of shock, *and* it was an expression of "lust" and "brotherhood."

Thompson ultimately seemed to settle on the position that the Hell's Angels were simply too menacing to be homosexuals, a position suggesting that the link between homosexuality and effeminacy continued to function as a loophole for straight, masculine men well into the 1960s. Thompson cautioned that to characterize the Hell's Angels as homosexuals would be a dangerous misrecognition of the threat they posed to society. He warned that "any attempt to explain the Hell's Angels as an essentially homosexual phenomenon would be a cop-out, a self-satisfied dismissal of a reality that is as complex and potentially malignant as anything in American society."[33] Even as a behavior-based sexual binary had already taken hold by the 1960s, the Hell's Angels's violence and fearlessness—qualities believed to be tethered to masculinity and irreconcilable with the image of the fag (even the leatherfetishizing fag)—confirmed that the Angels were best understood as *not* gay.

One of the more striking facets of these accounts of the Hell's Angels is the extent to which the defiant homosexual behavior they describe—especially the spectacular same-sex kissing—so closely mirrors the behavior of young women in the early twenty-first century. Much ado has been made in recent years about heterosexual college-aged women kissing, grabbing, and hooking up with one other—activities often described as a form of attention seeking. When enacted by young women, homosexual kissing is cast as both erotic and defiant, as a form of youthful salaciousness that titillates as much as it provokes concern. Corollary behaviors can clearly be found among straight white men, in both the past and the present, and yet these similarly defiant and lustful encounters are all too often forgotten, ignored, or dismissed as purely a prank—emptied of all their erotic meaning—under the now prevailing logic of male sexual rigidity. The performative kissing of the 1960s Hell's Angels marks an important moment in the history of straight white male homosexuality, one in which homosexual contact is presented to the public as an expression of such extraordinary hetero-masculine rebelliousness that it defies categorization as gay. Chapters 4 and 5 of this book trace this very logic into the present, revealing a set of erotic possibilities that are both everywhere and nowhere in contemporary straight white men's lives.

The Tearoom

While the Hell's Angels represent a working-class example of the homosexual behavior of straight white men, the best evidence of homosexual contact among middle-class, straight-identified white men comes from Laud Humphreys's 1970 study of homosexual encounters in public men's restrooms, also known in gay slang as "tearooms." In his controversial book *Tearoom Trade*, based on research conducted in the 1960s, Humphreys revealed

Figure 2.2. Police documentation of tearoom raids, Mansfield, Ohio (from *Tearoom*, a film by William E. Jones, http://lafilmforum. wordpress.com/2008/ 06/04/june-8-tearoom-a-document-presented-by-william-e-jones/).

what appeared to be a widespread practice of straight-identified, married men giving and receiving blowjobs in semi-isolated public restrooms, in or near parks, subways, and rest stops. The study is now best known for its use of unethical research methods; namely, Humphreys knew about the heterosexual identities and marital statuses of the men he studied because he covertly followed them home—a practice that would never be allowable today. And yet, Humphreys's method allowed him to document a subculture organized around homosexual activity that had little, and often nothing, to do with gay life. Over the course of his fieldwork, Humphreys observed straight white men visit bathrooms for sex on their way to and from work, and he noted that many were regulars at particular restrooms. Though Humphreys was reluctant to estimate the percentage of the adult male population who participated in "the tearoom trade" (he guessed 5 percent), his observations and interviews attested to the high volume of homosexual sex in many bathrooms: Some bathrooms were known for long lines, were in use around the clock, and were the site of dozens of blowjobs each day.

Humphreys pointed to the hetero-erotic culture of homosexual sex in public-use bathrooms, which were valued locales among straight men precisely because of their disconnection from gay bars and other places where gay men might congregate. He explained:

> Tearooms are popular, not because they serve as gathering places for homosexuals but because they attract a variety of men, a *minority* of whom are active in the homosexual subculture. When we consider the types of participants, it will be seen that a large group of them have no homosexual self-identity.[34]

Mirroring the norms dictating male interaction in restrooms more generally, Humphreys's study revealed that sexual encounters between men in public bathrooms were impersonal, emotionless, and often silent. Typically men's bodies did not come into any contact beyond the contact of mouth and penis. Encounters were anonymous, and carried no across-the-board presumption that participants were gay or lived gay lives. While gay bars were certainly available to men in the city in which Humphreys undertook his research, tearooms operated as an important alternative—a place to make homosexual contact that was *not* gay.

Unlike the Hell's Angels, the participants Humphreys observed in tearooms were "respectable" men; they were, to use Humphreys's term, and a term with great resonance in the 1960s, "the people next door." In fact, Humphreys offered a quite detailed and class-inflected profile of the men he met in tearooms and subsequently interviewed: They were white (all but one), mostly middle-class men in their thirties and forties, happily married to women, politically conservative, and involved in their churches and communities; they were ministers, carpenters, clerical workers, students, executives, truck drivers, and servicemen.

> The tearoom participant is just another neighbor—and probably a very good one at that. He may make a little more money than the next man and works a little harder for it. It is likely that he will drive a nicer car and maintain a neater yard than do other neigh-

bors in the block. Maybe, like some tearoom regulars, he will work with Boy Scouts in the evenings and spend much of his weekend in church. It may be most surprising for the outsider to discover that most of these men are married.[35]

Here Humphreys paints a vivid picture of white, middle-class heteronormativity at mid-century.

Not surprisingly, tearooms of the 1960s were, by and large, racially segregated spaces,[36] where white men could expect to interact sexually with other white men. Though Humphreys offers no consideration whatsoever of the significance of whiteness within tearoom encounters of the 1960s, some of his findings reveal white solidarity to be a central organizing principle of tearoom subculture. For instance, white male informants provided Humphreys, a white male researcher, with tips about where to find the best and most "active" tearooms, including the following tip from a surprisingly helpful white police officer in plain clothes: "Look, fellow, if you're looking for sex, this isn't the place. We're clamping down on this park because of trouble with the niggers. Try the john at the northeast corner of [Reagan] Park. You'll find plenty of action there."[37] Humphreys provides no analysis of this telling remark, except to say that tips often came from unexpected sources (e.g., police). And yet, we can surmise from the white police officer's comments that white solidarity was at work within the tearoom circuit to such an extent that even a police officer—whose typical role would be to break up tearoom activity and possibly arrest participants—would *facilitate* tearoom encounters when doing so provided the opportunity to close ranks on black men and affirm his allegiance to whiteness.

The clearly important but nonetheless ignored role of whiteness within Humphreys's study stands in stark contrast with the ways that the homosexual behavior of men of color has, and still is, almost always attributed to race, including in contemporary analyses of the down low. Like black men on the down low, the white male participants in Humphreys's study participated in a racially exclusive subculture of their own making, wherein contact between male bodies of the same race was eroticized and protected.

It is worth also noting that Humphreys was only minimally interested in *why* straight-identified tearoom participants engaged in homosexual sex in public bathrooms; his project was centered far more on *how* they did it. He confessed that he could only speculate about their motivations, and offered the suggestion that a high degree of Catholicism among his research subjects meant that wives who were unwilling to use birth control, and who also wished to avoid having numerous children, were less interested in sex than their husbands. Tearoom participants spoke of their wives in "glowing terms," but many reported having insufficiently frequent sexual experiences inside their marriages. For married heterosexual men dissatisfied with the amount of sex available to them, but not wanting to pay for sex with female prostitutes or enter a complicated extramarital relationship with another woman, sex in public bathrooms offered a "quick, inexpensive, and impersonal" alternative, "a form of orgasm-producing action that is less lonely than masturbation and less involving than a love relationship."[38] Humphreys further suggested that the disappearance of affordable and easily accessible whorehouses in the United States might have been largely to blame for the emergence and popularity of tearoom encounters among men who would otherwise prefer sex with women.

Importantly, however, Humphreys seemed to waiver in his analysis of whether participation in tearooms indicated some repressed truth about the sexual identity of the married men he studied. In some passages of *Tearoom Trade*, he described tearoom participants as men uninterested in homosexuality for its own sake (men looking only for quick and uncomplicated orgasms), while in others moments he seemed to contend something else, such as in his assertion that "closet queens and other types of covert deviants . . . are the persons most attracted to tea-room encounters."[39]

Though Humphreys acknowledged that a majority of the men in his study had no interest in gay subculture, even when it was available to them, he was also writing at a time in which the logic of the closet had already become firmly entrenched in the social sciences. Laying out an argument resembling the now-familiar claim that homophobia often signals repressed homosexuality, Humphreys dedicated an entire chapter to analyzing the moral righteousness of the men who frequented tearooms. Here he reported that the straight-identified men in his study, as compared with the smaller number of bisexual and gay-identified men who frequented tearooms, were more likely to be conservative, highly moralistic, and to openly express racism, homophobia, and support for U.S. military interventions. Though this political orientation was certainly consistent with the broader white supremacist and homophobic culture in which straight white men were situated in the 1960s, Humphreys interprets the strong conservatism of homosexually active straight white men as "a protective shield of superpropriety," a performance designed to deflect attention away from their deviant behavior and set the stage for future indignation should they be exposed.

While not exactly explicit, this analysis hints at what would later become a familiar sexual repression narrative, one in which conservative righteousness and homophobia are imagined to be fundamentally at odds with homosexual activity and therefore function primarily as decoys for a more authentic, homosexual self. This may well have been true for some of the men in Humphreys' study. And yet the emphasis on repression, in Humphreys's work as elsewhere, also glossed over a decades-long and fairly harmonious relationship between normative manhood—with all its disdain for "true" homosexuality and/or effeminacy—and homosexual behavior.

Scandal! Spiritual Crises and Hetero Redemption
in the Late Twentieth Century

The late twentieth century marked a shift not so much in the quantity or form of homosexual encounters among straight white men, but in the way that these encounters were perceived by the broader American public, including a now more visible and mobilized population of "out" gay men and lesbians. On the one hand, there is compelling evidence that straight-identified men continued into the late twentieth century, as they do today, to engage in precisely the kind of impersonal, non-identitarian, public homosexual sex described by Humphreys. The tearoom circuit remains alive and well, for instance, with police continuing to arrest straight-identified men—including some high-profile Republican politicians, as I will soon discuss—for engaging in transactional homosexual sex in public restrooms.

On the other hand, the emergence of a modern gay rights movement in the 1970s, and its tendency to subsume all homosexual activity under the banner of gay or bisexual identity, shifted the meaning of straight men's homosexual encounters. Homosexual acts that were "normal" in the 1930s and "deviant" in the 1960s took on far greater identitarian significance by the 1980s and 1990s. With the demands of the gay rights movement, the devastation of the AIDS epidemic, and the arrival of a conservative "family values" campaign all looming large on the American stage, the same homosexual acts that were normalized in earlier parts of the century became the material of great psycho-spiritual crisis and collective moral panic. A spate of sensationalized "gay sex scandals" in the late twentieth century arguably epitomizes this transformation, with most of these scandals following a similar narrative arc beginning with exposure and remorse, and ending with self-reflection and religious salvation. According to this late-century morality tale, straight white men could "lose their way" in, say, the glory hole of a bathroom stall,[40] but find it again through Christ's love and their wives' stalwart devotion.

John Howard's *Men Like That*, a study of homosexually active men in Mississippi between 1945 and 1985, offers a brilliant account of these shifts as they occurred in the state of Mississippi. Howard shows that prior to the mid-1960s, homosexuality was a common and visible feature of life in the South, not as an identity anchored in lesbian and gay communities, but as a set of sexual practices dispersed through space, from churches to country roads, living rooms to highway rest stops. While many queer historical accounts have attempted to point to the precise moment of homosexuality's transformation from a set of behaviors to an identity category, Howard's study suggests that, for most of the twentieth century, both meanings have operated simultaneously, varying across race, class, and place (with men of color and working-class men retaining a less identitarian understanding for longer than white, middle-class men). As Howard so clearly articulates, the twentieth century was home to "men like *that*—which is to say, men of that particular type, self-identified gay males—as well as men *who like* that, men who also like queer sex, who also engage in homosexual activity or gender nonconformity, but do not necessarily identify as gay."[41] Howard finds evidence of both groups of men as late as the 1980s.

Howard's case studies also mark the evolution of queerness from a kind of "nebulous eccentricity" at mid-century, to a fixed, dangerous, and often hidden sexual constitution by the 1980s. Foreshadowing the growing prominence of homosexual sex scandals on the eve of the twenty-first century, Howard offers a close reading of the case of John Hinson, a white, straight-identified, Republican Mississippi congressman arrested for lewd conduct in the late 1970s and again in 1981. While a number of scholars have analyzed more recent cases of straight-identified politicians and religious leaders engaged in homosexual sex, the commentary surrounding Hinson's case offers an important example of the line being drawn in the 1980s between forgivable homosexual behavior, on the one hand, and unforgivable homosexual selfhood, on the other.

Although Congressman Hinson's 1970s tearoom participation had flown under the public radar, Howard notes that Hinson nonetheless called a press conference in 1980 to confess his involvement in two "incidents . . . in areas frequented by some of Washington's homosexual community,"[42] one at the Iwo Jima Memorial (a popular gay cruising spot) and one in a gay porn theater—both outside the state of Mississippi. In Hinson's statements to the press, he pointedly disavowed homosexuality, describing himself as someone who had been in the wrong place at the wrong time and had succumbed to temptation. Hinson explained that he had made mistakes while suffering a "spiritual crisis," had sought the forgiveness of God and his wife, and had finally put the entire episode behind him. He stated plainly to reporters, "I am not, never have been, and never will be a homosexual. . . . I am not a bisexual."[43] Howard points out that more significant than whether or not Hinson himself would later identify as gay (which he did)[44] was the fact that otherwise homophobic white Mississippians stood behind him, allowing Hinson's anti-affirmative action track record and his "primary identification as a God-fearing Mississippian . . . [to] dismiss his potential queerness."[45] White conservatives rallied around Hinson and his wife, Cynthia, praising him for his capacity to turn his past sins, and his vulnerability to urban temptations, into an opportunity for a renewed commitment to God, family, and the state of Mississippi. As Hinson's former fifth-grade teacher put it, "I know he did that thing, but we all make mistakes. He was a little country boy who got up there and got into something he couldn't handle."[46] Enacting in a public forum what countless Mississippians did in church every Sunday, Hinson had confessed his sins, and repented.

Howard argues that the enthusiastic support for Hinson was possible because, even as late as the 1980s, the presumed links between homosexual behavior and gay identity were not fully established in Mississippi, or to the extent that they were, they could be undone with the overriding logic of sin and redemption. As Howard explains, Hinson's "audience did not necessarily conceptualize homosexuality as a state of being for a distinct, definable minority—or if they did, they cast homosexuality as elsewhere, as an other-worldly urban phenomenon."[47]

And yet, there was certainly a limit to how far Hinson's white supporters would go to forgive his homosexual transgressions, and Hinson crossed that line in 1981, when Washington, D.C., police arrested him for giving a blowjob to a black employee in an office restroom. The response from white Mississippians departed dramatically from their previous stance of forgiveness, with many calling for Hinson's resignation. Howard notes that this difference can be explained not only by the fact that Hinson's sins had been revealed to be matters of the present (and no longer sins of the past), but also by the particular details of the encounters themselves:

> The sex acts contrasted sharply. [In the first incident] former Marine reservist Hinson attempted to engage in penetrative oral sex. . . . He was an overworked, stressed-out young man looking for any receptacle for his pent-up desires. Such male profligacy was understood and often accepted in Mississippi. . . . [But in the second incident] Hinson's homosexuality was now undeniable. His gender nonconformity—his feminization and consequent degradation—complete. Not only was he [orally] penetrated. Not only was he the receptive partner in the sex act. He was [orally] penetrated by a black male, someone still viewed by many white Mississippians as his inferior—if not racially, then professionally and economically. Moreover, Hinson's cross-racial intercourse

discounted his conservative racial politics as it evoked the sixties cultural amalgamation of queer sexuality and African American equal rights.[48]

Hinson's loss of support following his "submission" to a black man and his relegation to the ranks of true homosexuals reveal the ways in which penetrative masculinity and white homosociality remained central alibis for white men engaged in sex with men in the 1980s. When imagined to have sought quick sexual release from a white gay man in an urban cruising locale (i.e., the first incident), Hinson was understood as having given in to an available temptation, signaling nothing permanent about his sexual constitution. But when it was discovered that Hinson, down on his knees, had fulfilled the sexual needs of a black man, he became unquestionably queer.

Since 2000, scandals in this vein appear to have proliferated, so much so that, according to sociologist Eve Shapiro, each new story "seems to bring a collective sigh among journalists, news anchors and cultural critics, as if to say, 'here we go again.'"[49] In some of these cases, like the "gay sex scandals" of politicians Mark Foley, Roy Ashburn, and James McGreevey, exposure has been the impetus for formerly straight-identified men to announce that, in fact, they *are* gay. In other cases, the men involved have responded to their exposure with repeated declarations that, in fact, they are absolutely *not gay*. For instance, in 2006, Christian mega-church pastor Ted Haggard was revealed to be in a sexual relationship with his male massage therapist, but after intensive counseling, Haggard was "cleared" by a bevy of Christian ministers, and by his wife, who all publically announced their certainty that he was now "completely heterosexual."[50] Similarly, in 2007, two Republican senators, Larry Craig and Bob Allen, were both arrested on charges related to sex with men in public bathrooms, but both men asserted that their bathroom behavior was simply misunderstood. Highlighting again the aforementioned links between white men's tearoom participation and their fear of black men (recall the police officer who warned Humphreys about "trouble with the niggers"), Bob Allen famously claimed he offered to give a black undercover police officer a blowjob because he feared that a threatening black man was trying to rob him.

Shapiro points out that what is noteworthy about the media's treatment of these scandals is the way that reporters and other commentators took for granted that these men's claims to heterosexuality were hypocritical, ludicrous, and tragic. By the mid-2000s, commentators could rely on the general public's agreement that any man who identifies as heterosexual, and who also has sexual encounters with men, must be lying to both himself and his family about who he really is. Such a view stands in contrast with earlier, more flexible and forgiving interpretations of sexuality documented by Chauncey, Humphreys, and Howard. Just a few decades earlier in American sexual history, these same scandalous encounters would likely have been understood differently, as momentary acts of deviance, as expressions of inexplicable eccentricity, and/or as mistakes that family and community members could agree to forget.

Into the Future: The Legacy of Normal Sexuality

This chapter has examined the features of white manhood that have rendered homosexuality "not gay" over the past century. Normative masculinity (that which is not effeminate), occupation of the penetrative role, working-class rebelliousness, middle-class respectability, and avoidance of cross-racial intimacy have been central among these features. And yet my point in offering these historical accounts has not been to tell an "old" story, but to provide vital background for what is very much a current story. These very same exceptionalizing logics are still in use today, regularly brought to bear as both experts and lay people attempt to make sense of straight men's seemingly incongruous encounters with homosexual sex. In the next chapter, I investigate contemporary

notions about the meaning of straight white men's sexual encounters with other men, and then move to a closer examination, in
chapters 4 and 5, of the ways in which white homosociality and
aggressive masculinity function to detach queer meaning from
the homosexuality of straight white men.

3

Here's How You Know You're Not Gay

The Popular Science of Heterosexual Fluidity

I F we are to believe contemporary sex commentators, the emergence of "the new heteroflexibility" is a sign of the times, a sign that points to the ever-increasing complexity of human sexuality in the twenty-first century. Sexual identities and erotic possibilities appear to be expanding exponentially not only for queers (as indicated by our swelling acronym, LGBTQQIAAP[1]), but also for heterosexuals, for whom identities like metrosexual and heteroflexible have gained some momentum. These terms describe the ostensibly new ways that heterosexuals can resemble lesbians and gay men—in their dress, their consumer habits, and their sex practices—without being "the real thing." As discussed in the previous chapter, the history of male sexual fluidity suggests that in actuality the lines between straight and gay (both as an affect and a set of sex practices) have always been blurry. Instead, what *is* new is the growing certainty that there is a "real thing," that a line can be drawn in the genetic or neurochemical sand between gay and straight.

The number of Americans who believe that sexual orientation is biologically determined has been steadily increasing, from 13 percent in 1977, to 31 percent in 1998, to 52 percent in 2010.[2] Much has been said about the political implications of the bioevolutionary science of sexual orientation, and in almost all of this commentary it is presumed that the biology/choice debate is of great significance for lesbians and gay men and largely irrelevant for heterosexuals. In this chapter I argue against this presumption, offering as evidence the centrality of a "born heterosexual" discourse within the popular and social-psychological justifications offered to explain straight men's sex with men. I argue that the story of heterosexuality in the twenty-first century is, in large part, a story about the hegemony of bio-evolutionary accounts of sexual desire. It is the story of heterosexuals who believe that they know who they really are, and what they can and cannot change about their nature. And, as such, it is also a story about the capacity of heterosexuals to pretend, to explore, to mess around and mess up, to be fluid and flexible—and then to return home to their presumed essence.

For many if not most gays and left-leaning heterosexuals, being "born this way," to quote Lady Gaga's 2011 gay-acceptance anthem, has become synonymous with gay rights, and with the project of sexual self-acceptance more broadly. This has not always been so. During the gay liberation era of the 1970s, gay activists in the United States, informed by a broad array of New Left movements, emphasized in their campaign literature that mutable differences such as religious beliefs and sexual orientation deserve political protection. However, as the religious right ramped up its attempts to repair homosexuals via violent conversion therapies, gay and lesbian activists revised their position. By the 1990s, a consensus was built among gay activists that homosexuality, like race and sex, is congenital and unchangeable.[3]

Tellingly, leaders of the lesbian and gay movement have been transparent about the strategic necessity of this position as a mode of gay self-defense. In 2011, the Human Rights Campaign, arguably the most powerful lesbian and gay organization in the United States, issued the following statement to its members: "Being gay is not a choice! . . . Implying that homosexuality is a choice gives unwarranted credence to roundly disproven practices such as 'conversion' or 'reparative' therapy."[4] Such statements infuse biological accounts with an obligatory and nearly coercive force, suggesting that anyone who describes homosexual desire as a choice or social construction is playing into the hands of the enemy. In 2012, the extent to which gay biology had become a moral and political imperative came into full view when actress Cynthia Nixon, after commenting to a *New York Times Magazine* reporter that she "chose" to pursue a lesbian relationship after many years as a content heterosexual, was met with outrage by lesbian and gay activists. As one horrified gay male writer proclaimed, "[Nixon] just fell into a right-wing trap, willingly. . . . Every religious right hatemonger is now going to quote this woman every single time they want to deny us our civil rights."[5] Under considerable pressure from lesbian and gay advocacy groups, Nixon revised her statement a few weeks later, stating instead that she must have been born with bisexual potential. Attempting to remain at least partially true to her original position, Nixon clarified that because she had the capacity to be attracted to both men and women, to be with a woman was, in some way, a choice.[6]

The controversy over Nixon's comments makes clear that the lesbian and gay movement has largely succeeded in linking gay pride and gay rights with adherence to sociobiological narratives, and conversely, and perhaps unintentionally, it has also succeeded in equating more fluid and/or queer accounts of sexual desire with homophobia and collusion with the religious right. As Rebecca Jordan-Young contends in the groundbreaking book *Brain Storm: The Flaws in the Science of Sex Differences*, to be critical of the notion that gay brains are "wired differently" from heterosexual brains (and male brains from female brains) is to be "cast as not only antiscience, but anitidiversity. . . . Once politically suspect, it is now often suggested that accepting these innate differences will encourage a more rational approach to equality."[7] And yet, in many of these debates, proponents of the "born this way" hypothesis suggest that it matters less what might be *true* about the constitution of sexual desire than what the political consequences of our speech might be. Many lesbian and gay activists, including the one quoted above, seemed to chide Nixon not for her belief about herself, but her willingness to tell the American public that sexual desire is fluid and that sexual orientations can change.

This is the cultural and political backdrop in which heterosexuals, too, are learning what to think and say about sexual fluidity. The many thousands of heterosexuals who followed the media firestorm over Nixon's comments learned, if they did not already know, that it is politically incorrect to think a gay person can change, and by extension, it is offensive to think a straight person who becomes gay- or lesbian-identified later in life was anything but unknowingly gay or bisexual in the first place. More to the point of this book, the science of sexual orientation also offers reassurances to those whose sexual behavior is "discordant" with their sexual identification. The logic of innate sexual orientation suggests that we can temporarily experiment, act out, or otherwise venture outside of ourselves. As Eve Kosofsky Sedgwick has argued, it is not only gay-identified men who are kept fearful of homophobic violence; at a much broader level, the very maintenance of the sexual binary is kept intact by keeping *all* men uncomfortably uncertain about the line between homosexual and heterosexual.[8] Here my aim is to trace the ways that biological accounts of sexual orientation—as the foundation of theories of sexual fluidity generally, and "situational homosexuality" specifically—work towards a resolution of this uncomfortable uncertainty.

Were You Born This Way? The Neuroscience of Sexual Orientation

This chapter offers a critical reading of popular and social-psychological explanations for the homosexual behavior of heterosexuals, and as such, it is beyond the scope of the chapter—or this book—to offer a thorough review and critique of brain organization studies as they relate to sexual orientation. That has been the project of feminist science and technology scholars such as Anne Fausto-Sterling, Cordelia Fine, and Rebecca Jordan-Young.[9] And yet, I *do* wish to argue that the ever-widening circulation of the "scientific news" that we are born with a core sexual orientation has produced an equally growing demand for accessible ways of conceptualizing what this means in everyday life, or what it means for the complex reality of people's sexual practices, desires, and identifications. With this aim, I begin by briefly introducing the basic premises of brain organization research here, as well as summarize Fausto-Sterling's and Jordan-Young's critiques. I rehearse this debate in order to draw attention to the ways that the gaps and contradictions in the science of sexual orientation produce trouble for average people—for those of us, like me, who are not neuroscientists—as we attempt to imagine our own gay or straight hardwiring, where it might live in our bodies, and how we might uncover it. What possibilities are we offered for personalizing or integrating the scientific evidence? What strategies do these scientists and their proponents offer us for translating this dense body of brain research into a set of simple ideas that can make sense—or not—of our sexual encounters?

At its foundation, most brain organization research begins with the presumption of an essential gender binary in which masculinizing and feminizing hormones produce masculine and feminine bodies and behaviors, including the masculine impulse to penetrate females and the feminine impulse to be penetrated, presumably by males.[10] According to this logic, high exposure to masculinizing hormones produces male-type sexual behaviors in women, including attraction to women; conversely, low exposure to masculinizing hormones produces female-type sexual behaviors in men, including attraction to men. Let's take one widely cited example of a study in this vein. In 2000, a team of researchers at the University of California, Berkeley, conducted a study in which they found that lesbians were more likely than heterosexual women to have a "masculine" hand structure.[11] According to the study, men have a longer ring finger (fourth finger) than index finger (second finger), whereas most women have the opposite or have index and ring fingers of approximately the same length. Lesbians, according to the study, are more likely than heterosexual women to have male-type hands, supporting the researchers' theory that lesbianism might be caused by a "fetal androgyn wash" in the womb, or an elevated release of androgyn to the brain before birth. That is, when female fetuses are exposed to greater levels of a masculinizing hormone, it shows up as various forms of female masculinity, such as male-typed hands and . . . attraction to women.

The study exemplifies the tendency to conflate gendered embodiment (hormonally produced signs of what we call "maleness" and "femaleness") with an array of factors that may be connected to, but are certainly not determined by, whether one has a masculine or feminine body. It goes without saying that many lesbians are quite normatively feminine, and many gay men normatively masculine. I must count myself among those whose queer desires cannot be substantiated by the research on lesbian fingers; I regret to report that I have but only normatively female hands to show for myself. I suppose researchers might point out that I am femme, and yet we would be left without an account for my homosexuality. The point here is that research on sexual orientation—itself a concept dependent upon the gender binary—begins from the heteronormative premise that masculine people (or men) are naturally attracted to femaleness and that normal (i.e., feminine) women are naturally attracted to men. It is through hormonal excess or deficiency that homosexual desire results.

But an even greater problem with the science of sexual orientation is that it seeks to identify the biological origins of gayness (and, by extension, straightness), as if we all agree about the meaning of these terms. To insist that one is born heterosexual or homosexual is to engage in science that hinges on a very historically recent and specifically European-American understanding of what being gay means. Is anyone who has ever experienced same-sex desire gay? What do we mean by desire? If one needs to act on such desires, how many times does one need to do so? How much do the circumstances or cultural contexts matter? Is the story different for women and men? Do the brains, hands, and other body parts of people who identify as bisexual, or of people who decide they are gay later in life, look like those of heterosexuals or homosexuals or some kind of hybrid? Do self-identification and political affiliation matter, or do only the body and its expert interpreters hold the truth about who we are? As Rebecca Jordan-Young illustrates, these are precisely the basic questions that have plagued the burgeoning field of "sexed brain" research, resulting in three primary measurement errors: overly simplistic and contradictory definitions of sexual orientation, which are often rooted in early studies of animal behavior and extrapolated to human sexuality; inconsistencies in the way homosexuality and heterosexuality are measured in men versus women; and lack of consensus about how frequently, or to what degree, one must be "homosexual" (in acts, thoughts, and desires) in order to qualify as homosexual for scientific purposes.

Another alarming trend in the science of sexual orientation, one especially relevant to questions of fluidity and flexibility, is to conduct research that measures genital arousal patterns. While perhaps not the intention of researchers, such studies have a "gotcha!" effect by pointing to discrepancies between who/what the research participants report to desire and to whom or what their genitals measurably respond. As you may have guessed, genital response is interpreted in this research to be true, or at least more true, than participants' self-reports. In a 2005 *New York Times* article titled "Straight, Gay, or Lying?: Bisexuality Revisited," reporter Benedict Carey cites a study in which men who identify as bisexual were shown images of both men and women by a team of psychologists. As if confirming the enduring stereotype that bisexual men are either "gay, straight or lying" (while women, as other studies suggest, are innately bisexual), the researchers found that nearly all of the men "were in fact exclusively aroused by either one sex or the other, usually by other men."[12] The article emphasizes the rigidity of male desire, missing entirely the opportunity to consider that arousal may take multiple forms, some of which are not genital, and that genitals may not be the ultimate barometer of people's desires nor the final authority on people's sexual subjectivity.

In addition to all of these concerns, and despite the fact that a growing majority of Americans believe sexual orientation to be innate and are now inclined to allude to scientific evidence to support this claim, there is no definitive and accessible test that you or I can take—at the local clinic, let's say—to determine whether we are authentic, hardwired heterosexuals, homosexuals, or bisexuals.[13] Instead, most people invoke the *idea* of this research, rather than, say, displaying their lesbian fingers as evidence. In other words, sexual orientation research has the power to affirm us, but only in the abstract. It encourages us to imagine the telltale signs of our sexual essence, signs buried in our bodies, or perhaps, if we are "lucky," legible on our hands or in our genital response. We might imagine being research subjects, placed under the microscope, so to speak, and then shown the evidence of our gay or straight or bisexual hardwiring—our gay brains, our normative (i.e., heterosexual) hormonal constitution, or, in the case of bisexuals, our balanced genital response to both women and men—which would ostensibly affirm and substantiate who we already believe ourselves to be. But the truth is that the vast majority of us will never acquire any of this evidence.

Presumably, most of us feel no need to seek out the biological evidence of our individual sexual constitution because we suspect the evidence would be in alignment with our sexual practices and identification. But what about those whose sexual practices blur the lines between gay and straight, and cannot be captured by the term "bisexual"? What about the straight-identified men who are the subjects of this book—men who prefer to be partnered with women, who are typically repulsed by the idea of a gay life, who feel no connection to gay or bisexual culture, and who, in various ways and for a variety of reasons, have sexual encounters with men? The possibility of substantiating one's heterosexual constitution has especially high stakes for straight men who want very deeply to know that they are congenital heterosexuals but find themselves concerned about what their homosexual encounters and/or desires might be signaling about their nature. These men's wives, girlfriends, and parents—when they suspect their partner or son of homosexual activity—also want some concrete answers. Gay? Bisexual? Straight? Heteroflexible? Fauxmosexual? Metrosexual? Telling the truth or lying? The demand to know seems increasingly reasonable in light of the scientific evidence that sexual orientation is fixed, and yet, given the proliferation of sexual possibilities, and the inaccessibility of neuroimaging or other means of viewing inside one's possibly homosexual body, how is one to really *know*? If only they sold gay tests at the drugstore!

In lieu of accessible screenings for sexual orientation, a growing field of expert psychologists, sociologists, sexologists, journalists, bloggers, and other lay people have developed tools that translate the elusive biology of sexual orientation into a series of diagnostic tools and social-psychological litmus tests used to distinguish the authentic, congenital homosexual from the merely fluid, or situationally constrained, heterosexual. These experts and commentators elaborate the seemingly countless circumstances, affective states, material needs, and cultural constructs that lead authentic heterosexuals to engage in homosexual sex. And, as I will show, they do the complex work of demonstrating that even the fluidity and unpredictability of sexuality stands as evidence of a natural heterosexual/homosexual binary anchored in immutable biology.

Beaches and Skyscrapers: The Diagnostic Imagination

As we move into the world of expert knowledge about the myriad reasons that heterosexuals might act out of accordance with their sexual natures, allow me to set the scene by introducing a frequently cited American commentator on the subject of straight men's homosexual desires. Joe Kort is a white gay psychologist and creator of the website straightguise.com,[14] a site dedicated to reassuring straight men who have sex with men that they are, as Kort declares repeatedly on the site, *not* gay. Kort, who is the author of self-help books for gay men such as *10 Smart Things Gay Men Can Do to Find Real Love*, has built a successful business offering webinars and teleconference workshops concerned primarily with men's sexuality and relationships—and with a focus on male sexual fluidity. Drawing on his experience counseling "thousands of sexually confused men" and their concerned wives, Kort believes that there are many reasons why straight men may have sex with men, none of which are about homosexuality. As he outlines on straightguise.com,[15] straight men have sex with men to work through early childhood sexual abuse; to make money; to experience sex acts presumably too kinky for most women's tastes (some of Kort's examples are anal sex, sex with dildos, and bondage); to satisfy youthful curiosity; to have a first sexual experience; to gain access to quick and emotionless sex; to fulfill a craving for fatherly attention; to be "worshipped and adored" by men; or to enable a sex addiction. Some straight men also have sex with men because they are exhibitionists or cuckolds;[16] others, because they are in prison or the military, and their need for sexual release requires that they turn to other men for satisfaction.

When faced with the apparent contradiction of straight men having sex with men, Kort's authoritative, no-nonsense approach helps to make practical sense of the confusion. Theories such as Kort's gained a remarkable level of mainstream media visibility in the mid-2000s, helping to shape the way that Americans would conceptualize sexual orientation. Kort has been quoted by MSNBC, the *New York Times*, the *Village Voice*, and other media outlets on subjects such as "Brokeback marriages,"[17] wives who find their husbands' stash of gay porn,[18] and the 2007 spate of sex scandals involving heterosexual politicians engaged in covert homosexual sex.[19] In interviews and on his website, Kort not only reassures men, their wives, and the general public that heterosexuality is a far more resilient condition than we might think it is, but he also clarifies the broader nature of sexual orientation along the way. "Straight men cannot become gay and gay men cannot become straight," he explains in a section of straightguise titled "It's Not a Gay Thing, It's a Guy Thing!" Having sex with men is as much a guy thing, to use Kort's parlance, as other late-modern male sexual imperfections like erectile dysfunction, premature ejaculation, or decreased libido brought on by aging. Yet unlike these sex problems, which can now be treated with a panoply of prescription medications, the desire for sex with men requires no treatment beyond simply understanding what it is, and what it is not.

For Kort, who is an avid reader of social science literature on gender and sexuality, the answer lies in the distinction among sexual identity, desire, and behavior. Sexual identity, he believes, is our solid and unchanging sexual foundation: "It's the alignment of affectional, romantic, psychological, spiritual, and sexual feelings and desires for those of the same or opposite gender. [It] doesn't change over time."[20] Following the consensus among research psychologists and others who conduct brain organization studies, Kort contends that we may experiment with different desires and behaviors, but our sexual identity, which psychologists often refer to as "sexual status," remains stable. Kort explains: "The reality is that from the start these straight men who have sex with men are not gay, and now we have research to prove it. . . . Orientation is innate." But in the absence of hard scientific proof about his individual clients, the aim of Kort's work is to help them determine whether their identity is (and has always been) heterosexual by using by using proxy measures, and if it is so determined, to help them recognize that this biological fact remains true despite any behavioral evidence to the contrary. Once men can stop worrying about being gay, they can address whatever other memories, desires, or feelings might be motivating their homosexual impulses. For instance, one of Kort's clients might eventually be able to say: "I see now that I'm not *gay*; I just want to occasionally be penetrated by a man who reminds me of my father."

How precisely does Joe Kort, or any other clinical practitioner, help men who have sex with men determine whether they are repressing their core gay essence or simply "acting out"? During an interview with Kort, I asked him this question:

> **Joe Kort:** It's not academic, but I call it the beach test. If you're sitting around on a beach, and you are distracted by images of men or women, who are you distracted by? Straight guys aren't interested in the bodies of other men. They'll say, "I'm interested in women. I'm all about women." But gay guys look at guys' faces, bodies, et cetera. Straight guys, they may have a penis fetish, or maybe they're into giving blow jobs . . . but it's not about the *entire* man.
>
> **JW:** So, if a client is truly straight, in your determination, does that mean he can have any amount of gay sex and still be straight? Like maybe even more gay sex than some of my gay friends?
>
> **Joe Kort:** Yes. You can have a straight person who has more gay sex than a gay person, because it's not the sex that determines the orientation. For gay people, it's about spirituality, psychology, emotionality, romance, and it includes sex.

For Kort, homosexual orientation is genetic in origin, and manifests in adults as a same-gender spiritual, psychological, emotional, romantic, and sexual gestalt. From this perspective, all or most of these elements must be in place in order to signal authentic, congenital homosexuality, and sex practices are perhaps the least important indicators of homosexual orientation. What Kort's "beach test" seems to be is an attempt at measuring the compartmentalization of homosexual activities and desires. Instead of emphasizing their quantity, as the Kinsey scale does, for instance, Kort draws our attention to the reach of homosexual impulses. Do they shape how one thinks, feels, and loves, or are they restricted to particular circumstances and discrete activities?

Kort's "beach test" may seem simplistic and arbitrary, but it mirrors other more scholarly but equally imaginative attempts to capture the difference between being sincerely gay or straight, on the one hand, and participating in a circumstantially homosexual or heterosexual act, on the other. In the 1980s, the famous sexologist John Money described another kind of test, one he termed "The Skyscraper Test." In Money's "test," which is more a parable about the immutability of sexual orientation than a test that could ever be administered in reality, a gay man stands atop the Empire State Building and is pushed to its edge by a heterosexual woman who is a "crazed sex terrorist." She demands that the gay man "perform oral sex with her," which he considers in order to save his life. According to Money, if the gay man agrees to the straight woman's demands, "he would have performed a heterosexual act, but he would not have changed to have a heterosexual status."[21] In both Kort and Money's accounts, sexual orientation does not preclude discordant behaviors, as long as such behaviors are compartmentalized and circumstantial.

Gay/straight diagnostic tests have their corollaries in popular culture, though rarely if ever do these versions acknowledge, as Kort does, the possibility that homosexual sex might be a circumstantial part of heterosexual men's lives. Dozens of "Is Your Boyfriend or Husband Gay?" quizzes can be found on the Internet, most of which ask women respondents questions about how their male partners feel about shopping and fashion, what kind of music they listen to, which films and TV programs they enjoy, whether they have gay male friends, and whether they are ever attracted to or have ever kissed men.[22] Some quizzes offer respondents an additional assessment tool in the form of pie charts comparing their answers to those of other respondents, presumably to establish a benchmark for normal straight boyfriend/husband behavior.

While the "Is Your Boyfriend Gay?" tests typically rely on time-worn assumptions about the link between gay male desire and female-typical interests, such as shopping and enjoyment of "chick films," tests designed for parents concerned about whether their sons might be gay add psychoanalytic considerations to their formula. For instance, in 2011, French developers introduced a downloadable Android app, in both French and English, called "Is My Son Gay?" The app, reportedly intended by its developers to be "humorous," asked parents a series of twenty questions, including several not-so-humorous inquiries such as: "Before he was born did you wish he would be a girl?"; "Are you divorced?" and "Is his father absent?"; "Is his father authoritarian?"; "Is his father close to him?"[23]

In many ways, the content of the "gay boyfriend" and "gay son" tests—that is, their presumption of a correlation between gender non-normativity, family trauma, and homosexuality—exemplifies an older sexual order, one that has seemingly little to do with current discourses on heteroflexibility, metrosexuality, and the significance of homo/hetero hardwiring. And yet, the viral popularity of these tools—in the form of smartphone apps and Facebook and Twitter "shares"—tells a late modern story, one in which the diagnosis of sexual orientation is no longer the sole purview of psychoanalysts and other mental health professionals, but also a form of do-it-yourself sexology to be taken up by curious or concerned wives, girlfriends, and parents. Arguably, hetero/homo diagnostic tests for husbands and sons have appeal precisely due to a consensus that men's sexual orientations are not obvious—an idea that has only recently found its way into the popular imagination. These tests, like Kort's and Money's, rely on the basic premises at the heart of the diagnostic imagination: (1) Male sexual orientation is hardwired; *but* (2) men's true sexual orientation may be masked by circumstantial factors; *however* (3) the truth can be gleaned with the right set of diagnostic tools.

Kort and Money, along with other inventors of hetero/homo diagnostic tools, are arguably working to clarify, albeit unintentionally, what academic theories of sexuality have left abstract. According to the constructionist approach that dominates queer scholarship, homosexuality and heterosexuality are not essential aspects of the self (biological or otherwise), but culturally and historically specific classifications used to explain and regulate sexuality and to produce docile sexual subjects.[24] Though constructionism provides us with a crucial understanding of the historical, economic, racialized and culturally embedded production of sexual difference,[25] it tells us remarkably little about why, within a given time and place, some people who engage in same-sex sexual practices can and do think of themselves as homosexuals (or bisexuals, or generally queer/different), while others can and do think of themselves as heterosexuals (or normal).

The diagnostic imagination, in contrast, aims to elaborate all of the conceivable circumstances in which men might, out of necessity or by accident or as a feature of homosocial bonding (in the case of straight men engaged in homosexuality) or as an adaptation to homophobia (in the case of gay men engaged in heterosexuality), act out of accordance with their true sexual natures.[26] It encourages us to understand that some homosexual encounters, like straight guys jacking off other straight guys, are a temporary and developmental part of young men's lives, or a means of learning about one's body on the path to adult heterosexuality. It also urges us to consider an array of intricate "what if" scenarios, situations in which homosexual sex could be a temporary solution to a situational problem: What if a straight man was in prison and no women were available? What if a straight man really needed money and someone would pay him to have sex with men? What if a hot woman would have sex with him if he had sex with another man first? What if his superior officer told him that he *must* do it? What if his fraternity brothers *made* him do it? What if a crazed sex terrorist threatened to kill him if he didn't do it? And the list goes on. Mirroring the explosive popularity of "Would You Rather . . . ?" books and games in the United States in the late 1990s, as well as reality game shows in which participants are pushed to their outer limits (by eating foods they find repulsive, for example), the diagnostic imagination plays to a contemporary fascination with the ways that people can and do break from their patterns, and even break from their presumed essences, under extreme or unusual circumstances. Its lesson is that people can and do stray away from their core sexual orientation, precisely because it feels more plausible than ever—in light of the evidence of sexual hardwiring—that doing so may be a wild ride, but it poses no risk to our basic natures.

Three Very Special Reasons That Straight Men Have Sex with Men

The rest of this chapter takes a close look at the three broad explanatory theories most frequently cited by social scientists and mental health practitioners to explain straight men's "discordant" homosexual encounters. My hope is to use these examples to demonstrate that such frameworks do not simply describe sexual behavior as it has been observed by social scientists. Instead, as these ideas about heterosexuality "trickle down" and circulate through popular culture, they also *shape* heterosexual behavior, becoming rhetorical resources or "sexual scripts" used to recuperate heterosexuality when it has been rendered suspect by homosexual contact.[27] At the individual level, these three scripts and their performances—the performances of necessary, homosocial, and accidental homosexuality—assist heterosexual men in repudiating any queer meanings that might be assigned to their sex practices, as well as assist in circumventing gay stigma. At the cultural and political levels, their circulation exceptionalizes heterosexuality as the domain of untouchable, inconsequential same-sex desire. This also has the effect of preserving queer sexualities as those in need of state regulation and moral intervention. The three scripts I describe here are not discreet but overlapping; they offer heterosexual men a range of complementary rhetorical devices that produce and authenticate male heterosexual subjectivity.

I also introduce the concept of *hetero-exceptionalism* here to refer to systematic efforts to protect and justify the homosexual behavior of heterosexuals. Hetero-exceptionalizing discourse frames some same-sex desires, namely those possessed by people committed to heterosexual normalcy, as exceptions to the general rule that homosexuality is punishable by law, social stigma, and/ or isolation. It supports, and is supported by, heteronormativity in that it expands the range of behaviors permissible within normative heterosexuality, while sustaining an underclass of queer outsiders subject to violence and discrimination. I return to these considerations, and how we might more adequately conceptualize the homosexuality of heterosexuals, at the end of this chapter.

Fuck or Die: The Performance of Necessary Homosexuality

The claim that homosexuality is occasionally necessary for heterosexual men is a dominant theme in psychological and sociological research, especially research on prisons and the military. In this body of work, men are reported to "engage in homosexual behavior only when [they have] no opportunity for heterosexual intercourse."[28] In 1950s sexology this behavior is referred to as "situational homosexuality," but also occasionally described by psychologists as "deprivational," "facultative," "functional," and "opportunistic."[29] As gay porn scholar Jeffrey Escoffier has argued, mid-twentieth-century research on situational homosexuality aimed to distinguish "the homosexual role" (i.e., authentic gay identity) from the situations that would compel non-gay-identified men to engage in homosexual behavior.[30] In line with sexological presumptions of the era, the situational nature of this behavior was believed to hinge on its temporal and spatial isolation to prison cells and military barracks where women were presumably inaccessible, and where the hydraulic force of male sexuality required release by whatever means necessary.

In his analysis of gay-for-pay porn performers, Escoffier builds on the work of historian Regina Kunzel and other sexuality scholars to "resuscitate" the concept of situational homosexuality. Kunzel and Escoffier aim to preserve the term's original focus on social context and non-identitarian homosexual behavior, but to replace the emphasis on male libido with attention to the evolving ways that particular settings permit or invite homosexual behavior while limiting access to heterosexual sex. For Escoffier, this reformulation allows for an expanded analysis of all non-identitarian homosexual behaviors, which have in common the feature of being "strongly conditioned by *situational constraints* whether physical (prisons and jails, ships at sea, barracks, men's restrooms), economic (porn actors, hustlers, homeless youth), cultural (immigrants) or social-structural (married men, adolescents)."[31]

Here Escoffier sheds some of the essentialist baggage that burdened earlier work on situational homosexuality. However, his attempt to broaden the term's reach also reveals the extent to which themes of heterosexual constraint and deprivation continue to dominate most thought about straight men's homosexual behavior. Once reserved for contexts in which heterosexual sex was not available or possible, constrained heterosexuality is extended in Escoffier's formulation to men's restrooms and even to heterosexual marriage itself. Situations we might call "constrained," like being on a ship at sea without access to one's preferred sexual object, and situations that are perhaps better understood as "opportunistic" (to use yet another dated term), like discovering a glory hole in the men's restroom, are largely collapsed here.

The characterization of all non-gay homosexual encounters as situational risks the suggestion that the homosexual behavior of heterosexuals is more circumstantial and rule-bound, and less identity-constituting, than the sexual behavior of gay men and lesbians (or heterosexuals who are not engaged in homosexual sex). A closer look at the elements that shape human sex practices—desire, opportunity, material/financial need, intimacy, scarcity, production and performance of selfhood/identity, etc.—reveals a far less dichotomous line between straight and gay motivations for homosexual (or heterosexual) sex. For instance, when heterosexual men invoke hetero-masculine scripts to account for their homosexual sex—male bonding, fraternal belonging, physical resilience, insatiable desire, and so forth—they, too, are engaged in identitarian sex; they are engaged in the production of heterosexual masculinity. Moreover, although institutions like prisons and boarding schools provide men with ready-made hetero-masculine scripts that make meaning of temporary homosexuality,[32] similar scripts exist outside of these institutional contexts. Creative and hetero-exceptionalizing scripts are imagined, reimagined, and put to noninstitutional uses in bars and bathrooms and living rooms and all other non-constrained (or less constrained) places where straight men choose to have sex with men. These less constrained environments are the subject of the next chapter.

Most importantly, research on situational homosexuality has largely missed the opportunity to distinguish between material constraint, on the one hand, and the performance of constraint and necessity, on the other. By performance, I am referring here to the *staging* of situations in which straight men ostensibly have little choice but to engage in homosexual encounters. This scripting of necessity is particularly salient for straight men who are unhindered by institutional isolation or heterosexual deprivation and who, nonetheless, seek male sexual partners. The idea—indeed, the fantasy—that same-sex encounters *must* occur in order to achieve a safe, normal, heterosexual end is prevalent within fiction, mainstream pornography, mixed-gender environments such as college campuses, and hetero-erotic discourse more generally.

The script of homosexual necessity dictates that straight men must sometimes endure sexual contact with other men in order to avoid death or violence, to prove their masculinity, to preserve their future access to women, and, ironically, to inoculate themselves against sincere, authentic gayness.

One way to begin thinking about the trope of necessary homosexuality is to examine how it manifests in the erotic imagination of slash fanfiction writers,[33] whose work is aimed at inventing plausible (or, as they call it, "canonical") reasons that heterosexual characters must engage in homosexual sex. Among the most longstanding plot devices used for this purpose is a trope called "fuck or die," in which two heterosexual male characters are forced by some unusual circumstance to have sex with each other in order to save their own lives. The trope dates back to the paradigmatic Kirk/Spock pairing from the 1970s television show *Star Trek*, in which Spock enters "pon farr," the eight-day mating period during which Vulcans must have sex or they will die from a neurochemical imbalance. Countless slash writers, working within *Star Trek*'s original description of pon farr, have used the concept to produce scenarios in which Spock—often stranded on a deserted planet with only Kirk, McCoy, or some other male character—enters pon farr and is forced to have homosexual sex to avoid death.

"Fuck or die" also appears in sexological research as a heuristic and diagnostic tool that is premised on the idea that all people are capable of acting out of accordance with their core sexual orientation should a desperate situation demand it of them. Recall Money's sex-crazed terrorist and the gay man who submits to her in order to save his life. Although death is clearly an extreme consequence that rarely appears outside of fiction and fantasy, "fuck or die" remains a useful metaphor for situations in which homosexual urgency is manufactured by heterosexual men and becomes an alibi for homosexual contact. Consider the following snapshots from contemporary heterosexual pornography. In the growing and popular genre of "cuckold" films, such as the series

Cum-Eating Cuckolds, a straight (and typically white) man discovers that his wife or girlfriend is cheating on him with a stronger, sexually powerful (and typically black) male rival. Feeling emasculated and undeserving of his female partner, the (white) man watches her have sex with his rival and is told that he must submit to both of them in order to keep his wife, ultimately by ingesting the other man's cum from his wife's vagina.[34]

This scenario is, of course, a pornographic fantasy, one in which white fear of black men lends credibility to the trope of homosexual necessity. However, the notion that white men must sometimes engage in cross-racial homosexual sex in the name of self-preservation is not without its counterpart in the narratives of real-life straight white men. For instance, in 2007, when white Republican Representative Bob Allen was arrested for offering a blowjob to a black undercover officer, he explained that he did so because he feared black men: "This [undercover officer] is a pretty stocky black guy, and there's other black guys around in the park that—you know!"[35] Allen appealed to the white male officers who arrested him with what he imagined was his strongest alibi: He needed to perform oral sex to save himself from what he must have believed was the widely recognized threat of black male violence.

Another example of presumably necessary intimate contact between men can be seen in *Shane's World: College Invasion*, the immensely popular series of college reality porn to which *Rolling Stone* has referred as "the new sex ed." In the *College Invasion* films, professional female porn stars arrive at college fraternity parties and refuse to have sex until the young male students, the "frat boys," have engaged in a series of feminizing and sexually intimate humiliation rituals with one another. Here, necessity is marked not by racial fear or threat of violence, but by the apparently undeniable need for sex with particularly desirable women. In *Shane's World*, frat boys strip naked, put on pink bras and panties, "bob for tampons," scream their assessments of their friend's penises (such as the chant "Big fuckin' donkey dick! Big fuckin' donkey dick!" that appears in *SW College Invasion*, episode 6), and stand side by side while receiving blowjobs (from the female porn stars), surrounded by a circle of male friends watching and cheering them on. According to feminist writer and adult film producer Tristan Taormino, similar instances of sexual contact between men in heterosexual pornography, such as the "double header," circumvent queer meaning, given their location within heterosexual sex.[36] As Taormino explains, the anatomy of the double header—in which two men penetrate one woman's vagina or anus, lubing up together, inserting together, thrusting together closely, rubbing their penises together, and ejaculating together—raises questions about which form of stimulation (the friction of two penises, or the friction of penis and vagina) results in the climax shown on film. In each case, the conceit in these films is that heterosexual men will "endure" a significant degree of sexual contact with other men as a matter of necessity, a sacrifice worth making to access sex with women.

Though such scenarios presume a degree of necessity, they are of course fictions manufactured by and for heterosexual men. The producers of *College Invasion* might just as well have cut to the sex between female porn stars and frat boys and bypassed the homoerotic contests and rituals. But this is not what happens, and there is evidence to suggest that the pairing of homoerotic humiliation with heterosexual sex is precisely what constitutes the sense of "reality" in these films. Sociologist Michael Kimmel's account of fraternity hazing rituals in his book *Guyland* suggests that *College Invasion* might be stopping short of revealing the full extent of sexual contact that takes place in fraternities, especially during initiation. Participation in fraternity hazing rituals, such as the elephant walk—wherein nude boys are required to walk in a circle, linked thumb-to-anus—is given credibility by the presumption of necessity. The hetero-masculine peer pressure is presumably too great to resist, the desire for male recognition and belonging, too profound to deny. In another example, in the "soggy biscuit" (or "ookie cookie") game, reported to be popular in schools in the United Kingdom and Australia, several male participants must quickly ejaculate on a cookie and the last to do so, the "loser," must consume it. Internet commentary about the game suggests a consensus among straight boys and men that the soggy biscuit, like the elephant walk, is "disgusting." Nonetheless, boys feel compelled to participate.

Regardless of the actual frequency with which such games occur in fraternities or elsewhere,[37] they are part of an evolving cultural narrative that elaborates the numerous circumstances in which heterosexual boys and young men may be called upon to penetrate one another (with fingers, penises, or objects) or to swallow each other's ejaculate. Given the youth of participants and their locatedness within educational institutions, empirical evidence of these rituals is somewhat limited (though see testimonials and photographic evidence in chapter 1). Far better documented is the ritualized deployment of homosexuality in military initiation and training. Numerous court records, investigative reports, and studies of the culture of the Navy, Coast Guard, and Air Force describe young American soldiers and military contractors urinating on one another, simulating anal sex and analingus, eating and drinking from each other's anuses, and inserting objects into anuses—acts committed in the name of toughness, unity, and boredom.[38] In chapter 5 I examine these practices in depth, with particular attention to the ways they are "necessitated" by masculine strength-building, national security, and, paradoxically, straight men's inoculation against real/sincere gayness.

What do all of these sex practices reveal about straight men's lives? Sociologists have offered them up as examples of the degrading, "gross and stupid" lengths that young white men will go in order to feel validated, powerful, and part of the male tribe.[39] Other scholars interested in the violent quality and institutional embeddedness of these encounters argue that they are better understood on a continuum of sexual assault behaviors sanctioned by male-dominated institutions.[40] And yet a third approach, and the one I emphasize in this book, is to consider their erotic underpinnings, or to pay attention to the creative ways straight men find to touch each other's bodies while working within the constraints of heteromasculinity, itself a construction arguably inseparable from dominance, violence, and grossness.[41] While I do not wish to diminish the problem of sexual assault between men, or situations in which straight men have sex with men out of true economic necessity, these situations may well account for only a small component of the full range of straight men's homosexual encounters.

The long history of straight men's sex with men, and the varied places where it occurs and the varied forms it takes, requires an expansive view, one that illuminates the all-too-often ignored probability that straight men, as a rule, want to have sex with men. *And* they want to live heterosexual lives. To make this same suggestion about women—"straight women want to have sex with women, but they want to live heterosexual lives"—has little impact these days. And yet, the myopia that clouds current understanding of male sexuality, and the hetero-exceptionalism that sets straight men's homosexuality apart from the presumably more consequential and subjectifying homosexual sex of gay men, has all but foreclosed this possibility.

The script of necessity is one way, and I believed the primary way, that heterosexual men negotiate the conflict between their heterosexuality and their desire for sexual encounters with men. They invent scenarios in which men must engage in homosexual sex in exchange for safety, access to women, or acceptance and belonging in heterosexual male groups. Necessity—in the form of self-preservation or a call to duty (as in the military)—is a construct with significant hetero-masculine currency. Far more multifaceted than narratives of situational constraint or deprivation would suggest, necessity involves the complex intersection of desire for sex with men, real and imagined external pressure, and the blurry line between the sexual, the violent, and the abject within hetero-masculinity.

The Bonds of Men: The Performance of Homosocial Homosexuality

Unlike the extreme and often desperate situations evoked by the trope of homosexual necessity, the trope of homosociality is casual and friendly, but also intimate. It too has become a primary rhetorical resource used by men to secure heterosexuality while engaged in homosexual sex, one organized around the belief that hand jobs are sometimes a "less gay" way to be close to men than the more intimate and feminized realm of friendship. Homosocial homosexualities have long been cast in developmental terms as a phase, a course of experimentation, a misdirected need for intimacy with other boys and young men, and a period of "acting out." The argument that homosexual experimentation is a natural part of adolescent male heterosexual development has a long history within developmental psychology and psychoanalysis, and has also long been acknowledged (and struggled against) by civic organizations for boys, such as the YMCA and Boys Scouts of America. Now, in light of scientific reassurances offered to heterosexuals about the immutability of sexual orientation, homosocial homosexuality is increasingly offered as a possibility for *adult* men who may have, in psychotherapist Joe Kort's words, a "deep longing to experience the physical intimacy with other men that they are denied in a sexist and homophobic world."[42] In Kort's view, if straight men can feel secure in the knowledge that they are innately heterosexual, and if they can understand that the craving for sexual contact with men is not only natural but "manly," they can embrace their sexual fluidity without a sense of discordance.

Joe Kort is not inventing this idea as much as he is synthesizing ideas and practices already present within the culture of white hetero-masculinity. As I demonstrate in the next chapter, one can find hundreds of online personal ads written by people claiming to be adult, white, straight-identified men seeking sex with other white men, an encounter they often frame in nostalgic terms, as a reenactment of youthful male bonding. The ads describe scenes in which straight men will get drunk or stoned, watch sports, reminisce about their youth, brag about heterosexual conquests, and give each other hand jobs and blowjobs. The ads explain that this is what "legitimate male bonding" looks like, not to be mistaken for "gay bullshit" marked by femininity, love, kissing, the anus, and a host of varied and sometimes contradictory gay signifiers. By drawing on the model of adolescent friendship, or the natural and presumably proto-sexual circle jerk, the ads reframe these activities as a kind of sex that bolsters, rather than diminishes, heterosexual masculinity. Some ads ask explicitly and longingly, "what ever happened to the circle jerk?" What happened to that time when mutual masturbation defined, rather than threatened, heterosexual masculinity?

In my interview with Kort, he explained that such desires and practices fall neatly within the list of reasons that straight men seek sex with other men. Straight men have a need for access to quick and emotionless sex *and* a longing for physical intimacy with other men. Such desires do not make men gay, Kort explains, but simply struggling to get off and achieve closeness with men in a world that makes both difficult. And yet, Kort's own explanation of these needs highlights the tensions between them. On the one hand, Kort views straight men's sex with men as impersonal:

> Straight men are not *attracted* to men. [They're] thinking, "I'm going to get off, get paid, etc." It's not personal. They are interested in the sexual behavior. It's not as easy to find women to do these things. Courting has to happen. And those women who will [have the kind of sex men want] are not attractive. . . . He's thinking, "I can't get a woman to just have sex with me in a bathroom," or "I don't want to pay [for sex]."[43]

On the other hand, though Kort assures clients that they can distinguish their heterosexuality from homosexuality by recognizing that their same-sex desires are motivated by purely sexual (and not emotional) needs, this assertion comes into conflict with Kort's explanation of the affective states that give form to men's sexual interactions:

> **JW**: If it's just about getting off, then why do these exchanges so frequently need to involve some kind of humiliation?
>
> **Kort**: Because boys aren't allowed to have intimacy with each other. Unlike girls, there's no going to the bathroom together, no dressing together, no affection, no vehicle for men to be soft, touch each other, etc. It comes out through sexualization and dominance. Feminizing other men allows them to explore that curiosity. They can sit back and jack-off with another guy, so they can be close with another guy. . . . Having a best friend is too gay, but sex is macho.[44]

Ultimately, Kort places male affection and intimacy at the center of his analysis of the underlying reasons that straight men sexualize their relationships with other men. From this view, both gay men *and* straight men want to have sex with men for erotic *and* emotional reasons. Given this slippage, the significance of biology comes as little surprise. It is only biology that distinguishes the two groups at the end of the day, given the absence of either a behavioral *or* psychic sexual binary.

In addition to speculation about men's need for connection with other men, another common feature of the homosociality trope is the presumption that sexual contact between straight men is driven largely by the patriarchal imperative to close ranks and preserve men's power over women. In fact, in most analyses of male homosociality, homosexual sex is understood to be a rare or ancillary part of the homosocial bond. Within the social sciences, homosociality describes the ways in which boys and men are socialized to respect and identify with men over women, to prefer to be in the company of men, and to practice a "bros before hoes" ethic of privileging substantive male bonds over the sexual function provided by women.[45] In this view, homosexual contact may occasionally be present within straight male bonds, but its primary purpose is to bolster the homosocial order. Queer studies has taken a somewhat different approach, wherein homosexual desire is understood to be present within homosocial relations, but largely suppressed by homophobia and therefore routed through women who become the triangulated objects of men's power and desire.[46]

In these approaches, the possibility that heterosexual men could engage in homosexual sex for the sake of sex itself drops largely out of view. And it is here that we see the force of hetero-exceptionism, whereby it is presumed that gay men have sex with men for the intrinsic pleasure it brings, while straight men have sex with men for largely instrumental reasons (e.g., to meet a suppressed emotional need, to move through a developmental stage, to secure power over women, and so forth). This view is so common that many of my savviest interlocutors have responded to this work with some version of the question: "Isn't this all *really* just about _____??" (fill in the blank here with sexism/anality/dominance/ homophobia). Setting aside the fact that we are rarely tempted to reduce straight women's sexual fluidity to a single asexual motive, we must consider whether *any* sexual pairing or fantasy is free of triangulated desires, third parties, and instrumental goals.

Previous investigations of homosociality have largely overlooked the ways that homosociality, like necessity, operates as an alibi or justificatory script for homosexual behavior. Straight men are arguably quite aware of the male-bonding imperative and its usefulness as a rhetorical device that elevates homosexual encounters out of the troubled waters of gay identity and into the realm of male solidarity. More than simply a description of men's subconscious and instrumental motivations for sexual contact with men, the homosocial narrative is also a fantasy and erotic script consciously taken up by straight men to seduce other men and to set hetero-erotic scenes. Within the circuits of dude-on-dude sex, sex with men is no more or less a "cover up"—or a side effect masking the real issue or impulse—than any other kind of sexual fantasy.

Drunk, Dumb, and Unexpected: The Performance of Accidental Homosexuality

A third though lesser common script that undergirds hetero-exceptionalism is the script of accidental homosexuality. Accidental homosexuality invokes a range of possible situations in which heterosexual men make sexual contact with men while intoxicated, dumb, or subject to other unusual conditions beyond their control. Though it may not seem plausible that such "accidents" occur with any frequency, the story of their occurrence is a common theme in films marketed to boys and men. Such has been the material of "bromance" films, which exploded on the scene in the early 2000s, and which depict homosexuality facilitated by drunkenness, amnesia, practical jokes, or the stupidity and goofiness of heterosexual men themselves. Film critics describe the bromance as a genre of American comedic films centered more on straight male characters' romance with one another than with the women they are presumably trying to seduce. Tellingly, the characters in bromance films are almost always white. For instance, in the 2000 bromance classic *Dude, Where's My Car?*, two straight white stoner dudes, played by Ashton Kutcher and Seann William Scott, share an extended French kiss in order to impress Italian male model Fabio. Though the kiss is neither brief nor lacking in passion, its accidental and meaningless quality is communicated by the fact that the two dudes are stoned, stupid, suffering from amnesia, and caught up in a science-fiction mess with "hot alien chicks" who are trying to destroy the universe.[47] Similarly, in

Ben Stiller's hit film *Zoolander* (2001), "very, very good-looking" but very, very dumb straight male models drink orange mocha frappacinos, prance about to George Michael tunes, and sleep together in bunk beds. In the mockumentary *Borat* (2006), two straight (white?) Kazakh men unfamiliar with American gender norms travel through the United States and happen to be nude when an argument breaks out between them, leading to several minutes of naked wrestling and face-to-scrotum contact. In *Superbad* (2007), two dorky and idiotic white high school boys hoping to get lucky with their female classmates end up together instead, cuddling in sleeping bags and whispering, "I love you . . ." And in *Blades of Glory* (2007), two equally idiotic straight white male ice skaters forge a best friendship while tenderly embracing each other—and each other's crotches—on the skating rink.

Bromance films arguably signal a widening range of ways that straight white dudes might inhabit intimate friendships with one another. In the next chapter, I closely examine the ways that whiteness animates this homosocial narrative, but for now suffice it to say that homosexual contact is made possible by the stupidity, zaniness, drunkenness, lack of cultural awareness (as in *Borat*), and general "loser" status of the straight (and almost always white) men involved. To ensure the heterosexuality of bromantic dudes, instances of sexual and romantic contact are structured to be the funniest moments in the films, the moments in which homosexuality becomes an accident that could only happen to losers and bumbling idiots.

In contrast with bromance films, television has offered some more complex representations of straight men's desire for other men, allowing these relationships to unfold without such overly simplistic justifications or slapstick resolutions. For instance, on NBC's long-running hit show *The Office*, the lead character, Michael Scott (played by the white male comedy actor Steve Carell), is the bumbling, racist, sexist, and homophobic boss at the Dunder Mifflin paper supply company. Though heterosexual,

Michael has an ongoing crush on Ryan, one of his straight white male employees. This attraction is conveyed over several episodes as Michael bestows Ryan with the "hottest in the office" award six years in a row, gives Ryan a $400 ipod during the office holiday gift exchange (despite an agreed upon $20 limit), and continues to employ and promote Ryan despite poor work performance. Michael's crush on Ryan—and the particular forms it takes (such as promotion)—signals the possibility that the "flip side" of racism, sexism, and homophobia is the admiration and desire that straight white men feel for their kind.

In a different vein, an episode of the F/X dark comedy television series *Louie*, starring the white male comedian Louis C. K., shows the schlubby Louie travelling to Miami for a stand-up comedy performance, during which time he meets, and develops a crush on, an attractive Cuban American lifeguard named Ramon. Louie is straight, and nearly every episode of the show centers on his (failed) pursuit of women, but in Miami, Louie and Ramon spend an unquestionably romantic day and night together, splashing and wrestling in the waves, riding around on a bicycle built for one, and taking in the sights and sounds of the city. The cross-racial romance and the clear differences between the two men's bodies (Ramon's strength and muscle tone versus Louie's vulnerable fleshiness) hint at a masculine/feminine binary, heightening the episode's feeling of "gayness." The episode ends with an intimate albeit very awkward conversation between the two, in which Louie struggles to express his attraction and Ramon gently rejects him.

Though these television depictions do not rely on the same level of over-the-top physical comedy that bromance films deploy to make clear that homoeroticism is the running "joke," they nonetheless suggest that homosexual desire is most seamlessly assigned to straight white male television characters whom viewers already perceive as idiots (like Michael Scott) or losers (like Louie). Homosexual desire is easily integrated into the list of tragic or bizarre qualities possessed by such characters, comfortably chalked up to their generally pathetic constitutions.

Though distinctly different from the light quality of bromance in film and television, similar themes of accidental or unexpected homosexuality appear in sexological research on straight men who have sex with men. A 2010 study published in *Archives of Sexual Behavior*[48] reports that some straight male participants described their homosexual behavior as "accidental," or beyond their personal control. One respondent blamed his homosexual sex on a combination of his methamphetamine use and an all-too-convenient bathhouse in his neighborhood. Another described having sex with men for drug money, a decision that unexpectedly became a kind of gateway to more and more homosexual contact. Some of the straight male performers interviewed in Jeffrey Escoffier's study about gay-for-pay pornography[49] echo these accounts, describing their pathway into gay porn as marked by a series of smaller steps unintentionally leading to a fulltime career of having sex with men on film.

The problem with the trope of accidental homosexuality is not that these scenarios never occur, but that their "accidental" quality is not unique to heterosexual forms of homosexuality. The fact that homosexual sex is unexpected, deeply ambivalent, or brought on by altered consciousness is intended in these narratives to exceptionalize straight people's homosexuality—to reveal its fundamental difference from the ever-so-natural, preordained, and epiphanic homosexual experiences of gay men and lesbians. And yet, as most queers know, to live under heteronormativity is quite often to have one's first homosexual experiences be marked by significant ambivalence, anxiety, awkwardness, or drunkenness (in addition, of course, to arousal, excitement, and other more positive sensations). This was certainly true of my own dyke coming of age, which began with a performatively accidental and one-time-only drunken experiment with a woman best friend, then a period of awkward bicurious identification and lesbian ambivalence, then a series of hot though troubled queer relationships, and finally, twenty years later, a blissful slide into an admittedly somewhat homonormative dyke marriage. Nowhere in the first several years of my queer history was there a profound moment of sexual "rightness" or self-affirmation. The structures of compulsory heterosexuality make this unlikely for the queerest of us. What I *did* experience, which gets closer to the heart of the difference between straight and queer engagements with homosexual sex, was the sense that my pursuit of queer sex was guided, at least in part, by my investments in queer politics, by my interest in queer ways of life, by my desire for a break with the boredom of heterosexuality, and by the exhilaration brought on by sexual "wrongness." My point here is that the fact that straight men (and women) are ambivalent about their homosexual experiences is not what distinguishes them from, say, a near-lifetime homosexual like myself. Instead, it is their investment in heteronormativity and their strategic and exceptionalizing deployment of the trope of homosexual accidents that marks them as truly "not gay."

The Binary Fails Again!

As these examples reveal, accounting for straight men's sex with men demands imaginative scenarios, elaborate frameworks, and lists of countless circumstances and situations that diminish male sexual agency, leaving men with little choice but to engage in homosexual sex. Aside from the evident problem of denying straight-identified men an agentic path to homosexual sex, these rhetorical maneuvers betray the pitfalls of the heterosexual/homosexual binary more generally.

For one, they illuminate the fragile and tautological construction of heterosexuality and homosexuality. Inventories of the exceptional reasons that straight men have sex with men are so lengthy and varied that they arguably cover the reasons that *all* people have sex, thereby losing most of their explanatory power. Kort's list of reasons that straight men have sex with men—to satisfy curiosity, to access quick and emotionless sex, to be worshipped and adored, to achieve financial security, to work through childhood issues, and so forth—sounds remarkably like the reasons that anyone has sex with anyone. What *is* sexuality, if not some complex mix of desire for "intensely arousing but (often) shameful experiences," the fulfillment of curiosity, the pursuit of opportunity/availability, childhood imprinting, narcissism, economic transactions, longing for parental affection, and/or addictive cravings? Most explanations of straight men's sex with men focus on the constraints and emotional and sexual needs that produce the context in which this sex occurs (such as Joe Kort's emphasis on straight men's need for access to quick and emotionless sex). But what of the needs and constraints—psychic, material, institutional—that structure *gay men*'s (or straight or lesbian women's) sexual encounters? Many a gay man has sought out quick and emotionless sex with men, or had sex with a man who reminded him of his father, or had sex for money, or to feel loved, and so forth. The difference here is not what or who is desired (e.g., quick and emotionless sex with men), but the presence or absence of a rhetorical triangulation with women, or more accurately, with heterosexual desire. In accounts of situational homosexuality, women are presumed to avoid quick or emotionless sex; men must turn to other men as a substitute. The triangulated presence of women, whether or not the story about women's availability is actually true, is what distinguishes the hetero-masculine account from the gay male account. In other words, when a heterosexual need or impulse is a man's primary alibi for homosexual sex, he is/ becomes heterosexual. *His heterosexuality is defined by his investment in heterosexuality.* Gay men, in contrast, are men who have sex with men without an alibi. Despite—but also because of—the tautological nature of this definition, it may very well be our most accurate and productive way to understand heterosexuality—as a construct accomplished not through acts of heterosexual sex, but through articulations of investment in heteronormativity.

Current explanations for straight men's sex with men also lead us in counterproductive directions by suggesting that gay male sex serves a subjectifying function that straight men's sex with men does not. Some accounts indicate that because homosexual sex is discordant with heterosexual identity, straight men's homosexual behavior is working against, and not towards, the affirmation of their heterosexual identity. Other accounts suggest that straight men's sex with one another has little to do with sexual desire, and more with establishing dominance over other men. In both views, homosexual sex is accomplishing something else, something other than the expression of sexual identity or sexual instinct, such as meeting a repressed emotional need or preserving male power. While these accounts are probably not without some descriptive merit, they also tend to elide the ways that the performance of discordance—or "acting like" something we believe we are not—operates to reinforce privileged subjectivities. Male forms of drag and white forms of black face come to mind here, though the subjectifying performance of "fag" behavior by straight men is also well documented. Sociologist CJ Pascoe, in her ethnography of a California high school, describes straight white teenage boys play-acting at being "fags" (by pretending to hump or kiss one another), followed by a sudden retreat from one another to express collective disgust and disidentification with the boys and men who would *really* do such things.[50] Paradoxically, this act of touching one another is an act of producing heterosexual selfhood. Such performances enable the expression of sexual desire and the experience of sexual contact between boys while simultaneously reinforcing heterosexuality. As I demonstrate in the chapters to follow, this dynamic extends to adult male encounters in which sexual contact is far more extensive and in which hyper-masculine, heterosexual narratives infuse the sex acts themselves. Sometimes it is precisely the endurance of homosexual sex that demonstrates men's heterosexual resilience.

Lastly, explanations of straight men's homosexual behavior take the awkwardness, shame, and ambivalence attached to these encounters as evidence of discordance between self and behavior, forgetting that these affectations characterize the terrain of sexuality more broadly. For example, among the many costs of sexism is that sex is often utterly scripted and unsatisfying for straight women, and yet straight women's sexual dissatisfaction is rarely taken as evidence that they are acting out of accordance with their heterosexual orientation. Similarly, the fact that straight people (or gay people) have uncomfortable feelings about, or dissociation from, their participation in homosexual sex probably tells us less about their core sexual orientations or embodied desires than it does about the effects of heteronormativity on people's sexual experiences.

Attempts to explain the homosexual behavior of heterosexual men have largely failed to point to any concrete differences between the motivations and identitarian functions of the sex that occurs between straight men, on the one hand, and gay men, on the other. The narrow and near exclusive focus on the *circumstances* in which straight men have sex with men—institutional, developmental, financial, and so forth—presumes, and then focuses on, a conflict between homosexual behavior and heterosexual selfhood, thereby obscuring straight men's agentic, subjectifying pursuit of homosexuality. Instead, if we view homosexuality as a constitutive element of hetero-masculinity, a central ingredient in the making of heterosexual men, we can then look closely at what homosexual sex *does for* heterosexual men, and for heteronormativity more broadly. We can illuminate the ways that heterosexual men, far from falling victim to an exceptional circumstance, learn to resignify homosexual sex as an act of heteronormativity. We can come closer, then, to understanding what actually sets straight and queer lives apart—not our bodies, or the homo or hetero sex they desire and experience, but the relationship of our bodies and desires to the pursuit of heterosexual normalcy.

4

Average Dudes, Casual Encounters

White Homosociality and Heterosexual Authenticity

IN the independent film *Humpday* (2009), written and directed by Lynn Shelton, two straight white dudes and best friends from college decide to do something radical for the sake of art: "bone" each other on camera. Since college, Ben, played by Mark Duplass, has married his girlfriend, Anna, bought a house and car, gained some weight, and is living a respectable middle-class life in Seattle. Andrew, played by Joshua Leonard, is an artist and an adventurer, freshly returned to Seattle after a long stint of "making art with the locals" in Chiapas, Mexico. The film opens with Ben and Anna awakened at two a.m. by the unexpected arrival of Andrew, the antithesis of their quiet and settled lives. Ever the hipster with his beard, tattoos, and fedora, Andrew shows up and begins to disdainfully survey his friend's staid life.

Humpday explores the ways that white hipster masculinity pushes back against heteronormativity without ultimately being able to untether from it. Andrew, though straight-identified himself, finds Ben's life, and heteronormativity in general, suffocating. And yet the film suggests that Andrew has little intrinsic material from which to craft an alternative. Like many a young white bohemian before him, Andrew resolves this dilemma through travel and cultural appropriation. In addition to making art with the indigenous people of Chiapas, he's spent time learning about herbal remedies in Machu Pichu and flirting with a princess in Morocco.

These allusions to indigenous and/or exotic ways of life establish Andrew's bohemian credentials, but the film focuses more closely on Andrew's relationship to yet another figure of Otherness, a different foil to Andrew and Ben's straight masculinity: Monica, the sexy queer/bi/polyamorous white woman (played by the filmmaker) whom Andrew meets at a café shortly after arriving in Seattle.

The pivotal moment in the film occurs when Andrew and Ben attend a queer party at Monica's house. Monica's party is every straight person's best and worst fantasy of queerness in Seattle— faggy men caressing each other, women with shaved heads, open displays of non-monogamy, trance music, lots of wine and weed, and a sign on the front door that reads "DIONYSIS." Andrew, who has developed a flirtation with Monica, relishes being in the middle of her queer Bacchanalia; Ben, on the other hand, is uneasy but finally settles in at the party, surrendering like a tourist in a foreign land. Later that night, when Monica and the other queer revelers reveal that they are submitting short films for Humpfest, the local amateur porn festival, Andrew drunkenly chimes in that he wants to make an "erotic art film," too. Ben scoffs at the idea, prompting Andrew to call attention to the drudgery of Ben's heteronormative existence: "Don't hate cause you can't play, because you're all fucking locked up, ball and chain, domestic style." After some drunken banter about what would constitute a "really radical" erotic art film, Andrew tells Ben, "I should just fuck *you*." Ben, also drunk and high and now invested in proving that he is as down-for-anything as he was in his college days, declares, while thrusting at the air, "*This* is what we're doing. You and me, two straight dudes, straight ballin'. It's *beyond* gay."

In the light of the next day, Ben and Andrew expect one another to renege. When Andrew speculates that Ben probably regrets their agreement ("you know, I fuckin' roll into town and all of sudden you're drunk and talking about fucking dudes and your wife is waiting at home with a cold dinner that she cooked for us."), Ben responds defensively: "I'm not as white picket fence as you think. . . . I would do it and I am not limited because I am married. . . . The idea is weird but amazing and it pushes boundaries and that's what good pieces of art should do." In the name of amazing art, the two men agree to have sex on film the next day, and in the awkward hours leading up to the big event, they share a tender moment reflecting on whether either of them has been repressing some latent queerness over the course of his life. Exemplifying the ambivalence within hipster heterosexuality, Andrew tells Ben that in his world, the world of "artists and travelers," he feels "almost embarrassed" to be heterosexual. "I wish I was more gay," he confesses with a chuckle.

One of the more instructive effects of *Humpday* is that the nature of the desire that compels Ben and Andrew to have sex is not entirely clear, as if often true in life. A *New York Times* reviewer described Ben and Andrew's motivation as platonic, and the film as "utterly lacking in titillation. . . . There is no intimation of any lurking erotic subtext in their friendship."[1] And yet, there are scenes in the film in which the characters, particularly Andrew, gaze extendedly at one another, their eyes glistening with longing, their dialogue nearing flirtation. Shelton, the film's director, has described the film as a reflection on the tension between straight men's attachment to their heterosexuality and their love for other men—a tension set within a changing culture in which homophobia is increasingly "not cool." The film takes advantage of the comedy and poignancy that emerges when straight men "want to breakout and be cool and try and sleep with each other," Shelton has stated.[2]

In the long and painfully awkward final scene of the film, Ben and Andrew meet in a hotel room to finally have the sexual encounter they have been plotting throughout the length of the film. The desire present between them in earlier scenes in gone, and each effort they make to begin fucking ends quickly, cut short by their endless chatter about whether the sex—and, more importantly, the art film they are making—is "working." They kiss and agree they don't like it. They take their clothes off, they put them on, they take them off, each time expressing concern over whether they are "pussing out." They try hugging without shirts. They analyze each step. They know they are being too cerebral. They agree "to let bodies take over." But ultimately their project, to fuck for the sake of art, buckles under the weight of their fear:

Andrew: Art is such a fucking *thing*. I just think if we're going to do it, it has to be like a fucking experience and not just like doing it to get through it. It's gotta be something we do because like, FUCK, we didn't think we could do it and we fuckin' did it! And I don't know how to actually get there and that's the tricky thing. It's the difference between doing this and fuckin' bungee jumping, dude. Bungee jumping you just walk to the edge and jump and you don't have to have a fuckin' hard-on to bungee jump.

Ben: I don't wanna be a pussy, I don't want to chicken out on this, but I can't help thinking what exactly about two straight dudes having sex on camera is a great piece of art?

Andrew: The fact that we picked this as this hurdle was almost arbitrary. . . . It could have been fuckin' anything, like hiking across Bhutan or something like that.

Ben: When you say something like "hiking across Bhutan," I don't even know what that is but I know that in the experience of doing that we would probably enrich our lives a lot more than fuckin' just trying to tag ass in a hotel room and force it.

Andrew: We're doing this because it scares us more than anything else. I'd be pretty amped to go to Bhutan.

Ben: There is nothing in this world that I want to do less than what we're talking about doing. And that's something.

Andrew: I guess the question is, is that a reason to go through with it?

Ben: Something just hit me. I think we might be morons. [Ben and Andrew laugh, they get dressed, they say "I love you," they part, and the film ends—with no sex.]

Figure 4.1. Ben (left) and Andrew, discussing whether or not to have sex, in *Humpday* (2009) (http://twitch film.com/2012/12/sun dance-2013—10-films-to-watch-before-the-fest—-dramatic-competition-edition.html).

Though Ben and Andrew do not follow through with their plan to have sex, *Humpday* nonetheless offers a useful map of the channels through which sex between straight white men becomes possible. While the protagonists may or may not desire homosexual penetration itself, what is clear is that they very deeply desire a radical break from heteronormative conventions (i.e., the picket fence, the ball and chain) and believe that humping another dude represents heteronormativity's coup de grâce. Andrew, in particular, wants to live on the edge and make intimate contact with difference, and as such, he locates his plan to fuck Ben on par with his travels in Chiapas and Peru, or the hypothetical trek through Bhutan. As Ben and Andrew's hump day draws nearer, they detach homosexual sex from its identitarian associations ("it's *beyond* gay") and imagine a new kind of sex—straight ballin'—which looks less like gay sex than it does like an extreme sport, a character-building hurdle, a foray into foreign territories where few straight white men dare to go. While the dominant culture may construct gay men as pussies, *Humpday* reworks the association between bravery and homosexual penetration. "Pussing out" means failing to face one's fear—of bungee jumping, Bhutan, and homosexual sex.

More importantly for our purposes here, *Humpday* illuminates the ways that race and class help to determine how straight men might temporarily break free of heteronormativity. For Andrew, in particular, the possibilities for homosexual desire are intertwined with a white, middle-class bohemian and imperialist ethos that not only compels him toward sexual exploration, but toward cross-racial and cross-cultural encounters as well. The force that compels Andrew to live among the indigenous people of Chiapas is the same force, or so we are led to believe, that compels him to bone his best friend. In fact, without Andrew's tales of living with the natives, which establish his credentials as an adventurer, the motivation that drives *Humpday* would be all but lost. It is Ben's envy of Andrew's recent exotic and seemingly life-changing experiences as a traveler that makes Ben willing to take his own leap and do something "amazing"—i.e., defy heterosexuality—while Andrew is in town and he has the chance. His desire for Andrew's way of life makes the impossible possible.

White Boys Gone Wild

Taking *Humpday* as a point of departure, this chapter takes a tour through the spaces—both material and rhetorical—where whiteness animates the homosexual encounters of straight white men. My aim is to demonstrate that whiteness sits at the very heart of white men's narratives about when, why, and how they might find themselves jacking off or boning another dude—to use their own parlance. Within popular culture, *Humpday* is hardly alone in its representation of the links between homosexuality and straight white male risk-taking. Themes of risk and adventure are also evident, for instance, in the prankster genre of reality film and television—exemplified by the *Jackass* television series and subsequent spin-off films by the same name—in which straight white "bad boys" engage in madcap stunts, often involving travel to the Global South *and* gratuitous dude-on-dude groping (which sometimes occurs between the white stars of the films and seemingly confused native men of color). The genre rests on the notion that idiotic and risk-taking white dudes, like *Jackass*'s white daredevils Johnny Knoxville and Steve-O, will do anything for a rush and a laugh, including homoerotic tricks involving their own and

Figure 4.2. The cast of *Jackass 3D*, from *Rolling Stone Magazine*, October 2010 (http://soul88. blogspot.com/2010_ 10_01_archive.html).

other men's anuses, testicles, and nipples. In *Jackass*, sexual contact between straight men is reconfigured as an extreme sport, akin to placing one's vulnerable genitals in the path of a hungry shark (a stunt that has, indeed, appeared in the films). The films invite viewers to celebrate homosexual play among edgy white dudes who are so reckless that their homosexual behavior reads as a macho display of endurance and self-sacrifice—a homosexual sacrifice made for the sake of our entertainment.

In some ways films like *Humpday* and *Jackass* appear to represent an old story in which straight audiences are invited to squirm with discomfort or laugh smugly at white men behaving stupidly and queerly, qualities often represented as one and the same. But as Jack Halberstam has argued, it is precisely the genre of low-brow white male "stupidity films"—exemplified by films like *Zoolander*, *Dude Where's My Car*, and *Dumb and Dumber*—that has the potential to disarm white hetero-masculinity by allowing it to be incompetent, ignorant, and forgetful of its own status and function. Consequently, such films offer us examples of straight white male figures who find themselves kissing and fondling other dudes, or otherwise open to the possibilities of sexual and gender transgression. As Halberstam explains, when white male idiots are left to their own devices—and not rescued by sympathetic women or by cultural frameworks that glorify white male stupidity (think George W. Bush)—then their stupidity stands to "disrupt, momentarily, the fortification of the white hetero male body and open it up to other forms of desire."[3]

Such representations also highlight the fact that straight white men's homosexual encounters typically have multiple layers of meaning. For instance, when *Jackass* stars Knoxville and Steve-O make intimate contact with each other's genitals and anuses for the sake of popular entertainment, their stunts offer to audiences not only a classic display of male physical endurance (they have *very resilient* penises and anuses), but also a remarkable display of white privilege. White male performers are arguably more likely than male performers of color to think they can appear on screen *as themselves* (as opposed to appearing in character) engaged in acts of personal humiliation, intimate homosexual touching, and full-body exposure, without severe consequences for their careers and reputations. And yet, at the same time, Knoxville and Steve-O's white male jackassery also models a way for young white men to disidentify with the knee-jerk homophobia of their generation. As Knoxville told a reporter for *Vanity Fair*, "We [the *Jackass* cast] always thought it was funny to force a heterosexual MTV generation to deal with all of our thongs and homoerotic humor. In many ways, all our gay humor has been a humanitarian attack against homophobia."[4]

Taken together, *Jackass* and *Humpday* suggest that homosexual encounters between straight white men flourish when adventure and physical endurance is valued over self-image; and conversely, that gender and sexual transgression is foreclosed when straight white men take themselves too seriously (thereby risking venturing into dangerous identitarian territory). To return to the final scene of *Humpday*—Ben and Andrew's extensive and obsessive reflections on the existential meaning of their proposed sex, as compared with the impulsiveness that fuels the homoerotics in

Jackass, rescues them from the homosexual experience they both admire and fear. Resonant with Halberstam's suggestion that certain forms of failure and stupidity may well represent straight white men's best pathway to gender and sexual transgression, *Humpday* offers an example of two white men for whom the suspicion that they may be "morons" ultimately shuts down the sexual encounter they have worked so hard to imagine.

Straight White Dude Seeks Same

Let us now turn from popular culture to the different but nonetheless performative world of online personal ads—ads written by people claiming to be "straight white men" seeking sex with other "straight white men." In 2005, some friends of mine brought to my attention some personal ads they had discovered in the "Casual Encounters" section of the online bulletin board Craigslist Los Angeles. The text of one such ad read:

> *Str8 guy wants to try BJ tonight. . . .–27*. Ok, I'll make this short. I'm up late tonight. I have a girlfriend. But I'm at home by myself now. I watch porn and I like when the women suck on big cocks. I've been thinking about it, and I think I'd like to suck one. I'm not attracted to guys so I'd rather not look at you much. Just suck your cock. I have a Polaroid and would like to take a pic with cum on my face. But this is really only for tonight cuz I'm horny! . . . I am Caucasian and prefer Caucasian.

Though my friends and I were/are all queer people of the poststructuralist persuasion, we marveled at the suggestion that this was the fantasy of a "straight guy." We imagined that its author was a kinky gay man posing as straight to enact his straight-dude fantasy. Some of us considered that perhaps this ad was the outcome of a sad and sexually repressed life in the closet. As we scanned through three days of Craigslist posts, we discovered dozens of similar ads in which "str8"[5] men were looking for sex with other men. A few weeks later, I revisited Casual Encounters, wondering if the impressive number of ads I'd seen earlier had been a fluke. But there they were again, seemingly countless declarations of desire purportedly written primarily by straight white "dudes"—dudes who were, as they repeatedly proclaimed, just average white guys looking to have friendly *not-gay* sex with other normal, average white guys. Photos of jocky looking white guys accompanied some of the ads, seemingly included to corroborate this description.

I had questions. Who were these white dudes? Exactly what kind of sex acts were they looking for? Why weren't gay men acceptable sex partners if what they wanted was to have sex with men? How would they know anyway? Did these men need to "prove" their heterosexuality to one another, and if so, what methods were they using to accomplish heterosexual realness while soliciting sex with men? And, perhaps most importantly, why had my friends and I been initially so invested in claiming as gay a cultural space so decidedly intent on identifying with heterosexuality? Motivated by these questions, research assistants and I collected and analyzed 243 similar ads in the Casual Encounters section of Craigslist Los Angeles over the course of 2005 and 2006.[6]

Perhaps what one first notices about the ads placed in Casual Encounters is that they are elaborate, often describing sexual scenes with a dazzling level of detail. The authors of the ads typically identify themselves as white, straight, in their twenties and thirties, and seeking sex with men, and then proceed to offer numerous hetero-authenticating details, from homophobic disavowals of gay men, to misogynistic references to violence against women, to hetero-masculine props: beer, sports, straight porn. Collectively, the ads assert that being straight or gay is not about the biological sex of participants, but about *how* the sex is done— the language that will be used (before, during, and after sex), the type of pornography that will be viewed, the types of alcohol and drugs consumed, and the agreed-upon reasons for the sex itself. The following ads are representative of dozens of similar others, in which sex between men is articulated as a casual act of "being free to be a man" that need not have any troubling/gay identitarian consequences:

Straight Dude Drunk and Horny.... Any str8 bud wanna jack?—27: Here's the deal. Went out drinking and clubbing, thought I'd hook up with a chick, but didn't pan out. I'm buzzed, horny, checking out porn. Is there any other straight dude out there who would be into jacking while watching porn? ... I'd rather hook up with a chick, but none of the CL [Craigslist] chicks ever work out.

What happened to the cool bi/str8 dude circle jerks?—33. What happened to a group of masc[uline] dudes just sitting around stroking, watching a game, drinking some brews, jerking, showing off, swapping college stories, maybe playing a drinking game and see what comes up?

STR8 for STR8 Dudes: I'm STR8 looking to mess around with another STR8 dude from time to time. Discreet and looking for more than one time hookups so if you respond, have the balls to follow through with this ad and meet up.

STR8 Drunk Dude Looking to Get Off: Hi there, Looking to lay back, have some beers, etc. and watch some STR8 porn this evening. I'm 5.10, brown hair, brown eyes white dude.

Str8 jackoff in briefs outside male bonding edging stroke—34. I am a tall blond built packin' jockman with a big bulge in my jockeys. Dig hanging in just our briefs man to man in the hot sun workin' my bulge freely. ... If you are into jackin' and being free to be a man, let's hang. If you have a pool or a yard to layout and jack freely smoke some 420 [marijuana] and just be men, hit me up. No gay sex, I am looking for legit male bonding, masturbating in the hot sun only.

$300 Bucks Cash If You're STR8 & Goodlooking!! . . .–27. Hey, are you str8, good-looking and broke? Are you Under 30 and hella cool? Like watching porn and talking bout pussy? You're in luck. 300 bucks every time we hangout. Be under 30. Honestly STR8. I'm mostly str8, great looking chill bro.

The ads depict a world in which body parts and sex acts (male mouths touching male penises, for instances) are not meaningful indicators of whether sexual participants are straight or gay. Instead, it is a willingness to identify with and consume gay culture that makes others queer, and conversely, it is str8 dudes' mastery of hetero-masculine culture and their capacity to infuse homosexual sex with heterosexual normalcy that makes them straight. This way of thinking about sexuality lends support to a consensus within queer studies that queerness is defined not by a presence of homosexual sex, but by a refusal of gender and sexual normativity, a position exemplified by Foucault's assertion that "homosexuality threatens people as a 'way of life,' rather than a way of having sex." Str8 dudes' straightness is constituted by their way of life; it is performed and substantiated through a hyper-masculine and misogynistic rejection of queer culture.

The scenes described in the ads—the props, the costumes, the dialogue—capture the drama and spectacle of white male homosociality. What do young straight white men do together when they are engaged in male bonding? They get drunk and stoned, watch heterosexual porn, and they talk about "pussy." The ads draw heavily upon the model of adolescent friendship, or the presumably meaningless and proto-sexual circle jerk. Nostalgic commentary about being buddies or "bros" and sharing "legit" male bonding experiences constructs dude-sex as a kind of sex that bolsters, rather than threatens, the heterosexual masculinity of the participants. Only those who are man enough (e.g., "have the balls") and "chill" enough will want dude-sex, or be able to handle it.

In his book *Guyland: The Perilous World Where Boys Become Men*, sociologist Michael Kimmel depicts "homoerotic" encounters between straight white men as developmental, or as a feature of a delayed coming of age process wherein the lives of straight white boys, from ages sixteen to twenty-six, revolve around binge drinking, repudiation of gayness, homoerotic hazing, casual sex, porn, and above all, the avoidance of adulthood. Kimmel's analysis suggests that, as a feature of white male adolescence and young adulthood, performative homosexual or homoerotic contact is ultimately abandoned as white men shift their attention to work, family, and ideally, cooperative adult partnerships with women (or gay men). And yet, most of the ads that appear in Casual Encounters are placed by adult men ranging in age from twenty-seven to thirty-five years old, many of whom express an arguably romantic sense of lost youth and a nostalgic yearning for hetero-masculine sex with other dudes. Indeed, *what happened to the circle jerks?* While young white men in high school and college are more readily provided with institutional contexts that facilitate dude-sex (competitive sports, dormitories, fraternities), adult dudes must find other channels for organizing dude-sex, and must work harder to recreate its mood, meaning, and ritual.

Like a married couple nostalgically recreating their first date, dudes set the scene with friendship, beer, weed, straight porn, sports, and talk of "bitches" who are out of town or otherwise unavailable. Unlike in similar websites for gay men (including those frequented by and for "straight acting" gay men), women are a central part of str8 dudes' erotic discourse. Dudes often describe their sex as a less desirable but easy alternative to sex with women, or suggest that dude-sex is a means of getting the kind of sex that all straight men want from women, but can get only from men—uncomplicated, emotionless, and guaranteed. In some ads, such as the following, dudes express desire to share in violent or objectifying talk about women during their sexual encounter:

> *Whackin Off to Porn*: STR8 porn. Gang bang. STR8, bi-curious masculine white guy lookin' for a masculine guy. Get into stroking bone with a bud, talkin' bout pussy and bangin' the bitch.

> *Any Straight/Bi Guys Want to Help Me Fuck My Blow-up Doll???*: Come on guys . . . we can't always pick up the chick we want to bone right??? So let's get together and fuck the hell out of my hot blow-up doll. Her mouth, her pussy, and her ass all feel GREAT. Just be cool, uninhibited, horny, and ready to fuck this bitch. It's all good here . . . lates.

Given the ways that sexual violence against women is woven through the culture of hetero-masculinity, it should come as little surprise that misogyny also registers within men's expressions of desire for other men. That fantasies of raping women are easily incorporated into dude-sex is, perhaps, one of the clearest illustrations of its embeddedness within structures of heteronormativity, as distinct from gay male subcultures in which misogyny typically manifests as the invisibility, rather than the violent sexual objectification, of women.[7]

But Who Are They Really?

Before looking more closely at the operation of whiteness in the ads, I feel compelled to briefly attend to the question of who these men are "in real life," a question people frequently raise when I speak about this research. As I confessed earlier in this chapter, my initial reaction to the ads was that they had either been written by closeted gay men or by "real" gay men pretending to be straight in order to satisfy a fetish for "real" straight men, or to mark their interest in particular masculine codes. These assumptions were fueled by my own default binaristic thinking at the time, as well as numerous stories I'd heard from gay male friends about their desire to seduce straight men—stories they told even as they bemoaned the hierarchy within gay male culture that glorified "straight acting" gay men. How can one be sure that Casual Encounters is not a site in which gay men seduce one another vis-à-vis a compelling hetero-masculine gender performance? Sexological survey research conducted with straight-identified men who post ads for sex with men on Craigslist suggests that, in fact, these men quite commonly report actual heterosexual identification.[8] But beyond this empirical substantiation, to claim with any certainty that these ads must be, or probably are, written by gay men commits the fallacy this book works against. To defer to this common suspicion is to foreclose the possibility that straight men *do* desire men in some of the ways expressed in these ads, and to disregard a growing body of research on straight men's homosexual contact and the discursive context in which it takes place.

Similarly, some might argue that the ads placed in Casual Encounters are expressions of bisexual desire, and that a failure to highlight the bisexuality of str8 dudes reproduces bisexuality's persistent invisibility. Although I agree with the spirit of this concern, and while it is true that a few men who post in Casual Encounters do use the terms "bisexual" or "bicurious," I also note that the broader context of their ads almost always suggests that "bisexual" is a label they use in lieu of a sexual vocabulary to describe the homosexual sex of heterosexuals. Consider this ad, for instance, where reference to "bi stuff" appears alongside "STR8" identification as a technical description of sex between two straight men:

> *Laid back STR8 guy seeks same for j/o (jerk off) buddy*: Easygoing STR8 Caucasian male seeks same—looking for a buddy to stroke with who enjoys STR8 porn and sex with women but who is cool and open minded. I'm not gay but do like to show off and have

done some bi stuff in the past. Interested in jerk off only. I'm in shape and attractive, and this is no big deal to me. Don't have girlfriend right now and wanted to get off today so hit me back if interested.

As I have argued in the preceding chapters, the primary litmus for what counts as heterosexuality versus queerness should be the cultural and relational investments of the participants: That is, are their same-sex sex practices anchored within heterosexual culture and conceptualized through the logics of heterosexuality? Or are the participants' sex practices shaped by queer ideas, queer subculture, and queer politics? Because I understand bisexuality as a mode of queerness, one marked by sexual desire that is not gender-specific (or that extends to masculinity, femininity, and genderqueerness), it would be troubling to conceptualize as bisexual the desires expressed in the ads, as their authors have gone to great lengths to circumvent the imposition of this kind of queer meaning.

Staging White Homosociality

Straightness in Casual Encounters is authenticated not only via expressions of homophobia and misogyny, but also through white dudes' disidentification with men of color, their refusal of cross-racial desire, and their deployment of white male archetypes—like surfers, jocks, and frat boys—which they use to evoke the normal, the average, the casual, and the friendly. As such, Casual Encounters is an instructive site for revisiting the relationship among whiteness, masculinity, and what Eve Sedgwick has called "the potential unbrokenness of a continuum between homosocial and homosexual."[9] In Sedgwick's theorization, homosociality refers to the continuum of male bonds aimed at promoting men's patriarchal interests and their control and exchange of women. Erotic desire permeates male homosociality, but is suppressed by homophobia, and therefore routed through women, taking the form of bonds between male rivals or homoerotic training on the path to heterosexuality. Sedgwick explains that, unlike the ancient Greeks, for whom the relationship between homosexuality ("men loving men") and patriarchy ("men promoting the interests of men") was apparently seamless, men in the modern period sustain male bonds via heterosexual triangulation, in which desire between men is disguised by the centrality of women within the popular erotic imagination. Implied in Sedgwick's analysis is that while homophobia was not necessary to maintain patriarchy in ancient Greece, the modern figure of the gay man also had no corollary within Greek society; it is with the nineteenth-century solidification of homosexual personage—and concomitantly, the arrival of the heterosexual who must repudiate homosexual desire—that the rupture in the homosocial/homosexual continuum is concretized.

In light of Sedgwick's account, what sense might we make of the erotic scenes crafted by straight dudes in Casual Encounters—scenes that cut directly to egalitarian homosexual sex and bypass any unfriendly rivalry between male participants or complicated triangulation (at least in the material sense) with women? What does it mean when homosociality does not mask or redirect desire between heterosexual men, but takes on the rhetorical and often theatrical function of naturalizing homosexual sex (or explaining why only the straightest of dudes are man enough to jack off, suck, or fuck another dude)? What mechanisms are now available to contemporary straight dudes to recuperate homosexuality within the bonds of mentorship and friendship, perhaps returning to something resembling the Athenian system, even as the modern specter of the fag is looming? And what, too, is the significance of whiteness for this project, and within a space like Casual Encounters, which is dominated by white dudes who "seek same" as their "jack off buds"? How, precisely, does white sociality—namely, white friendship, white fetishism, and white forms of racial appropriation—imbue homosexuality with heterosexual meaning?

Sociologist Michael Kimmel has suggested that when homosexual contact occurs within homosocial spaces, the sexual nature of these connections is largely incidental.[10] From this perspective, when men add sexual contact to their "boys will be boys" tomfoolery, sex is but one form of glue that bonds men together for the higher purpose of preserving gendered power arrangements (i.e., establishing male unity, male hierarchy, and power over the feminine and the queer). In sum, sex is a means to a homosocial goal. But another and I believe more productive way to read sex between straight white dudes is to consider the reverse causality, or the ways that men deploy the *idea* that sex can be an innocent or incidental part of heterosexual male bonding—an idea widely circulated within developmental psychology—to fulfill a homosexual longing. It also stands to reason that if possible, straight dudes will try to achieve *both* goals—to make intimate contact with their friends' penises *and* to make it look like an act of homosocial necessity. It is in this effort to achieve both—to fuck and to bond—that the performance of homosociality is vital. Heterosexual men have a limited repertoire for enacting homosexual sex outside of the homosocial script; when it comes to homosexual sex, there is the gay way, and there is the straight-dudes-bonding way, and anything else arguably sits outside of most men's imaginations. But the homosocial imperative, or the taken-for-granted presumption that men must bond and that these bonds are often (temporarily or circumstantially) sexual, lends heterosexual credibility to dude-on-dude encounters. It enables homosexual contact while drawing its meaning from heteronormative logics.

The Idealized Homosocial Subject: White
Surfers, Skaters, Jocks, and Frat Guys

For a homosocial script to do the work of resignifiying homosexual sex as heterosexual sex, it must be convincing. It must be firmly couched within understandings of normal friendship and developmental necessity. And it is here that whiteness, or white realness, is an important player in establishing heterosexual realness for white men. In Casual Encounters, straight dudes craft ads in which archetypes of youthful white masculinity—jocks, skaters, surfers, and frat dudes—are presented as paradigmatic "average guys," and as the most natural subjects of homosocial bonding. The ads employ the hetero-masculine codes discussed previously (beer, straight porn, fantasies about sex with women), but they also specify the particular white male types that complete the scene:

Any HOT White jocks lookin to get sucked off???—*23.* Hey guys, I'm just a chill good looking dude heading down to the area for a BBQ and I'm looking for any other HOT Str8 or bi white dudes looking to get sucked off. Just sit back and relax and get drained. I'm especially into sucking off hot jocks, skaters, surfers, and frat dudes. If you're hot and if you're into a hot no strings blow job, then hit me up.

Seeking a MASCULINE JACK OFF BUD to STR8 PORN—- 29. Hot masculine white dude here . . . looking for another hot white dude to come by my place, and work out a hot load side by side. Straight Porn only. Prefer str8, surfer, etc. Not usually into gay dudes.

EX FRAT JOCK (seeking) JOCK as J/O BUD or MORE. Alpha straight jock, 6 feet one. . . . Always horny, big shooter, looking for a cool str8 dude to kick it with, chill, have a beer, watch some porn, maybe stroke our cocks, maybe a massage after a work out. Just wanting to check out what messin' with another hot guy is like. (with figure 4.3)

Figure 4.3. Original cropped photo included with text of personal ad.

The ads convey the friendly and casual mood of dude-sex, a mood that is neither romantically intense (as "dates" often are) nor particularly raw and kinky (as gay leather bars might be, for instance). Dudes relax, they chill, they "shoot the shit," and they kick back. There is no stress or pressure, as pervades the military and fraternity hazing rituals I discuss in the next chapter. In some cases, dudes give or receive blowjobs or engage in penetrative sex, but often they describe a desire for a more egalitarian, friendly, "side-by-side" encounter exemplified by the concept of the "jack off bud."

In ads such as these, heterosexual realness hinges on the believability of the homosocial motivation: Is this a *gay* encounter, or a meaningless extension of a naturally occurring male friendship? Racial sameness, or white sociality, helps to resolve this question by infusing the friendship narrative with credibility. Who are white boys' friends? White boys. What do white boys in California—this is Craigslist *Los Angeles*, after all—do together? Surf, skate, hang out in the frat house. Surfers are a particularly desired type, not likely due to the importance of surfing skills during the sexual encounter or the desire to actually surf together. Instead, surfers (and frat boys) evoke the youthful, heterosexual, white boy next door, the kind of white masculinity that is utterly normal, deeply American, and decidedly not gay. The surfer or frat boy—unlike cops, leather-clad bikers, or even the cowboys fetishized by gay men—carries little association with dominance or queer kink, at least not in the contemporary period.[11] Surfer dudes and frat dudes are simply buddies; their interaction is facilitated by the homosocial context of shared sport or fraternal membership, not the willful pursuit of gay sex.

Some of the ads in Casual Encounters accomplish hetero-masculine realness by delineating precisely what will be worn, uttered, consumed, known, and felt by the participants. For instance, the ad below, placed by a "str8 guy" who "lives a very str8 life," included a much longer script from which I have excerpted only a small segment. While whiteness is not explicitly named in this ad, its author makes use of many of the white-fetishistic tropes that appear in Casual Encounters (i.e., dudes in flip flops, tank tops, and shorts; friendship, stupidity, and need for initiation).

> You come to the hotel in loose shorts with no underwear on, a tank top and flip flops, and when you get there we just kick back and maybe have a few beers and shoot the shit to get to know each other a little bit and feel more comfortable, then we start talking about our girlfriends and girls that we have fucked before or the best blow jobs we have had, etc., the whole time acting like we are just good friends that are horny. I am kind of dumb and don't have a lot of experience with chicks and you want to teach me and help me learn more. You then tell me that you are getting really horny thinking about all the hot sex you have had and ask me if I have any porn we can watch. I put one on and as we watch the porn, you are

> constantly grabbing your dick and playing with it as it gets harder and harder. . . . Then you sit down right next to me and you say, "dude, you gotta hear this story about this one chick that I made suck my dick until I blew my load in her," then you tell me the story about it. While you are telling me the story you act it out with me.

As in this ad, which makes reference to the beloved white-boy costume of tank top and flip flops, the demographic and socio-political landscape of Southern California is clearly significant to the particular imagination of white masculinity that appears in Casual Encounters. Los Angeles, simultaneously one of the world's most racially diverse cities and the place where white surfer-boy dreams were born, is a rich site for analysis of what is possible—what is centered and what is eclipsed—within straight white men's desires for, and fantasies of, heterosexual masculinity. For those who actually live in Los Angeles, it takes considerable effort to imagine men, and Los Angeles itself, in such narrow and homogenous/white terms (e.g., one ad reads: "looking for surfers, [and other] LA-types")—a consideration that is itself an indication that straight dudes are engaged in a racial project in which white-ness is serving various ideological and representational ends, not the least of which is eliding the possibility of cross-racial desire. White archetypes are not referenced in these ads simply to iden-tify a desired physical type; they also provide an entire cultural universe from which to draw heterosexual costumes, scripts, and countless other codes for normal male bonding between white male subjects.

Appropriating Black Masculinity: White Bros and Thugs on the DL

While the film *Humpday* discussed at the beginning of this chapter offers an example of upper-middle-class white bohemian forms of cultural appropriation, Casual Encounters is a world where white men appropriate black masculinity to bolster a working-class expression of heterosexual realness. Some of the white straight dudes who place ads in Casual Encounters—like a growing number of young white men in general—imagine their hetero-masculinity through the lens of "white thuggery," or the white appropriation of urban black style. Borrowing on the notion that working-class male bonds are among the least likely to be gay bonds, many of the ads achieve heterosexual legibility by positioning sex between straight men as a display of hyper-masculine resilience and as an opportunity to strengthen the bonds of white "thugs."

Writers critical of the mainstreaming and white ownership of rap have pointed to the ways in which its consumption by white youth has bled into other forms of cultural appropriation.[12] Since the 1990s, white executives have marketed mainstream rap to white male youth. As Jackson Katz has argued, part of what is being sold in this transaction is a compelling model of masculinity, one ostensibly embodied by black men and characterized by hyper-heterosexuality and the capacity to threaten and intimidate other men. Accordingly with marketers' plans, white boys have eagerly consumed rap music and imagery, learning to mimic the narrow representation of black masculinity conveyed within it.[13] Sex between straight dudes, like other currents of white masculinity, is shaped by the wide circulation of images that link heterosexual authenticity with black men. While many ads in Casual Encounters draw on white archetypes to construct friendly heterosexual realness, others borrow from dominant representations of black male style to construct street realness, or male bonds organized around toughness and invulnerability. In these ads, straight dudes commonly use words and phrases such as "sup?," "hit me up," "aiite," and "thugged out," which have been identified by African American studies scholars as black slang:[14]

> 23 y/o white dude party in Hollywood—Hey guys, I'm partyin right now at home and have plenty of stuff to share. . . . I'm lookin to meet a cool str8 thugged out white dude around my age, who

would wanna come over, kick back, watch a lil porn, smoke a lil, and stroke off together. I might even be down to deepthroat some cock so if you love getting awesome head you should definitely hit me back! I'm lookin for someone chill & masculine so hit me up if this sounds like you . . . LATE

Str8 curious on the DL. Lookin' to chill—23. Sup? Just looking to chill with another str8/ bi dude, into young or older bros type . . . to mess around, not into perverted shit. . . . Please be in shape. I'm sort of skinny, curious here and haven't really acted on it. Just regular sane dude. Discretion a must. Aiite, late.

As with many forms of cultural appropriation, the black slang used by white dudes is fast becoming associated with whites, and with young white men in particular. For instance, according to the American Heritage Dictionary, "bro," a term commonly used in Casual Encounters, is a slang term for "brother" with etymological roots in African American vernacular English. However, its popular and contemporary usage by young white men in California has transformed its local and contextual meaning. Contributors to urbandictionary.com, for example, define "bros" as: "white frat guys," "stupid white trash guys," and "usually white young males, found commonly in places like San Bernardino County in California, as well as Orange County."

In this vein, the working-class version of dude-on-dude sex is themed around a kind of Eminem-inspired white working-class "thuggery," constructed through an in-your-face reclamation of "white trash" and homophobic, or anti-gay, sexuality. While some ads express desire for "average" working-class men (e.g., "carpenters, carpet layers, plumbers, construction workers, mechanics, truckers, cable guys, delivery guys, overall just a hard working guy as I am. NO GAYS sorry"), others eroticize aggressive "white trash" masculinity, such as the following personal ad, which appeared with figure 4.4:

Figure 4.4. Original photo included with text of personal ad, cropped by author to protect anonymity.

Str8 fuck a guy in his briefs, masc(uline) man to man fuck, hiv neg only. Hey fucks. I need to fuckin lay the pipe in some tight manhole today. I am hiv neg [HIV-negative] fuck with rubbers only. I want to have a hot packin guy in some tighty whities bent over and on all fours takin my dick like a champ. No fems or tweeking pnp ["party and play"] dudes. I hate that shit. Only 420 and a hot packin butt. Hit me up with your pix and your contact info.

The author of this ad amplifies his heterosexuality through a synthesis of working-class whiteness and what is arguably the appropriation of black masculinity through hip-hop slang ("hit me up"). White male friendship takes a less relaxed and friendly form here, where dude-sex is described as a hyper-masculine ("man to man") daredevil behavior to be endured like a "champ." Mirroring the focus on anal resilience in films like *Jackass*, sex between dudes is constructed in the above ad as an extreme sport, an exhilarating stunt. Though white male friendship does not completely fade from view here (a similar ad states: "lookin for str8, bi, surfr, sk8r, punk, military, truckers, skinhead, rough trade. . . . I'll give you the best head ever, buddy"), the homosocial is conceptualized differently in these ads. White male bonding takes the form of challenge and dominance, and working-class white male archetypes—such as truckers, punks, and skinheads—are added to the list of potential not-gay types.

Less Str8, More DL: Desiring Black Men

Public discourse on "straight men who have sex with men" has been highly racialized since the 2000s, a context that undoubtedly informs how straight dudes—such as those posting ads in Casual Encounters—can imagine and articulate their desire for homosexual sex. The mainstream media's attention to the subject has focused almost exclusively on black men "on the down low" (the DL), or black men who have sex with men but do not identify as gay. Following the publication of a high-profile *New York Times Magazine* article by the white reporter Benoit Denizet-Lewis in 2003, titled "Double Lives on the Down Low,"[15] everyone from HIV outreach workers to daytime talk-show hosts (such as the hosts of *The View*) began debating the causes and effects of black men's purported refusal to be "honest" about their sex with men. As word of "the down low phenomenon" spread through the media, the sexual fluidity of black men was blamed for rising rates of HIV infection among heterosexual women of color,[16] a claim that persists today despite the U.S. Center for Disease Control's official position that "there are no data to confirm or refute publicized accounts of HIV risk behavior associated with [men on the down low]."[17] One effect of the media's attention to the down low is that men of color have become the new public face of the closet, inviting speculation among scholars and reporters about greater levels of homophobia in black (and Latino) culture.[18] Black men on the DL have been repeatedly described as "a new subculture of gay men" who are constrained by rigid gender norms and hyper-heterosexuality within African American culture.[19]

Critics of these discourses have pointed out that the down low has the all too familiar ingredients of moral panic: "concealed non-normative sexualities, . . . a pandemic caused by a sexually transmitted agent, *innocent victims* (heterosexual women), and a population often accused of misbehavior (men of color)."[20] Black gay activist and writer Keith Boykin argues that the term "down low," applied almost exclusively to men of color, evokes a dark and frightening underworld—imagery that reinforces a long history of white supremacist ideas about the dangerous or predatory character of black male sexuality. White men who have sex with men are typically accused of being in the closet, but they are not attributed the additional layer of ominousness associated with the down low. To illustrate the racialized framing of heteroflexibility, Boykin has noted that in only one of over four thousand published news stories about the 2005 hit film *Brokeback Mountain* did critics use the term "down low" to refer to the film's main characters.[21] In commentary surrounding *Brokeback Mountain*, sex between straight white men was attributed greater human complexity and romantic depth, and approached with greater forgiveness, than that of black men:

> If these characters had been black, they would have called this movie a film about the down low. Instead, they're calling it a classic love story. . . . But make no mistake about it. *These men are on the down low.* The term "down low" is commonly used to refer to "men who have sex with men but do not identify as gay." . . . If the cowboy boot fits, then wear it. The reason why we don't say they're on the down low is simple—they're white. When white men engage in this behavior, we just call it what it is and move on. But when black men do it, then we have to pathologize it into something evil called the "down low." Therein lies the double standard.[22]

Boykin's juxtaposition of the fear surrounding black men on the DL with the celebration of the white romance depicted in *Brokeback Mountain* offers a compelling example of the ways that white dominance and black racial oppression have long converged to cast black sexual fluidity as pathological, and white sexual fluidity as progressive.[23] It offers a window into the reasons that straight-identified white men may feel greater permission than black men to conceptualize their homosexual experiences through the lens of normal homosociality.

Boykin's critique further draws attention to the challenges of giving *name* to the racial and cultural differences that shape straight men's sexual encounters with other men. Indeed, the white cowboys in *Brokeback Mountain* certainly conform to Boykin's definition of being on the down low, but Boykin himself acknowledges that the concept is deeply fraught with pathology; in light of this, widening the term's usage seems a counterproductive goal. And yet, by some accounts,[24] the down low is a vital channel for the expression of black pride and an important black subcultural formation that resists the whiteness of the lesbian and gay movement. But, of course, being on the DL is not the only way to embody black pride while having sex with men. What distinguishes black men on the DL from black gay men is not likely a more developed political critique of whiteness, but an increased comfort with black heteronormative culture and the primacy of sexual relationships with women (or at least the appearance of this primacy).

This racial and political context—and its implications for the language straight white men use to describe their desire for sex with other men—is evident in the ads straight dudes post in Casual Encounters. In some rare but nonetheless significant ads, white dudes' appropriation of blackness takes the form of reference to "the down low." Just as white men's uses of African American slang correspond with a less friendly and egalitarian formulation of dude-sex in the examples above, the introduction of the DL shifts the encounter even further away from the elaborately scripted scenes of white friendship and towards an encounter that is quick, secret/closeted, and silent:

STR8 DUDES . . . White boy lookin for a NO CHAT suck . . . u lemme suck u . . .—29. Hot dude on ur dick . . . u fuck my throat and bust it. . . . we never talk. Come over, kick back, pull ur cock out and get a kick ass wet deepthroat BJ. Love to deepthroat a hot str8 dude on the DL . . . bust ur nut and split. I'm a very goodlooking in shape white dude . . . totally on the DL . . . just wanna suck a hot str8 dude off, take ur nut . . . that's all. My place is kewl.

SECRET SERVICE HEAD—28. Sup? Looking for bi/ str8 bud who is just looking to crack a nut . . . Just walk in kick back watch a porn and get blown . . . Cum and go . . . That's all I am looking for . . . Be white, under 30, masculine and discreet. This is on the DL . . . Have a girlfriend . . . but new to town.

Here white men do not express cross-racial desire: The first ad does not specify a racial preference, and the second ad specifies that the respondent should "be white." But they deploy the DL—however inaccurately, given its far more complex meaning in black and Latino DL subculture—as a code for quick and meaningless sex between straight men.

In another small set of ads, however, some white dudes describe scenes in which they wish to have "no strings attached" sex with black men on the DL. In contrast with "white seeking white" ads that imply sameness, reciprocity, or egalitarianism (let's stroke together, watch porn together, "work out a hot load side by side," etc.), the presence of cross-racial desire, or even black cultural formations like the DL, disrupt the homosocial narrative. The ads in which white dudes express desire for black men do not use terms like "buddy," "bro," or "man-to-man." They do not involve leisurely exchanges in which dudes will kick back, drink beer, and chat about bitches. Instead, they are centered on themes of difference, hierarchy, and service, primarily characterized by white men seeking to perform blowjobs for big, muscular black men.

The ads also highlight the relationship between race and body size (e.g., "big BLACK cock," "nice big meaty Black guys"):

> *Discreet White Deep Throat 4 DL Black—-Size Matters—44.* Discreet 44 yr old white guy lookin' to service hot Black guys on the DL. I'm hairy, good shape. I'm lookin' for very hung Black guys who love to kick back, watch porn and get their cocks serviced. I really like to deep throat big BLACK cock. If you are interested, hit me back with your stats and a pic if you have one. . . . I really love very tall skinny men, hung huge.

> *Looking to suck off big black men, on the DL*—White guy here looking to suck off big muscular black guys. I like them big, over 250lbs and muscular. No strings attached. Hoping to meet some men on the DL. Got my own place, it's private and discreet, no strings, no hassles, etc. Just want to suck off some nice big meaty black guys.

> *Muscled Guy Looking for Str8 or Bi to Service on the Down Low*— Meet me at the construction site. I will be there waiting for you [in the?] dark, service you and leave anonymous. . . . Send pic must be hot like me . . . [with figures 4.5 and 4.6].

In the images pictured in figures 4.5 and 4.6, white submission and Black dominance is also a central theme. An image is included that reverses the master/slave relationship (a dominant black male, and a shackled white male) and that has likely been taken from BDSM-themed[25] gay porn. While race is not mentioned in the text of this ad, the figure of the dominant black male (and the submissive white male body) is used to represent the queerer—or less normal and natural—white fantasy of the down low. The ads suggest that in the black-white encounter, black men are always dominant; they receive sexual service, but they do not provide it. Within Casual Encounters, friendship, equity, and "normal and natural male bonding" are represented as either undesirable or

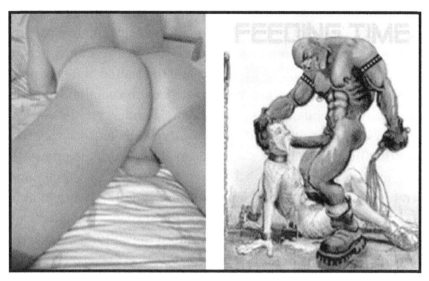

Figures 4.5 and 4.6. Original photos included with text of personal ad.

impossible across racial lines. The DL requires anonymity, discretion, and meeting in "dark" places like the "construction site." In straight white dudes' representations of the black-white encounter, cross-racial sex is not an organic expression of homosocial bonding or "just being men." The presence of (or desire for) racial difference produces a darker, less natural encounter permeated with difference and inequality, and concomitantly, queerness.

Between White Men

As the late critical sociologist Lionel Cantú elaborated, the social science of sexuality has long placed emphasis on the ethnoracial and cultural meanings of sexual fluidity among people of color, to be contrasted with the structural and circumstantial meanings attributed to white sexualities. Particularly within the disciplines of anthropology and sociology, the sexualities of people of color, especially outside of the United States, has been attributed to both hyper-rigid (i.e., homophobic) and hyper-fluid (i.e., not adhering to a natural hetero/homo binary) cultural formations. In contrast, culture is treated as generally irrelevant to

European American sexualities, which are largely understood to have evolved in relation to political and socioeconomic developments. This can be seen in scholarship linking the emergence of modern queer sexualities in Europe and the United States to processes of industrialization, urbanization, and social movement mobilization, while, in contrast, the most widely cited research on Mexican sexualities, for instance, typically emphasizes the way that the particularities of Mexican culture result in an exotic system of sexual roles (such as *activo/passivo*). As Cantú demonstrates, such characterizations not only elide the political and socioeconomic conditions that shape the sexualities of people of color; they also remain generally blind to the cultural and racial elements of European American sexualities.[26]

Straight white men's sex practices, including their homosexual practices, are shaped by the culture in which they are situated: namely, the culture of white hetero-masculinity.[27] Scholars within critical whiteness studies have identified several key elements of "white culture": Internalized racial superiority, political and economic entitlement, self-perceptions of normalcy and rationality, and ethnoracial appropriation are among its defining features.[28] Cultures of masculinity are also defined by rules and signifiers that guide social relations among men and that are interconnected with processes of racialization. In the United States, normative heterosexual masculinity is signaled by the performance of invulnerability, the repression of emotions other than anger, attempts to establish dominance over women and other men, and the glorification of men's physical strength and authority.[29] Taken together, these aspects of white male subjectivity certainly have structural and institutional foundations, but they are also cultural to the extent that they are passed down from white parents to their white male children, reproduced within white art and media, and woven through white men's psychic, social, and sexual lives.

The ways that these elements of white masculinity shape white men's sex practices is remarkably understudied, with most exceptions focusing on straight white men's cross-racial desires, or their desire for women of color. While I have considered here the cross-racial desires of white men, my broader concern has been with the ways that straight white men—the paradigmatic figures of the normal, average, every man—express desire for the mirror of idealized white masculinity. In popular culture—such as the films I discussed at the outset of this chapter—as well as within straight white men's personal ads, we see what may well be an effort to repair the break between homosexual sex and male homosocial bonds. This project of restoring the harmony between male homosexual contact and male cultural and political dominance—the "unbrokenness" Sedgwick describes as characteristic of earlier periods in sexual history—requires a return to yet another feature of premodern sexuality: namely, the delinking of homosexual acts from homosexual personage. For straight white dudes, the path to "homosexual sex without homosexuality" is marked by dis-identification with gay men, affirmation of men's investments in misogyny and gendered violence, and deliberate deployment of a nostalgic homosocial narrative that (re)situates the sexual within the realm of normal male bonding. But this project is a tenuous one that demands as much supporting evidence as possible, and harnessing all signs of normal friendship—especially racial sameness—is at its core.

Archetypes of white heterosexual masculinity—the jock, the surfer, the frat boy—appear in Casual Encounters not simply in the context of white men's attempts to establish their own "average dude" subjectivity or to express a preference for white male types; they also signify a particular quality of relation *between white men*, one marked by shared normalcy, collective non-Otherness, and the *not-queer* feelings of home, comfort, friend-liness, and sameness. Jocks and frat boys are not autonomous white male subjects; they evoke "team sports" and "brotherhood" as much as they evoke personhood. They suggest also an institutional context that facilitates, if not requires, homosocial (and homosexual) contact between men. Sexual forms of male bonding that occur in the name of sport and fraternity can hardly be blamed on an individual male subject; they are a functional part of a time-honored tradition. They foster white male unity.

Given the ways in which systems of white racial dominance construct whiteness as natural, invisible, and non-racialized, sex between white men is de-racialized by extension, so that it seemingly possesses none of the difference or racial fetishism expressed in cross-racial sexual encounters. Despite misguided pronouncements of a "post-racial" era, cross-racial encounters are not *casual* encounters, nor are they encounters in which it can be presumed that white men are invested in promoting the interests of men of color (nor the reverse, though clearly for different reasons). While racial appropriation of blackness by whites may appear to be an attempt at cross-racial homosociality, actual sexual contact between white male bodies and male bodies of color disrupts the staging of natural male bonding and unity and denotes a distinctly queerer space "down low."

This chapter has delved into some of the friendly and egalitarian features of straight white male relationality—namely, the casual, nostalgic, and adventurous modes of white male bonding that facilitate, rhetorically, if not materially, not-gay homosexual contact. The next chapter takes a dramatic turn toward themes of force and humiliation, the arguably less friendly channels of homosexual contact among straight men. Taken together, both this chapter and the next demonstrate the remarkable range of rhetorical tools available to straight white men to create and sustain utterly normal, totally straight, nothing-gay-here environments where *real men* can touch, lick, and penetrate other real men.

5

Haze Him!

White Masculinity, Anal Resilience, and
the Erotic Spectacle of Repulsion

Acommon refrain about hazing in male-dominated institutions, such as college fraternities and the military, is that the homosexual encounters that occur in these contexts are not primarily sexual in their motivation, but are instead acts of dominance and violence that make strategic use of homosexual activity in order to heighten straight men's experience of humiliation and repulsion. Especially in the military context, such an interpretation appears logical given the fact that there is indeed a blurry line between homosexual penetration that falls under the banner of routine hazing of new soldiers, on the one hand, and what we would likely agree are cases of actual male-male rape in military zones, on the other. Fleshing out the erotic meaning of homosexual behavior within hazing is a complicated task then, because violence, repulsion, and humiliation run through both experiences—those that we would likely characterize as generally consensual and those we would characterize as assault.

Research on military hazing suggests that when male soldiers are commanded to eat objects out of other soldiers' anuses or are anally penetrated with hands and objects during initiation ceremonies, they are compelled to endure these acts with visible displays of homophobic repulsion and hetero-masculine resilience. They take penetration like a champ, to use the straight-dude parlance introduced in the last chapter. Even as hazing implies a degree of consent on the part of participants who have temporarily abdicated their comfort and dignity in order to gain access to the group, the staging and performance of "force" remains integral to the experience. The shared understanding that participants are being required, in some form or another, to endure something to which they would not otherwise willfully agree is a central theme within hazing. Akin to the contention by some feminists that rape is about power and violence and not sexual desire, one might argue that homosexual contact within hazing—presumably forced, or at least falling within the previously discussed rhetorical framework of "fuck or die"—tells us little about the sexual fluidity of straight men and more about men's impulse or socialization to dominate one another by any means necessary (including homosexual touching).

And yet, in this chapter I argue for a more nuanced reading of homosexual behavior within hazing, one that recognizes the complex interplay of desire and repulsion within the circuits of white male heterosexuality. My aim here is to show that the presence of power, repulsion, and disgust do not, in and of themselves, signal the absence of eroticism or sexual meaning, even as these affective states are often used—by men themselves and by commentators about male sexuality—to dismiss or obscure the sexual content of straight men's homosexual encounters. Indeed, whether or not one "likes" or is "turned on" by same-sex or opposite-sex sexuality is typically believed to constitute the evidence of one's sexual orientation. But what sense can we make of situations in which intimate contact is both arousing and repulsive, infused with desire and disgust? To consider this complexity, we need look no further than heterosexual, male-female attraction itself. At the heart of misogyny lies the tension between heterosexual men's ostensibly hardwired desire for women and their simultaneous contempt for women's perceived weakness and inferiority, including the unmodified and unclean female body (e.g., women's "nasty" body

hair, "foul-smelling" vaginas, and so forth). Misogyny, or men's hatred of women, and heterosexuality, which presumes men's desire
for women, coexist more harmoniously than would at first appear
logical, in large part because constructions of masculinity allow
sex acts to have a far more complex set of meanings for men than
for women, extending beyond pleasure and intimacy to include
dominance, dehumanization, ownership, and violence.

Central to misogyny is also the construction of women as especially easy to defile, always potentially abject. One apt example is
the figure of "Susie Rottencrotch," a common euphemism in the
Marines for girlfriends left behind during deployment.[1] The term
purportedly has its roots in the U.S. military's venereal disease
propaganda films, but Marines now conceptualize Susie Rottencrotch more broadly as the name for women back home who are
simultaneously objects of love and longing, hatred and disgust.
According to Rottencrotch lore, once-beloved girlfriends, when
separated from their boyfriends by distance and time, degenerate into manipulative and disloyal sluts, filthy and unclean, "filled
with cock," dangerous in their capacity to distract men from survival in the trenches.[2] Extending well beyond the military, this
slippery slope between desire and repulsion runs through adolescent boys' stories about sex with girls,[3] adult men's accounts
of the reasons they abuse women,[4] gender imagery in countless
music videos,[5] and male philosophers' accounts of women's basic
nature.[6]

The point here is that to be armed with an historical, feminist
view of male (hetero)sexuality is to recognize that it has long
taken the form of that which is both desirous of, and repulsed by,
its object. Of course I am not suggesting that men don't feel genuine love and respect for the women, and men, they have sex with.
Instead I am arguing that straight men's sexual track record points
to a dynamic tension between desire and disdain for that which is
being fucked, and hence, straight-identified men's sincere repulsion with homosexual sex and with other men's bodies does not

signal innate heterosexuality any more than straight men's sincere misogyny signals innate homosexuality. That straight men are grossed out by men's bodies, that they appear especially obsessed with what is grotesque about their own and other men's anuses, and that they use homosexual sex to humiliate and demean and dominate one another are all important pieces of information for analysis, but they are not evidence that these acts are nonsexual. Instead, as I will argue, dominance, humiliation, anality, and repulsion are more productively read as having a fetishized quality within white hetero-masculinity, one that infuses homosocial settings with the hetero-erotic. In this sense, hazing—which entails all of these elements—is not simply a practice; it is also a hetero-erotic trope, one that facilitates access to homosexual activity while inscribing this activity with heterosexual meaning.

To uncover the hetero-eroticism within homosexual hazing activity, this chapter begins with a review of research on U.S. military hazing rituals long known for their use of humiliating and "homoerotic" tests of endurance and allegiance. I look closely at the nonsexual meanings other researchers and commentators have attributed to homosexual contact sanctioned in the military, and expand on these analyses by (re)introducing the erotic—and more specifically, the hetero-erotic—to our understanding of homosexual activity in military hazing. The chapter then follows militaristic hazing as it circulates beyond the bounds of the military, starting with drunken "hazing parties" held by privately contracted security guards stationed at the U.S. embassy in Kabul (a setting arguably within the military industrial complex even as it sits outside the formal boundaries of the military itself), and then shifting to the representation of military-style hazing in the popular series of Internet hazing porn, HazeHim.com. These settings, though not subject to the same conditions, nonetheless recreate virtually identical scenes, borrowing on military traditions and imagery to establish their own heterosexual meaning. "Hazing porn," I will argue, offers a particularly powerful example of hazing as an erotic trope that facilitates homosexual contact without disrupting heterosexual realness. In *HazeHim*, as in the military itself, homophobic outbursts and expressions of disgust and repulsion signal heterosexuality, offering gay fans of the films the opportunity to eroticize what is rarely marked and made visible—the sexual culture of straight white men.

The hazing rituals I discuss in this chapter have been, for the most part, created by and for white men. Consequently, the chapter attends to the ways that sadistic, grotesque, and anus-centered hazing mirrors the culture of white American hetero-masculinity more broadly, as exemplified by the remarkable popularity among white male viewers of TV shows centered on these themes, like *South Park* and *Jackass*. To the extent that white male entitlement, aggression, and grossness have been normalized within popular culture, so too has the erotic significance of white men's hazing practices been all but erased or subsumed under the unexamined category of "boys being boys." As a corrective to this erasure, this chapter attempts to bring both hetero-masculinity and whiteness into view as we consider the meaning of homosexual activity within the hazing practices of straight white men. Once largely normalized and invisible, the cultural underpinnings of white hetero-masculinity—including entitlement, violence, obsession with the grotesque, and the nexus of homophobia and homosexual desire—have recently been placed under the spotlight by numerous writers attempting to understand mass shootings and other forms of violence committed almost exclusively by young white men.[7] This chapter builds on these developments.

Crossing the Line: Homosexual Encounters in Military Hazing

The figure of the male soldier is fraught with contradictory meanings in the American imagination. Within nationalist discourse, he is an exemplar of idealized American masculinity: brave, strong, patriotic, ethical, and until very recently, heterosexual and white. Alongside this imagery, countless blockbuster war films and media exposés have revealed male soldiers to be tragic victims of post-traumatic stress, callous rapists and homophobic torturers, and racists capable of demonizing even the young children of the enemy. According to political scientist Aaron Belkin, the status of the male soldier is equally riddled with contradictions within the ideals and practices of the military itself. While most research on the culture of the armed forces has pointed to the military's insistence that troops disavow all forms of femininity and vulnerability, Belkin illustrates in his provocative book *Bring Me Men* that in fact service members are compelled to engage in practices coded by the military as both masculine and feminine, normative and queer, pure and polluted, vulnerable and resilient. The blurring of these dualisms, and soldiers' concomitant confusion and anxiety about their meaning, has long functioned as a tool central to the military's control and discipline of troops, Belkin explains.

For example, while the armed forces glorify impenetrable bodies, pristine uniforms, and spotless barracks, they sanction initiation ceremonies—such as the Navy's "crossing the line" ceremony—involving filth, anal penetration, and rimming (analingus). According to anthropologist Carrie Little Hersh, a standard element of the crossing the line ceremony is to have "garbage, sewage and rotten food . . . poured over the wogs (sailors crossing the equator for the first time) and into every orifice of their bodies, including their anuses."[8] Hersh explains that wogs are also frequently required to retrieve objects from one another's anuses, initiating analingus. Military researcher Steven Zeeland describes crossing the line as a "time-honored, officially sanctioned initiation ceremony in which sailors traversing the equator for the first time may experience cross-dressing, sadomasochistic rituals, and simulated anal and oral sex."[9] Zeeland elaborates that the Navy's position on acceptable forms of hazing during the ceremony has evolved in response to external pressures. For instance, follow-

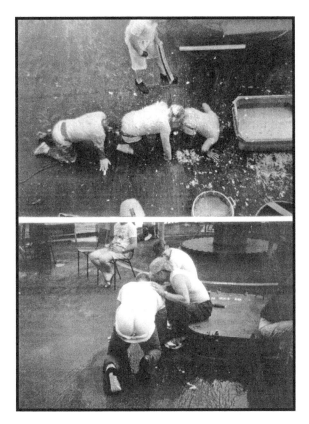

Figure 5.1. The Navy's crossing the line ceremony (Zeeland, *Sailors and Sexual Identity*).

ing the Tailhook sexual assaults in the early 1990s,[10] Navy guidelines were revised so as to prohibit dressing in drag and spanking, though they retained the time-honored traditions of lathering wogs with Crisco, chocolate syrup, grease or other lubricants and ordering wogs to simulate anal intercourse. Other Navy initiation rituals described by Zeeland involve sucking olives from the belly button of the ship's fattest petty officer and inserting grease guns into shipmate's anuses (now a banned practice).

Both Belkin and Zeeland make a persuasive case that the meaning of homosexual contact in the Navy is fluid, contextual, and contested. Drawing on interviews and documents from Naval Academy investigations, Belkin concludes that in late twentieth century,

Male American service members penetrated each other's bodies "all of the time." They forced broom handles, fingers, and penises into each other's anuses. They stuck pins into flesh and bones. They vomited into one another's mouths and forced rotten food down each other's throats. They inserted tubes into each other's anal cavities and then pumped grease through the tubes. . . . Penetrating and being penetrated have been central to what it means to be a warrior in the U.S. armed forces. And yet . . . rape and other forms of penetration have implied a range of meanings. In some cases, being penetrated is a marker of weakness, subordination, and lack of control. In other cases it is an indication of strength, dominance, and power. In some cases, it signifies infantilization. In others, maturation. . . . Some military practices construct being penetrated as the ultimate taboo . . . others construct it as central to what it means to be a real man."[11]

Belkin goes on to explain that in many cases, these competing meanings are operating simultaneously, resulting in confusion and increased compliance among soldiers who are not certain whether they have engaged in the right, or hetero-masculine, form of homosexual penetration.

In Belkin's view, military-sanctioned homosexual contact is imposed on men by military institutions, therefore falling somewhere on the spectrum of sexual assault. The driving force in Belkin's analysis is not men's impulse toward, or desire for, intimate contact with other men. Instead, Belkin argues that it is the military itself, which incites soldiers to participate in ambiguous acts of queerness and then ensures soldiers' confusion about the meaning of these acts. Tellingly, Belkin argues that "U.S. service members have confused gay and straight, love and hate, rapist and rape victim, anus and mouth, expulsion and retention, rape and hazing, friendship and loneliness, literal and symbolic penetration, and gay identification and same-sex erotic experience."[12] Though perhaps not Belkin's intention, this line of thinking implies a world outside of the military in which the distinction between "gay" and "straight" behavior is quite clear—an idea I hope to have cast considerable doubt upon by now.

But more to the point at hand, the slippage between "rape" and hazing in Belkin's analysis masks the erotic forces at work as men manufacture opportunities to touch, lick, and penetrate one another's anuses. Throughout this book, I make the case that such activities occur in too broad a range of contexts to be accounted for by the particular logic of any given institution, a point I return to later in this chapter. But for now, let us consider for a moment how we might interpret "crossing the line," or any other ritualized form of "simulated anal and oral sex," if these behaviors were enacted by a group of women service members, or perhaps a group of sorority sisters. Let us imagine scenes in which women pour chocolate syrup on one another's anuses and demand that the least powerful women among the group must lick it off, or scenes in which a row of women are "simulating" cunnilingus as part of a time-honored initiation ritual. Even as power is operating in such scenes, the absence of a masculinity alibi and the presence of women's purportedly "fluid" sexuality allow the erotic possibilities of these scenes to come into clearer view. Such has not been the case in analyses of straight men's ritualized homosexual contact, as pervasive notions about male sexual rigidity and aggressive homophobia have all but foreclosed any reading other than rape, or perhaps "closeted" homosexual identity (often attributed to men in the Navy, for instance).

In contrast with Belkin, Zeeland, whose research is based on interviews with gay former sailors and Marines (only some of whom were "out" during their period of service), gives attention to the pleasurable sensations made possible by hazing rituals like crossing the line. While some of Zeeland's interview participants are emphatic that having Crisco applied to their anuses or being "humped" by other men was not a sexual experience (but an act of submission to a team-building tradition), others found these rituals erotic. Men in the latter group felt sexual excitement about "getting fucked," being dominated, and even engaging in gross-out contests, but explained that this sexual response was not *gay*, as it might appear in civilian contexts, but erotically charged precisely because of its association with hyper-heterosexual masculine endurance. One of Zeeland's interviewees, Eddy, reports that he found crossing the line "fun," in part because he could not be "broken," as was the intention of the ritual:

> I thought I was going to hate it, but I had fun. Some people quit, the people who couldn't take it anymore, men who were crying . . . it's really degrading. I had food all over me. I had Crisco oil poured on my face. . . . Everyone thought I was going to break down. Everyone. All the straight people. "We're going to break you." . . . [A guy] was behind me . . . humping me . . . this supposedly straight guy. . . . But that wasn't unusual, because everyone was doing that that day. Wog day is a day for everyone to have fun, and if anyone ever thought about any kind of homosexual tendency, they could do what they wanted to do without anyone even thinking about it.[13]

Mirroring some of the narratives explored in the previous chapter, such accounts illuminate the powerful ways in which hetero-masculine brotherhood rituals recode intimate bodily contact appearing to be both "gay" and "repulsive," repackaging it as a potentially pleasurable opportunity to display one's masculinity.

Although Zeeland's research subjects are men who identify as gay and bisexual, their accounts of sex with straight men while out at sea suggest numerous nonobligatory and consensual scenarios in which straight men seek out sex with men. Stories such as the following appear over and over again in Zeeland's research:

> If he didn't want it he could have really beaten me up, and I don't know whether it was the fact that he was drunk that he let me come on to him. . . . But we did have . . . oral sex. He gave me oral sex,

I gave him oral sex. It was great. . . . We still keep in touch. . . . He's engaged to marry this girl he's been dating for a while. (Anthony)

One of my good friends . . . is married and has children, and . . . is totally straight . . . in fact, he looks down on gay people. . . . We went to a port in Australia and he didn't want to sleep with a girl because he thought it would be cheating on his wife. So he had sex with another man. . . . We all saw it happen. He didn't think twice about it. (Eddy)

There was a lot of [straight guys] I had to say "no" to cause I was like, "what do you all take me for?" . . . I knew their attitude toward gays, or fags, or whatever they'd say. Then when they got drunk they want to come back and get their dick sucked. (Trent)

In fact, in many cases, when homosexual contact was coerced, it was gay men who felt pressured by straight men to have sex. As Anthony explained, "when you're the sea bitch, or what some guys also called the sea pussy, it's expected of you to perform sexual favors . . . whether you feel like it or not. You're going to suck their dick or jerk them off. . . . Straight guys, married guys."

In contrast with Belkin's account, Zeeland's research lends itself to viewing the military as a kind of opportunity structure, a term used by sociologists to describe external factors that converge to create conditions for collective action. From this point of view, the military does not incite homosexual contact to confuse troops, but rather it provides a logic (masculine resilience) and a setting (isolation, such as while at sea) that facilitates and recuperates homosexual encounters, for both straight and gay service members. As one of Zeeland's interviewees, a Navy lieutenant, explains, "on submarines they have a joke that 'it's only queer if you're tied to the pier.' In other words, out at sea sex is okay, but once you're in port, you can't talk about that, or they'll throw you out for it."[14] Viewing the military as a sexual opportunity structure recognizes the significance of the circumstances in which men engage in homosexual activity, but does not foreclose straight men's erotic agency as pursuers of homosexuality.

Regardless of how one interprets rituals like crossing the line, the normalized, military-sanctioned role of penetration within military contexts remains remarkable given the simultaneous existence of a powerful penetration taboo within the Armed Forces. Belkin convincingly demonstrates that this taboo is rooted in timeworn discourses linking warrior masculinity with sealed-up, leak-proof, impenetrable bodies, to be contrasted with the vulnerable, leaky, penetrable bodies of women and the enemy. Impenetrability carries more than sexual meaning; it is also about safeguarding the body from bullets, shrapnel, and other penetrating objects with lethal consequences. And yet, as Belkin illuminates, the penetration taboo is "flexible" in the presence of two forces: first, violent forms of initiation, and second, extreme and performative grossness/repulsion (such as is central to the crossing the line ceremony). Zeeland's research suggests the additional force of isolation: It's not queer when one is out at sea or in the trenches, presumably without access to women sex partners.

These forces have the power to resignify homosexual contact as hyper-masculine, resilient, and exceptional. With these forces in operation, being penetrated takes on new meaning as it is imbued with the power to toughen up the male body and put the male character to an extreme test. It offers men the opportunity to endure homosexual penetration and then stand up, unbroken. At its best, penetration by one's fellow soldiers inoculates men against the ever-looming threat of truly queer penetration by the enemy.

Understandably, military researchers like Belkin and Zeeland do not address the extent to which these resignifying narratives—-i.e., homosexual sex is not gay when it occurs in the context of force or hazing; homosexual sex is not gay when it is paired with rotten food and all things vile; homosexual sex is not gay when it happens under conditions of isolation—have rhetorical power beyond the military context. Like most researchers focused on the institutional contexts in which heterosexuals engage in homosexual sex, both Belkin and Zeeland exceptionalize the military, viewing straight men's engagement with homosexuality as a sign of the military's unusually complex and contradictory gender and sexual order, or its uniqueness as an institution providing just the right material and rhetorical conditions to bring out men's potential for homosexual desire.

Here I take a more expanded view that it is not male-dominated total institutions like prisons and the military that are particularly contradictory and complex in their conceptualization of sexuality, but that it is heterosexuality itself—including and especially male heterosexuality—that is contradictory and complex. Total institutions do not teach straight men how to behave homosexually, just as straight women do not need to go to prison to learn how to kiss other women on the dance floor at their local club. Straight boys and men, I believe, already have all of the information and proclivities they need to manufacture situations that facilitate homosexual (and heterosexual) activity. Institutional hazing—wherein one sets up the opportunity for powerful men to order less powerful men to touch each other's anuses, for instance—is but one of the justificatory tropes that facilitates these encounters and divorces them from gay/identitarian consequences. As discussed in previous chapters, to "endure" abject homosexual penetration, to take it like a champ or a warrior, to surrender to blood, shit, and penises so as to demonstrate one's allegiance to a male group or to display one's masculine autonomy—all of these are tropes that circulate well beyond the hetero-masculine confines of the military, appearing in fantasies posted on the Internet, in college fraternities, in prisons, in straight and gay porn, in living rooms, in public bathrooms, at truck stops, and a range of other contexts.

Much needed attention has been given to the role of power, humiliation, and violence in institutional hazing, but all too often these factors subsume the erotic components of hazing, which take place in the context of power and hierarchy but are nonetheless "real" sex acts not unlike those that boys and men experience outside hazing contexts. As stated at the outset of this chapter, the nexus of sexual desire, disdain, and repulsion is arguably a mainstay of heterosexuality itself, directed at girls and women as much as, and probably more than, other men. For instance, in her study of teenage boys in a California high school, sociologist CJ Pascoe documents the central role of abjection in boys' stories about sex with girls. Pascoe finds that boys' accounts of heterosexual sex were frequently detached from any conventional erotic meanings, including their own personal pleasure or orgasm, and instead emphasized the conquering of girls' abject bodies, with common reference to "ripping vaginal walls" and making girls bleed and fart and shit. Such findings point to the role of violence, humiliation, and disgust, at least rhetorically, within even the most heteronormative expressions of male sexual attraction.

I draw these parallels—between the seemingly extraordinary abusiveness of military initiation rituals and the violence that runs through the mundane heterosexuality of high school—to shed light on one of the underpinnings of hetero-exceptionalism. I am referring here to the flawed tendency to believe that power and disgust trumps the presence of sexual pleasure, or indicates that sexual pleasure is somehow distorted or discordant. Institutionalized hazing—involving rigid rules, homosexual degradation, and evident repulsion—has been posited as a clear-cut example of extreme and sexualized bullying, wherein young men are forced to act out of accordance with their normal sexual impulses. But there is another way of viewing hazing, not as a purely abusive practice that forces straight men to "stray" from their natural sexual constitution, but as one expression of the nexus of power and pleasure that undergirds hetero-masculinity more broadly.

Taking our lead from feminist theorist Gayle Rubin, we can see that one of the challenges inherent in analyzing sex within hazing is that like any sex practice, it is subject to multiple interpretations that are largely informed by the sexual tastes and values of the interpreter. From a queer perspective, the one I bring to this book, hazing scenes look easily like kinky sex play, like the kind of consensual soft-core BDSM at which most queers would hardly bat an eyelash. From a more mainstream perspective, the very presence of food or objects shoved in anuses raises a red flag immediately, marking the scene as humiliating and abusive.

Added to this complexity is the fact that there is clearly a cultural interplay between the normative U.S. imagination of kinky and humiliating sex practices and the truly violent and sexualized forms of torture enacted upon enemy prisoners by American soldiers. For instance, highlighting this relationship in the context of American soldiers' torture of Iraqi prisoners at Abu Ghraib, philosopher Slavoj Žižek has written, "When I saw the well-known photo of a naked prisoner with a black hood covering his head, electric cables attached to his limbs, standing on a chair in a ridiculous theatrical pose, my first reaction was that this was a shot of some latest performance art show in Lower Manhattan. The very positions and costumes of the prisoners suggest a theatrical staging, a kind of tableau vivant, which cannot but bring to our mind the whole scope of U.S. performance art and 'theatre of cruelty.'"[15] Žižek goes on to argue that the distinctly performative acts of torture enacted at Abu Ghraib cannot be understood apart from the U.S. obsession with degrading, anus-focused initiation rituals, which white American men impose upon themselves—offering themselves a "false free choice" of whether or not to participate—and then extend to their enemies, who have no choice but to endure them. Žižek's analysis is perhaps misdirected at the representational realm of performance art and a bit too quick to judge anus-related degradation, but it is nonetheless a useful framework for considering the ways that performative humiliation, anal penetration, and "false free choices" are constitutive of white American masculinity, rather than unusual deviations.

Raising similar concerns, feminist theorist Jasbir Puar offers a powerful critique of the way U.S. commentators made sense of the nexus of torture and homosexuality at Abu Ghraib. In the groundbreaking book *Terrorist Assemblages*, Puar highlights the contradictory U.S. obsession with committing acts of (homo) sexual torture, on the one hand, *and* imagining itself as a nation characterized by greater levels of sexual freedom and tolerance relative to Islamic societies, on the other. Astonishingly, as American commentators constructed Muslim detainees as victims of an especially repressive and homophobic Muslim culture, they crafted a narrative in which U.S. acts of racist and homophobic torture at Abu Ghraib became an occasion for self-congratulation. According to this narrative, any soldier would be traumatized by the humiliation of homosexual sex (the American torturers shouldn't have done what they did . . .), but "our" soldiers would find these acts "less torturous" given elevated levels of tolerance for homosexuality in the United States. Echoing Žižek, Puar demonstrates that "the [American] use of sexuality—in this case to physically punish and humiliate—is not tangential, unusual, or reflective of an extreme case," but is central to the U.S. construction of itself and its difference from those cultures that ostensibly cannot tolerate forced (homosexual) penetration quite so well.[16]

Feminist theorist Judith Kegan Gardiner has also shed light on the relationship between white American masculinity and grotesque anality, or the "raucous delight in noise, mess, evacuation, and expulsion."[17] Long associated in psychoanalysis with working-class defiance against middle-class mores (consider, for instance, the excrement-focused folk humor central to medieval and Renaissance popular culture), anal eroticism and its links to hetero-masculinity arguably reflect the socioeconomic conditions and constructions of gender and sexuality in operation in a given time and place. In the modern U.S. context, Gardiner observes a shift from the anal retentive masculinity of the early and mid-twentieth century to an explosive anality in the late twentieth century brought on by a media culture that encourages increasing amounts of male passivity and conformity. Young white men can maintain the appearance of defiance and autonomy in the face of the onslaught of prepackaged corporate media by consuming television programs like *South Park*, in which the celebration of the male anus and its excrement is offered up as a kind of populist masculine rebellion. For Gardiner, contemporary white hetero-masculinity can be understood, then, as "a new configuration that has many qualities at once—an apparently childish, homoerotic but homophobic, racist, cynical, and paranoid form of anal eroticism."[18] Gardiner adds that childishness, the notion that even adult men are always potentially boys, is a centerpiece of contemporary manhood, constructing men as infinitely capable of a defiant embrace of a pre-adult sexuality—a sexuality that is implicitly heterosexual but primarily male-bonded, sometimes sadistic, and oriented toward an aggressive enjoyment of grossness and the anus. Here again, we are invited to consider that the orientation toward grossness, anality, and the homoerotic is not a departure from normative white hetero-masculinity, but among its central ingredients.[19] Taken together, Žižek, Puar, and Gardiner each highlight in different ways the obsessive entanglement of white hetero-masculinity with fantasies of anal penetration and homosexual degradation.

Lord of the Flies: "Deviant Hazing" at the U.S. Embassy in Kabul

With these considerations in mind, let us move now to the site of another example, in what we might call an extra-military zone, the United States embassy in Kabul, Afghanistan. In 2009, the U.S.-based independent watchdog organization Project on Government Oversight (POGO) released findings from their investigation into "security failings" at the embassy in Kabul. The noted failings centered primarily on problems with guards and supervisors employed by the North American security contractor ArmorGroup, including ongoing understaffing, fourteen-hour shifts, chronic sleep deprivation, high staff turnover, and poor decision-making. Exemplifying this chaos, the report explained, were allegations (alongside photographic evidence) that Armor-Group supervisors and guards were "engaging in near-weekly deviant hazing and humiliation of subordinates." Addressed to then Secretary of State Hillary Clinton, the report describes the situation as dangerous and volatile, especially given that the Kabul embassy had been a target of two Taliban attacks in 2009, resulting in seven deaths and ninety-one wounded. The men hired to protect the embassy from such attacks were busy, it turned out, drinking and eating from one another's anuses.

Although the report describes nearly identical activities as those that occur in the Navy-sanctioned crossing the line ceremony, here hazing is framed as a signal of a breakdown in the chain of command and a threat to national security. The report describes the scene as follows:

> Numerous emails, photographs, and videos portray a Lord of the Flies environment. One email from a current guard describes scenes in which guards and supervisors are "peeing on people, eating potato chips out of [buttock] cracks, [drinking] vodka shots out of [buttock] cracks (there is video of that one), broken doors after drnken [sic] brawls, threats and intimidation from those leaders participating in this activity. . . ." Photograph after photograph shows guards—including supervisors—at parties in various stages of nudity, sometimes fondling each other. These parties take place just a few yards from the housing of other supervisors. Multiple guards say this deviant hazing has created a climate of fear and coercion, with those who declined to participate often ridiculed, humiliated, demoted, or even fired. The result is an environment that is dangerous and volatile.

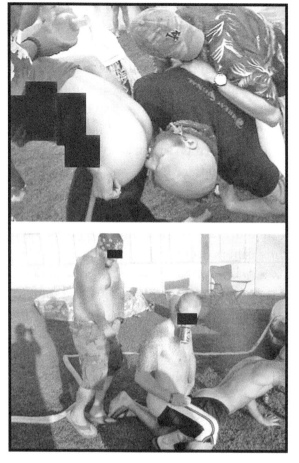

Figures 5.2 and 5.3. A "deviant" pool party hosted by American Guards of the U.S. Embassy in Kabul; with original censor bars (photos provided to *Mother Jones Magazine* by the Project on Government Oversight, http://www.mother-jones.com/mojo/2009/09/embassy-guards-gone-wild-pictures-nsfw).

That the author of the report opens the discussion of hazing at the embassy with a reference to William Golding's 1954 novel *Lord of the Flies* tells us a good deal about how the context of U.S. occupation in Afghanistan might shape American perceptions of the guards' behavior. An allegorical story of a group of young, white, upper-class British boys who are reduced to brutality and group-think after their plane crashes on a deserted island during a time of war, *Lord of the Flies* offers an image of the ways that harsh conditions can harden and pervert even the most normal of white boys and men. The report's reference to the novel provides a ready-made interpretive frame to viewers who may be shocked by the content of the photos and who may wonder how young, white, ostensibly heterosexual American men could find themselves eating potato chips out of one another's butts. The report calls for an end to the "lewd hazing" behavior of the guards, but it avoids assigning blame to them. Instead, it implies that the terrible circumstance—long hours, little sleep, poor working conditions, and isolation from home—is what causes these young men to lick each other's nipples while wearing plastic Hawaiian leis (see figure 5.5).

The POGO report, likely due to the spectacular photographs accompanying it (see figures 5.2–5.6), received the attention of the international news media. Many reporters picked up the *Lord of the Flies* framing, while others drew parallels to more familiar male behavior, such as a *Mother Jones* reporter who described the guards as engaged in "Animal House–like antics" and behaving like "depraved frat brothers" hosting "drunken parties."[20] Indeed, the images, filled with smiling, drunken, mostly young white men holding red plastic cups, depict a scene familiar to anyone who has been to a party hosted by white college students. The photos show no visual evidence of violence or abuse. This fact is likely what prompted Danielle Brian, the executive director of POGO and the author of the report, to clarify to a CNN reporter: "This is well beyond partying. . . . [They are] facilitating this kind of deviant hazing and humiliation, and requiring people to do things that made them feel really disgusted. . . . This is not Abu Ghraib. We're not talking about torture, we are talking about humiliation."[21] Brian reports that more than twenty whistleblowers, mostly embassy guards, filed unanswered complaints with ArmorGroup about harassment and intimidation at the embassy, including threats that if they did not participate in the pool parties, they would not be promoted.

POGO's report also highlights language barriers between ArmorGroup's American guards and Nepalese and North Indian guards, the latter of whom are described as constituting nearly

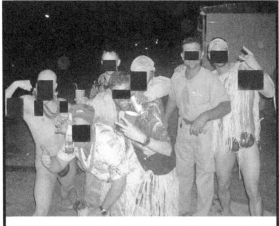

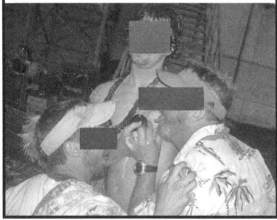

Figures 5.4 and 5.5. American guards of the U.S. embassy in Kabul; with original censor bars (photos provided to *Mother Jones Magazine* by the Project on Government Oversight, http://www.motherjones.com/mojo/2009/09/embassy-guards-gone-wild-pictures-nsfw).

two-thirds of the guard force, but notably, are not named in the report's description of the pool parties and are not evident in the photos released with the report. Some of the photographs do depict Afghan men drinking alcohol and embracing American guards (see figures 5.4 and 5.6), a scene the POGO report describes as "victimization of Afghan Nationals," given Muslim prohibitions against alcohol consumption and public nudity. Not surprisingly, the report does not take issue with the U.S. occupation in Afghanistan, but relies instead on the premise that there are more culturally sensitive ways to engage in occupation, which include attention to Muslim norms guiding modesty and bodily contact.

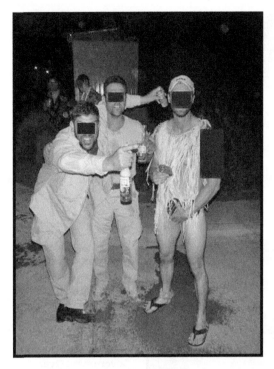

Figure 5.6. Afghan nationals and American guards of the U.S. embassy in Kabul; with original censor bars (photos provided to Mother Jones Magazine by the Project on Government Oversight, http://www.motherjones.com/mojo/2009/09/embassy-guards-gone-wild-pictures-nsfw).

What can we learn from juxtaposing the Navy's "time-honored, officially sanctioned" crossing the line ceremony with the scandal-worthy parties held by guards of the U.S. embassy in Kabul? While the male participants' behavior in each case is nearly identical, crossing the line has the weight of military-sanctioned tradition on its side, a tradition rooted in the more or less explicit belief that subjecting young men to intimate and humiliating homosexual contact strengthens their characters, their bodies, and the bonds of brotherhood. In this narrative, hazing is kept in check by Navy guidelines, and all acts of anal penetration, rimming, and so forth, can be traced back to these goals. New sailors, as they approach the equator, also know their initiation is impending, and they know they will most likely endure it only once.[22]

By contrast, the subcontracted security guards at the U.S. embassy in Kabul "fondle one another" in a more ambiguous context of their own creation, characterized by ongoing parties and a general "boys gone wild" atmosphere. They are not soldiers, but employees of a privately owned security contractor; they are stationed at their place of work and they party in their off hours at their camp nearby the embassy. There is no evidence that the guards are facilitating initiation rites or conforming to any set of rules; they seem to be drinking vodka from each other's butts to pass the time and for its own sake, for the pleasure in it. They intimidate and punish the guards who do not want to join their party—an actionable form of workplace harassment, as the POGO report rightly points out. And yet the language of the POGO report is not the language of a workplace sexual harassment complaint; it is the language of fear in the face of deviance and perversion.

These differences help to account for the characterization of the security guards, and not the sailors, as engaged in dangerous behavior. In the absence of an institutional logic to explain and justify their homosexual activity, the guards are imagined to have surrendered to their baser instincts, descended into chaos, and to have possibly lost their sanity, given their challenging workplace conditions. Without a clear circumstantial justification for their homosexuality, a circumstance that could explain why they would act out of accordance with hetero-masculinity, the guards are imagined to have "gone wild." That their sexual deviance takes place on foreign soil and is witnessed by Afghan men amplifies its danger and queerness. Mirroring Gardiner's analysis of the relationship between masculinity and childishness, the guard's apparent childishness, their capacity to behave like the young boys in *Lord of the Flies*, is posited as their only alibi, the only reasonable explanation for their homosexual behavior.

The POGO report describes the treatment of Afghan men as "victimization," which is no doubt true in more ways than are captured in the report. But it is also useful to return to Žižek's and Puar's suggestion that when young white American men degrade Muslims with homoerotic gestures, they are in fact sharing something of themselves, something core to white American hetero-masculinity, rather than conjuring up a wholly external source of shame. In this view, the elements familiar to hazing scenes—dominance and submission, humiliation, filth, anality, and so forth—are not simply "circumstances," but desires woven through the fabric of white hetero-masculinity itself. Disgust, for instance, rather than a signal that straight men are simply "not into" touching other men's bodies, is also a fetishized and performative mode of encountering men's bodies, its own mode of sexual relating. These are insights long known to practitioners of BDSM, and sometimes applied to straight women as we make sense of their attraction to wealthy and powerful but conventionally unattractive men. And yet, remarkably little headway has been made in understanding the nexus of desire and repulsion in straight men's lives, in part given the hyper-agency attributed to straight men, and in part because any movement in this direction is often clouded by the far too simplistic assertion that men who display extreme disgust with homosexuality must actually be "gay." To be clear, abject disgust is one way—and it turns out a very common hetero-masculine way—of engaging in homosexual activity, but it tells us remarkably little about the course of people's sexual desires, practices, and identifications. Both straight men and gay men (as I discuss in the next section) eroticize what is, or can be made to be, disgusting or repulsive about homosexuality.

Hazing as Fetish: The World of Internet Hazing Porn

Research on sexualized hazing has focused on the strategic use of sex to enhance what are often perceived as nonsexual motivations, like the motivation to humiliate. Let's call this "sex as hazing." But to flesh out the ways that hazing itself is fetishized, which we might call "hazing as sex," I now turn to a realm in which the erotic value of forced homosexual contact and hetero-masculine disgust is made quite explicit: the world of internet hazing porn. The pornographic website HazeHim.com describes its mission on its welcome page as follows:

> Welcome to Haze Him, the official site for straight college frater-
> nity guys getting hazed into gay sex. This is just how the cookie
> crumbles on hazehim. You get your pledges to do gay sex acts and
> we give you a chance to win $10,000 cash. . . . The crazier the video,
> the better your chances at winning. So what are you waiting for?
> Watch and enjoy real frat boys sucking and fucking cock.[23]

As the site's introduction explains, the conceit in *Haze Him* is that
straight frat boys, who are probably already engaged in sexualized hazing, may go the extra step to film and submit their hazing
activities for the chance at $10,000. For a monthly membership
fee, viewers can watch scene after scene of young, purportedly
straight white boys in baseballs caps and flip flops, laughing and
drinking beer, packed into frat house basements and dorm rooms,
screaming at pledges—also white, seemingly straight young
men—to suck and fuck each other.

Exemplifying the dynamic relationship between militaristic
hazing rituals and the pornographic imagination, many of the
scenes of *Haze Him* follow the military script to the letter, as frat
brothers scream at pledges about how homosexual sex will turn
them into men and secure their place in the brotherhood. For instance, in one scene, pledges are shown being dragged out of bed
in the early morning, while a frat brother yells:

> "Get up! Let's go! You aint seen shit! It's called the initiation. It's
> an important tradition. We're gonna teach you honor, commu-
> nity, and brotherhood! You wanna be part of this fuckin' fraternity,
> you're gonna fuckin' touch each other's dicks! I'm gonna make you
> jerk off in a cup and drink it! . . . [the film cuts to another scene in
> which pledges are giving each other blow jobs] You wanna be a
> man, be a brother, keep going, suck that dick!"

Haze Him's success as "reality porn" is dependent upon the legibility of hazing as an erotic trope, one with familiar ingredients

Figures 5.7, 5.8, 5.9, and 5.10. Assorted screenshots from HazeHim.com.

and cultural resonance in the United States. Chief among the ingredients of the hazing trope is the use of homosexual contact to produce states of humiliation and, ultimately, group belonging and resilient manhood. But where does this notion originate? *Haze Him* arguably owes a debt to the United States Armed Forces for the films' capacity to feel real to viewers or to resonate with their sense of what is possible in the real world. The films "work" because they tell a now familiar story about the extreme circumstances in which straight men are forced to act out of accordance with their heterosexual nature. Though Hollywood has been shy to explore these themes, even mainstream engagements with the hazing trope spotlight a military logic in which perverse and violent acts—which would likely shock the general American public—are the necessary work of building strong men. Recall, for instance, Jack Nicholson's now infamous declaration that the American public "can't handle the truth!" about the necessity of military hazing, in the 1992 film *A Few Good Men*.

And yet, just as we might wonder about the authenticity of the Craigslist ads analyzed in the previous chapter, so too does the question of authenticity quickly arise for fans and scholars of "reality porn" sites like *Haze Him*. The question is worth exploring here, as it points us to the layered and mutually constitutive performance of both hetero and homo masculinities. Fans of the site, for instance, want to know whether *Haze Him* offers its viewers video footage shot by actually straight frat boys who submitted their films for cash, or whether the films are "gay" performances carefully scripted and staged by film producers. In many ways, the allure and brilliance of the site is that the answer to this question is not completely evident. Flaccid penises, expressions of disgust and repulsion, homophobic outbursts, beer-chugging, and tits-and-ass-obsessed dudes all lend credibility to the films (indeed, the gay male scholar who first introduced me to the site assured me the videos are "REAL!," which he communicated with more than a glimmer of excitement in his eyes).

Much of what feels "real" about the films is in the affective quality of the scenes, especially the expressions of heterosexual disgust and fear upon which the *Haze Him* storyline rests. In some of the films, the on-camera frat dudes—the ones ordering or observing the hazing of the ostensibly unfortunate pledges—become visibly repulsed at the sight of the forced homosexual penetration they themselves have ordered, and they dramatically exit the scene in disgust. They cringe, they look away, they squirm uncomfortably, they whisper to their friends, "Dude, sorry, but that's all I can take of this shit." And as for the pledges being forced to suck and fuck one another, they appear paralyzed with fear, nauseous, sometimes on the verge of tears, just waiting for the homosexual torture to end. In this way, many of the scenes read as real-life rapes, without any of the safe/sane/consensual negotiation or explicit pornographic staging that might otherwise invite view-ers (at least, queer feminist viewers like me) to freely eroticize them. The films end when the pledges are covered in cum, thor-oughly fucked, and appear utterly dejected. Borrowing heavily on rape discourse, the frat dudes often accuse the pledges of having "asked for it" and ridicule them for having just engaged in a "gay" sex act. The only good news, we might imagine, is that they are now secure in the knowledge that they have earned their access to the fraternity of their choice.

While these performances lend a sense of the real to *Haze Him*, many of the films' other features—set lighting, multiple camera angles, and the occasional appearance of identifiable gay porn performers—point to their staging. HazeHim.com is now one among many cinéma vérité–style porn websites specializing in videos of "real people"—usually teenage girls, but also straight men—being baited with cash into sex with apparently unappeal-ing partners.[24] Of course, these are regulated pornographic pro-ductions featuring professional performers posing as amateurs, all of whom sign release forms consenting to the use of their im-ages. And yet, authenticity is key to the success of such films. In gay fan forums for *Haze Him*, some fans express disappointment that the films are "probably fake," while others proclaim the films "hot either way." As one porn-savvy fan points out to his more naïve interlocutors, "Cameras for professional filming require certain lighting requirements that every *Haze Him* video just magically seems to have. . . . The biggest issue of all is the liability factor. Every 'frat' you see in the video must sign a release form. . . . Do you really believe they are going to sign-off on a model release form for their humiliation to be used as public gay porn? . . . It's fake, but entertaining nonetheless."[25]

Like the consensus among many fans that it doesn't much matter whether the films are staged, from a cultural studies standpoint, the authenticity of *Haze Him* is less relevant than the fact that there is a growing demand for eroticized representations of the nexus of homophobic repulsion and homosexual sex, and that performers in these films are familiar enough with the hazing trope, and with the look and feel of homophobic heterosexual masculinity, to be able to deliver convincing "not gay" performances even as they are having sex with one another. The boys in *Haze Him*, most likely gay or "gay for pay" actors, know enough about the exceptionalizing logics that facilitate sex between straight men to be able to engage in believable not-gay sex on screen. The films make explicit that not-gay homosexual sex is constituted by a set of dudely and homophobic gestures, the staging of a heteronormative scene bound by hetero-masculine logics, and an emotional landscape marked by repulsion and resilience. The reliability of this trope enables gay porn performers to take up the formula with relative ease. In this way, the films highlight the fluid and performative construction of white heterosexual masculinity, offering viewers the opportunity to eroticize what is rarely marked and made visible—the erotic culture of straight white men.

The whiteness of the majority of *Haze Him* performers also contributes to the frat-house realness of the films (in the seventy-six *Haze Him* films I viewed for this project, fewer than five men of color appear among hundreds of performers). The world of college fraternities, in most of the United States, is a racially diverse but segregated one characterized by separate African American, multicultural, and white fraternities with distinct histories and organizational cultures. But it is the symbolic and practical order of *white* fraternities—wherein preppy, upper-middle-class white boys spend their time getting drunk or high while also developing the networks that will deliver a lifetime of professional opportunities and cultural capital—that is most visible in the U.S. imagination of college fraternities. The association of frat boys, or bros, with middle-class whiteness means that white hetero-masculinity is a central ingredient in the production of frat-house realness in *Haze Him*.

In one film, for instance, a group of white frat brothers rouse a young, skinny white pledge named Brad from his bed. It is his birthday, and the frat brothers tell him that they have arranged for a very hot stripper named Ramona to give him a lap dance. They tell him she has "the best titties you've ever seen. Tits in your face!" They blindfold Brad, who appears none the wiser when in fact a gay-male, leather-clad Latino stripper named Ramon enters the scene. The white frat boys cheer Brad on as he caresses Ramon, all the while believing he is touching Ramona. When Brad finally touches Ramon's penis and jerks away with disgust, the frat brothers remove his blindfold and the scene shifts from friendly to aggressive and threatening. The frat brothers bark orders at Brad, who appears scared and nauseous: "On your knees bitch! We don't care if it's your fuckin' birthday! You wanna be a brother? On your fuckin' knees! . . . Now touch those nuts [Ramon's testicles], bitch! Like a fuckin' squirrel!" They demand that Brad give Ramon a blowjob and ultimately force him to submit to penetration by Ramon (if he wants to be in their fictional fraternity, that is). They yell, "How do you like Ramona now? . . . Happy fuckin' birthday! . . . Pull those fuckin' nipples bro!" The scene ends shortly after one of the white performers says, "Happy Birthday Brad. You're *gay*! Nine inches of brown dick for ya!" A shot of Brad's face shows him looking violated and dejected.

Men of color are invisible in the vast majority of *Haze Him*'s films, with the Brad/Ramon scene being one of only two in the entire series in which a man of color is a central figure. When Ramon, a Latino figure, does appear, he is used to amplify the white figure's humiliation: As the dialogue in the Brad/Ramon scene makes explicit, to be a white straight dude fucked by a white dick is one thing, but to be fucked by a brown dick adds an additional dimension of degradation and queerness. While nearly all the *Haze Him* films depict two equally ashamed straight white pledges being forced into a sexual interaction with one another, the Brad/Ramon scene departs from this formula sig-

Figure 5.11. Brad, Ramon, and another pledge being hazed (screen shot from HazeHim.com).

nificantly in its acknowledgement of a queer world that exists beyond the bounds of the heteronormative fraternity. Ramon is both an outsider and a queer whose shaved body, plucked eyebrows, and leather fetish gear invokes the perverse and gender-bending world of queer men. The casting of a Latino performer as this leather-clad queer figure, the source of Brad's moment of hetero-masculine horror, stands out in a series in which men of color do not otherwise appear.

Of course for gay male fans of the site, homosexual degradation—the moment when the seemingly innocent white straight boy is subjected to the most naughty of gay sex acts—is presumably the very thing that makes the films hot. Porn in which white boys are sexually dominated by men of color constitutes its own immensely popular genre, a fact not lost on the producers of *Haze Him*, who, not incidentally, send weekly email messages to all members of *Haze Him*, including myself, with teasers for related porn websites centered on white men being fucked by "huge black dicks." Such messages provide a telling window into *Haze Him*'s apparently white target audience, as well as into the use of men of color by porn producers to invoke themes of submission and humiliation.

Ultimately, how might we make sense of hazing porn and its relationship to the real world? Being hyper-masculine and "straight-acting" has long been fetishized among gay men, and hence one could argue that *Haze Him* is a genre of gay porn that simply extends this fetish by eroticizing heterosexual masculinity. But it is significant that in *Haze Him*, the scenes revolve less around the dominant figures who are barking orders and more around the boys being "forced" to engage in homosexual sex, the boys whose averageness is marked by their especially pale-skinned, scrawny, and nerdish appearances. The films depart from the glorification of hyper-masculinity, a gender arguably overrepresented in gay porn, eroticizing instead the fear and submission of boys who appear to be, like many nineteen-year-olds, socially and physically vulnerable. In many ways, *Haze Him* gives a far more nuanced treatment to heterosexual masculinity than is typical of gay porn, as it shows straight men to be both dominant and submissive, powerful and weak.

Though *Haze Him* is consumed by gay men and likely cast with gay performers, there is a sense in which to call it "gay porn" misses the mark, in the same way that calling films populated with straight performers, like *Milk* (Sean Penn) or *Monster* (Charlize Theron), "straight films" would miss much of their complexity. Considered alongside military hazing, *Haze Him* offers us a fairly accurate representation of a feature of straight white male sexual culture. It provides us a view into the world of straight men's sex with one another, as seen through the eyes of gay men. To understand the films purely as products of gay subculture or gay fantasy is to miss what George Chauncey, Steven Zeeland, and many others demonstrate in their research on the points of contact between gay and straight men (see chapter 2): namely, that gay men and straight men do not live in separate worlds, but instead witness, perform, and even sometimes inhabit what is ostensibly one another's relationship to homosexuality.

Reading hazing porn alongside the military hazing practices discussed at the outset of this chapter allows us to consider the ways in which both straight men and gay men borrow on the kinds of gender performances and sex practices typically attributed to the other. We might say that straight male soldiers and sailors, for instance, "borrow" homosexual sex practices to enact rites of passage (such as crossing the line), even as they know that these practices have queer meaning when not aboard ship. In many cases, it is precisely the queer meaning of the sexual activity that straight men are borrowing, using it to amplify the humiliation or "grossness" of the encounter. Many gay men, in turn, eroticize normative hetero-masculinity, including the male bonding rituals that enable intimate contact between men in heteronormative environments. Gay men observe straight men's gender performances, integrating them into a gender repertoire that includes possibilities like "acting straight." In this vein, we could argue that *Haze Him*—to the extent that it offers us gay men who are performing as straight men who are behaving like gay men—highlights the social construction of both straight and gay subjectivities, revealing gender and sexual orientation to be scripted and easily copied.

And yet, even this analysis is not quite right, as it risks positing an ownership of homosexual sex by gay men (and heterosexual sex by straight men) by implying that straight men must borrow homosexual sex acts not actually their own. As discussed in chapter 2, most historical accounts suggest that homosexual activity has long been a feature of the lives of "normal" men, men who are sexually oriented toward women. The assignment of same-gender and opposite-gender sex acts to closed groups called "homosexuals" and "heterosexuals" is a historically recent phenomenon, one characterized by a persistently blurry and permeable line between the two categories. Hence, a more productive reading of the relationship between hetero-masculine and gay approaches to homosexuality recognizes that homophobic disidentifica-

186 | Haze Him!

tion and dramatic displays of repulsion and endurance are what imbue homosexual activity with heterosexual meaning, and that these theatrics are up for grabs, so to speak—available not only to straight men but also to gay-identified men who may put them to erotic uses. In sum, what gay and straight men borrow from one another are not sex acts themselves, but their rhetorical and subcultural meanings.

Lifting the Haze: Toward a Deeper Analysis of Hazing

Returning to the military examples discussed at the beginning of this chapter, let us recall that, in the U.S. military, men's intimate contact with one another's genitals and anuses is divorced from gay meaning vis-à-vis the location of these acts within a context of hierarchy and obligation—i.e., situations in which less powerful men are obligated by their superiors to participate in degrading and repulsive acts that would have homosexual meaning in almost any other context but are here understood as necessary compliance. What else, but to comply, might we expect of a young heterosexual sailor, for instance, who is many hundreds of miles out at sea, being ordered to simulate anal sex by a superior officer? Or, in the case of the drunken parties in Kabul, what is an entry-level guard to do but comply with his supervisor's demand that he engage in analingus, when his job is on the line? These are serious questions, not to be taken lightly, as they point us to what may well be a prevalent occurrence of sexual harassment and assault within all-male contexts.

And yet, there are two problems that arise when we exclusively apply a sexual assault or "no other choice" framework to hazing, as if these analyses alone can tell us everything we need to know about the meaning of homosexual activity between straight men positioned in a hierarchical relation to one another. First, and somewhat obviously, these analyses, when overgeneralized, mask the multiplicity and complexity of straight men's experiences of hazing and being hazed. It is likely that many straight sailors who have undergone the crossing the line ritual, for example, took no pleasure in it, and perhaps related to the ceremony largely as a trauma, an experience they would not wish on future sailors. This is likely true of many gay sailors as well. It is also likely that, for others, perhaps the same straight men who seek out occasional sex with gay men aboard ship, the ceremony is a worthwhile tradition, an honorable and thrilling experience, an opportunity for an intense and pleasurable form of physical intimacy—a pleasure that cannot be *queer* precisely because one is out at sea, playing by a different set of rules than are at play when one is tethered to the pier. But as I have also argued here, even men's repulsion with a sex object or encounter and/or the apparent consensus among men that a given sex act is "gross" and unappealing do not in and of themselves preclude men's desire or erotic engagement. After all, the complex intermingling of desire and misogyny has long structured heterosexuality itself.

A second problem with the tendency to view sexualized hazing as extreme sexual harassment or assault is that such analyses tend to make sense when applied to isolated contexts, but fail us when we look to the full range of environments in which men haze other men. College fraternities, for instance, are sites to which the "no choice but to comply" frame is frequently applied, and yet the stakes of non-participation in fraternity hazing, as great as they may seem to young men at the time, arguably fall quite short of job loss or whatever violent or institutional consequence sailors out at sea might suffer should they refuse to participate in the "crossing the line" ceremony. In the case of fraternity hazing, most scholars agree that the stakes of hazing are more psychological and less structural—a function of the culture of masculinity more broadly, which trains men to desire to degrade others, on the one hand, and to be validated by enduring degradation, on the other.

In this vein, sociologist Michael Kimmel has argued that manhood itself is what's on the line when fraternity brothers participate in an "elephant walk" (when pledges walk naked in a circle holding each other's penises), or get "teabagged" (when a fraternity brother rubs his scrotum on a pledge's face), or eat the "ookie cookie" (when pledges eat the cookie on which older frat brothers have ejaculated), or in other now well-documented initiation rituals. Kimmel contends that "such initiation rituals provide ample evidence that hazing is less about younger males trying to impress their elders, and far more about the sense of entitlement that the older males have to exact such gratuitously violent and degrading behaviors from those more vulnerable than they. . . . It is a way for them to reassure themselves that they belong to a group so worthy that the other guys are willing to suffer just to join them."[26] Kimmel goes on to explain that straight guys "put up with it" because they want to be liked and validated by other men.

Kimmel's analysis is helpful to the extent that it reveals hazing to be an expression of normative hetero-masculinity itself, rather than aberrant behavior occurring only in extreme or isolated situations. And yet, here again, the forms of intimate contact that occur between young men who impose and endure them in the name of manhood—hands on penises, scrotum on faces, ejaculate in mouths—are exceptionalized as "gratuitously violent," even as they are the stuff of everyday sex for straight women and gay men. Arguably, many young women also take scrotums to their faces and ejaculate into their mouths in order to be liked and validated by men. Whether interpreters like Kimmel attribute a primarily erotic or primarily violent meaning to these acts too often rests on an a priori assumption about the sexual proclivities of the participants. Stated more plainly, hazing is viewed as especially violent and degrading when it is imagined that the sexual acts in question are discordant with the sexual nature of participants.

Returning again to the hypothetical scene in which young women are engaged in the same hazing behaviors as young men (i.e., touching each other's vaginas, rubbing labia on one another's faces, swallowing one another's vaginal fluids), we might consider these acts distasteful or degrading, but gratuitously violent? Probably not. At the heart of these divergent interpretations of male and female "homoeroticism" (a term rarely applied to women) is the implicit presumption that few sex acts are fundamentally discordant for women given the nature of female sexual fluidity. In contrast, the belief in men's inherent sexual rigidity results in a bizarre circular logic: Men's sexuality is rigid, hence heterosexual men do not engage in the same kind of homosexual contact that is possible for women; and when they *do* engage in homosexual contact, it must not be "sexual" because . . . men's sexuality is rigid!

In keeping with the broader claim of this book that homosexual encounters are not in fact discordant with heterosexual masculinity when they are approached through the most recognizable circuits of hetero-masculinity, here I have argued that hazing creates one "obviously not gay" context for hetero-erotic encounters to occur between men. In this way, it is useful to view hazing as a kind of hetero-masculine festish, one characterized by homophobia, the presence of dominant men barking erotic orders, and a shared agreement among male participants about the necessity of testing one another's anal endurance and resilience. The rising popularity of what Gardiner describes as anal explosive white masculinity in the United States, exemplified by gross-out reality TV and anus-focused cartoons marketed to adult white men, helps to normalize the hazing fetish, to position it as an effective heterosexual alibi in the face of questions about hazing's erotic meaning. The films published on HazeHim.com capitalize on this fetish, reducing straight men's homophobic engagements with homosexual sex to a ready formula, a formula reproduced in dozens of films marketed to gay men. The films highlight that the script of white hetero-masculinity and its ostensibly reluctant engagement with homosexuality is now a familiar trope, available to be taken up by anyone, including gay men. In the next and final chapter, I extend this analysis of the relationship between evolving constructions of heterosexuality and queerness, looking closely at the ways that fluidity discourses construct homonormative and romanticized gay subjects as the straight dude's foil.

6

Against Gay Love

This One Goes Out to the Queers

I came to my own interest in heterosexuality, and in this project, as I observed straight-identified people compulsively pointing to queerness, like a compass always pointing in the same direction. Straight boys and men, in particular, persistently call on fags to occupy the earnest, immutable, congenital, and often tragic space of ostensibly unchosen and unwanted homosexuality. When gay boys and men occupy this narrow space, presumably the space of "real" homosexuality, the possibilities for heterosexual engagement with same-sex sexuality expand. In many ways, gay men and lesbians perform a kind of unpaid labor for straights, embodying the symbolic and romanticized position of sincere gayness and amplifying the normalcy of those whose homosexuality is insincere and "meaningless."

I began this study because I felt heterosexuality calling me to do something, repeatedly hailing me, flagging me down to tell an obligatory and erroneous story about myself. This compulsory narrative goes like this: "I was born this way, and of course I'd rather be like you. I would be you in a heartbeat if I could. But I love women, and it's simply out of my control." Later, I will discuss how and why this story fails to account for my experience, and for that of many queers, and what all of this means for heterosexuality. For now, I want to note that I was moved to write this book not from a singular interest in straight white men's sexuality, but from an interest in the way that narratives about heterosexual fluidity (or not-gay homosexuality) depend on very particular constructions of gay identity and gay life. In large part, straight homosexualities lay claim to their ostensibly ephemeral existence—their presumably inconsequential, circumstantial, and non-identitaritan nature—through contrast with those "other" homosexualities, the "real" homosexualities deemed culturally and politically meaningful, hardwired, and subjectifying. While the dominant narrative is that heterosexuality doesn't want much to do with homosexuality, and doesn't give gay or queer subjectivities much thought, I want to close this book by suggesting that quite the opposite is true.

In this spirit, the aim of this chapter is to draw attention to a largely unexamined aspect of the relationship between straightness and gayness—namely, the way that straight people imagine what it looks and feels like to be deeply, authentically, and congenitally gay, and in so doing, help to *produce* normative gay personhood, to call us gays into being, and to co-create the evolving standards for authentic gayness to which all non-straights are held accountable. The preceding chapters have examined the remarkable effort straight white men invest in distinguishing between queer forms of homosexual contact, on the one hand, and those that are normal (heterosexual), on the other. As straight men engage in this project, they do far more than simply observe or react to queerness, as if queerness is something wholly outside of their purview. They do more than look at gay people, or gay ways of life, and say, "that's not me." They do more than adjust their own behaviors to substantiate their claims to a "not gay" sexual constitution, or to embody the apparent opposite of all things fag-inflected. In addition to these projects, they also work at *defining* normative gayness through their obsessive involvement in identifying the line where normal ends and queer begins. As they point to their heterosexuality, they exercise their imagination of gay subjectivity, gay love, and gay life by telling stories about what it means to be really and truly gay—to be the thing that they believe they are not, or that they wish not to be.

As I have shown, the line straight people draw between "actually gay" and "merely joking/hazing/experimenting/getting off" is only minimally about specific sex acts. Instead, it is the *circumstances* of our sex acts—the different subcultural, institutional, affective, gendered, and racialized contexts in which homosexual encounters occur—that have long sustained the hetero/homo binary and have, in many cases, trumped the raw facts about same-sex bodies engaged in sexual touching. As I have shown, *setting* is central to this formula. The act of placing male tongues on male anuses has gay meaning when it occurs in gay men's bedrooms and straight meaning in Navy initiation ceremonies and at drunken parties outside the United States embassy in Kabul. The act of placing male fingers in male anuses has gay meaning when it occurs in gay porn and straight meaning during an "elephant walk" in a college fraternity. Homosexual penetration often has straight meaning in prisons or aboard ship and gay meaning beyond the walls of these ostensibly constrained or situational environments (as they say in the Navy, "It's only queer if you're tied to the pier"). I have demonstrated that *gender*, too, has long been a vital part of the distinction between gay and straight engagements with homosexuality. For much of the twentieth century, when masculine men engaged in penetrative homosexual acts or when tough-guy gang members engaged in homosexual kissing, these encounters did not carry the same queer associations as did the homosexual behavior of fairies and fags. I have also argued that *white homosociality*—or preserving the brotherhood of white men—bolsters the friendly, casual, and inconsequential meanings linked to straight white men's homosexual contact, while cross-race encounters are perceived by white men as "more queer." And lastly, I have shown that the stated *motivation* or intent is equally significant when men touch each other's genitals and anuses. For instance, if men can reasonably claim that the sexual encounter was beyond their control, that either social pressure or sexual deprivation or the need for quick and impersonal sex *made* them do it, then their heterosexual constitution arguably remains intact.

How do we come to know that these circumstances make all the difference—that they are the most meaningful signals of circumstantial homosexuality, on the one hand, or of gay personage on the other? The answer is that, with a few gay exceptions, straight white men—white men who understand their sexuality to be normal—have told us so. Straight white men constituted the bulk of physicians, psychologists, sexologists, and sociologists who mapped these distinctions throughout the twentieth century, providing us with templates for diagnosing sexual encounters as circumstantial, and therefore normal, or subjectifying, and therefore queer. Still today, our efforts to think about the homosexual behavior of straight-identified men remain utterly over-determined by this false dichotomy between circumstance and identity. Recent efforts to incorporate heteroflexibility into the sexual binary suggest that straight people find themselves in very particular situations that facilitate homosexual contact, whereas gay people need no "situation"; gays are homosexual to their core and would be gay even if they ejaculated in a forest and no other gays were there to hear them make a sound. Of course the now widely accepted sociobiological premise that people are born with a core sexual constitution—heterosexual, homosexual, or bisexual—has given this logic a significant boost.

More constructionist approaches, of which I am a proponent, suggest that the way out of this essentialist dichotomy between circumstance and personage is to see that sexual personages (like straight or gay) do not exist outside of the cultural circumstances that give name and shape to them. As illustrated in chapter 2, both heterosexual and homosexual subjectivities resulted from decades of medical, legal, and cultural efforts in the late nineteenth and early twentieth centuries to draw the line between normal and deviant sexuality, a line drawn differently for men and women, for whites and people of color. Throughout the twentieth century, this line shifted in response to changing ideas about gender, race, sexual desire, and immutability. As I have shown, the history of the hetero/homo binary includes a remarkable catalogue of circumstances believed to be more important than the sheer fact of sexual contact between people possessing the same or opposite genitals—circumstances that have included where and when the contact occurred, the gender normativity of participants, and whether homosexuality was imagined to be congruent or incongruent with other features of participants' lives.

Still today, the line between straight and gay is subject to an array of cultural contingencies. This point is beautifully illustrated by my students at the University of California, Riverside, when each year I lead them in an exercise called "Gay or Straight?" In this exercise, which I employed most recently in an "Introduction to Gender Studies" course of approximately four hundred students, I describe various "circumstances" and ask students to shout out how they make sense of them—or to tell me whether the people involved are gay or straight. I ask, what about straight-identified women who kiss each other at parties while men watch and cheer? (Like a unified chorus, the students yell out: "Straight!" A few students subvert my intentionally dualistic framing and yell, "Bisexual!" or "Bi-curious!"). What about straight-identified men who kiss each other at parties while women watch and cheer? ("Gay!!" they laugh and scream. "Does that ever happen!?" others shout, laughing hysterically). Young boys who touch each other's penises while playing? ("Gay!" many yell, to my surprise. "Gross!" some say. "Straight!" others call out. "Normal!" say a few psychology majors—almost always young women—attempting to add their developmental perspective. "Who knows?" one yells). Men who have sex with men while in prison but not when they are on the outside? ("Straight!" "Gay!" "Fucked Up!" The students are divided on this one). Two women who have lived together for thirty years and sleep in the same bed but do not identify as lesbians? ("Straight!" "Spinsters!" "Sad!") Two men who have lived together for thirty years and sleep in the same bed but do not identify as gay? ("Gay!") A young woman who has sex with two women in college, and then marries a man after she graduates? ("Straight!" Bisexual!" "Confused!" "LUG!") A young man who, while being hazed by a fraternity, strips naked and puts his finger in other guys' anuses? ("Gay!" "Straight!" Some men in the room have worried facial expressions . . .).

In many of these examples, the students are utterly divided on where to draw the line between gay and straight, and many consistently apply one set of standards to women and another to men. What most *do* agree on is that the circumstances are meaningful. In fact, they are everything. Sometimes they feel that my short description is all the information they need to make a confident assessment of whether the people involved in the scenario are gay or straight. In other cases, they want to know more about the circumstances ("How many times did it happen?" "How old are the boys you are talking about?" and so forth). Ultimately, they all get the point: We don't agree about the exact line between a gay constitution and a straight one because this line has always been a moving target, one subject to people's culturally and historically located beliefs about gender, sexuality, age, and race, and one deeply bound by the circumstances in which homosexual sex practices occur.

Paradoxically, even as the students get the point about the cultural construction of sexual identities, most also seem certain that there is a real answer and that they know the real answer, that they have all the qualifications they need to decide which circumstances are gay, and which are straight. Many will shake their heads and proclaim, "I'm sorry, but that's just *gay.*" This is especially true of the straight students, who come to the exercise with a remarkable sense of authority. By contrast, I have found that queer students are more likely to hesitate, to tilt their heads and look confused or ambivalent, to call out words like "fluid!" or "queer!" or to assert that we simply do not know.

What I am getting at here, as I have illustrated in the preceding chapters, is that straight people generally have a lot of confidence that they know the difference between gay and straight circumstances. Straight-identified white boys and men, in particular, fashion themselves experts at being able to document and verify their normal sexuality, to harness the evidence of their not-gay constitutions, and to expand or contract the circle of normal (not gay) homosexual activity as it suits their interests. And as they do this, they also weave together a story about the boundaries of queerness: They imagine not-gay forms of homosexual contact to be most "at home" in public and institutionally constrained spaces, while queerness, by contrast, resides in domestic, private, and presumably less contingent corners. They validate the not-gay quality of their homosexual contact by pointing to its meaninglessness and/or its abject and power-inflected forms (eating potato chips out of anuses, for instance), while casting queerness as that which is sincere, love-based, and, in the minds of more liberal heterosexuals—beautiful. They keep their not-gay homosexual contact largely among white men, imagining interracial homosexuality as telling evidence of essential queerness.

Straight Stories of Gay Love and the Misrecognition of Queerness

Increasingly central to contemporary discourse about the difference between heteroflexibility and authentic gayness is a romanticized story about queerness as same-sex *love*, as opposed to "meaningless" same-sex *sex*. The former is reserved for the real gays, while the latter is available to heteroflexible straights as well. This distinction operates on multiple registers. On the one hand, in homophobic accounts, gay men trigger straight men's disgust precisely because homosexual activity is not confined to the impersonal and the corporeal; instead, it is imagined to be attached to earnest and feminized feelings of love and tenderness between men. On the other hand, gay love is also central to stories of heterosexual "alliance" and support for gays—exemplified, perhaps, by the earnest tale of gay male love told by straight white male rapper Macklemore in his 2012 hit song "Same Love," a song applauded by countless gays and lesbians invested in the politics of sameness. In both the homophobic and the "pro-gay" versions, straight men imagine gayness as essentially a matter of same-sex love, romance, and tenderness, a notion that reinforces the immutable heterosexuality of straight men (and women) who, regardless of their homosexual activity, feel no attachment to *gay love* and its subcultural expressions. Macklemore, for instance, announces within the first few moments of "Same Love" that he is not gay, which he knows because he "loved girls since before pre-K," an utterance that, as any lesbian or gay man will tell you, seems to preface most straight people's declarations of LGBT alliance ("*I'm straight*, but I support gay rights . . ."). Using Macklemore as an example of this interweaving of heterosexual authentification with alliance to gays and their love, sociologists CJ Pascoe and Tristan Bridges explain:

> Macklemore's profession of his heterosexuality in "Same Love" actually bolsters his heterosexuality rather than calling it into question. . . . This sort of "bro-ing" of anti-homophobia stances does not necessarily have the effect of challenging the naturalness and inevitability of sexual and gender categories. . . . [These] gender and sexual practices and proclamations reinscribe . . . heterosexuality as so powerful and inevitable that even an anti-homophobia stance can't call [it] into question.[1]

Conventional wisdom would suggest that straight men give little attention to matters of gay love and domesticity; but in fact, attention to the boundaries of gay love—or of the imagined realm of earnest, unstoppable, and lifelong gay yearnings—are vital to men's heterosexual identifications, especially given the frequency with which straight men find themselves touching each other's penises and anuses for apparently non-loving reasons. Indeed, it is in telling stories of gay true love, whether of the homophobic or the pro-gay variety, that proclamations of heterosexuality find one of their more compelling outlets.

This late twentieth-century turn to love, domesticity, and family-making as defining features of gay life was clearly a joint effort, one embraced by gays and straights alike. Gay people and straight people both stood to "gain," at least superficially, from suppressing images of leather-clad BDSM practitioners, radical fairies, angry lesbian feminists, trans people, street punks, AIDS activists, diesel dykes, and other queer freaks who were giving "good gays" a bad name. As historian Lisa Duggan has described, this homonormative turn, paired with growing acceptance of sociobiological theories of sexual orientation, swelled the ranks of complacent neoliberal subjects and shifted gay and lesbian attention away from revolutionary projects and toward middle-class aspirations and allegiance to the nation.

But beyond this investment in turning gays into legible and complacent subjects, straights have arguably benefitted in other ways from gay subjectivity's detachment from its earlier associations with promiscuous, impersonal, abject, transactional, performative, and experimental homosexuality. With gay identity now tethered to love and biology, these other forms of homosexual relating can be more easily taken up by straights, as they are increasingly believed to be distinct from the true meaning of gayness: monogamous same-sex love and the gay and lesbian families presumed to ultimately result from this love. The recent reduction of gay politics to the rights of the romantic couple is evidenced by the nearly exclusive focus on same-sex marriage in the last decade—a focus that, while perhaps temporary and strategic, has nearly subsumed popular discourse about what it means to be gay. In sum, while the field of queer erotics has narrowed with this turn to homonormative love, the field of hetero-erotics is ever-expanding to include performative same-sex hook-ups, drunken homosexual accidents, mouth-to-anus games and rituals, bromantic stunts and homosexual derring-do—all of which carry no identitarian or structural consequences.

I am not suggesting a direct causal relationship between the cultural turn to gay love and the emergence of heteroflexibility discourses, but rather a convergence of mutually complementary forces. As the gay movement continues its transformation into a PAC-funded celebration of homonormative love, it becomes more difficult to conflate naughty, casual, and disavowed homosexual encounters with gay identity, as gay identity is now so commonly represented by the image of out, proud, and respectable gay couples.[2] The other side of this relationship is that discourses surrounding heterosexual fluidity feed into the production of the homonormative homosexual, who, in contrast with queer sex radicals, gender outcasts, and other revolutionaries, is imagined to be motivated by a complex of sincere gay feelings—namely, the desire to fall in gay love, to have a gay family, to be out and proud.

In an unexpected turn, heterosexuality has arguably co-opted much of what is "naughty" about homosexual sex, casting heterosexuality as the domain of the masculine, the erotic, the unfettered, and even the forbidden, while homonormativity and genetics converge to redefine "gay" in affective, domestic, and often sexless terms. The problem with this isn't simply one of bad public relations, requiring our rejoinder "Queers are not bad in bed!" but part of a broader trend of keeping queer life contained within domestic space, where queers are distracted from more imaginative political projects by their pursuit of middle-class respectability. The overwhelming emphasis on mainstream gay equality politics (or the politics of sameness) distracts us from queer ways of life that are fundamentally different from—and in revolutionary opposition to—the ways that most straight people fashion their bodies, their relationships, and their cultural and political investments. Not only is this a political loss, to the extent that potential queer radicals are being absorbed into the machinery of equality and sameness, but it also misrecognizes queerness, as narratives about love, biology, and immutability are projected onto people, like me, who enrolled themselves in queer subculture in order to escape the sexism and boredom of heterosexuality.

As I hinted at the outset of this chapter, the notion that a genetic predisposition accounts for my presumably authentic lesbianism (I have been a dyke for nearly twenty years, after all) and marks my difference from straight-identified people who engage in homosexual sex has never resonated for me. The idea that I was born with a sexual orientation toward "women" (to vaginas? breasts? estrogen? female energy? Precisely *what* was I born desiring?) erases what is a far more specific—and not reducible to any gendered body part—accounting of what arouses me. A little backstory: I had a nice long run with boys and men throughout high school and college and into graduate school, but later I became aware that the sexism I had taken for granted in those relationships was not actually sexy to me. Men's bodies, and masculinity more generally, were hot, but sexism had become repulsive. I looked around for genuinely feminist men and found few or none. I was attracted to several gay men, but most were uninterested in sex with me. One drunken night, I had sex with a close female friend, who was also one of my main feminist comrades. This was my first "lesbian sex," and the absence in that encounter of the heavy overlay of heterosexual culture and its erotic scripts was incredibly sexy.

Soon after, I started going to queer dive bars, completely exhilarated by the idea that I had no idea what sort of bodies, genders, and sexual possibilities awaited me there. I fell in lust with these bars, and with the kinds of performance (abject drag, weird performance art, BDSM demos, etc.) and performativity, including my own, they facilitated. I went to queer sex shows in San Francisco, where leather dykes with shaved heads penetrated each

other with vegetables on stage, inciting swarms of dyke spectators to then fuck each other in the bathrooms and hallways of
the dark venues where these events took place. I went to BDSM
play parties where sadistic leather daddies of various genders
performed for those of us watching how to take a bottom from
almost unwatchable pain to the most tender forms of comfort.
In these spaces, I had discovered my sexual "orientation," so to
speak: I was undeniably, viscerally attracted to the unexpected,
the unruly, and the risky. I was attracted to the bodies (masculine
female bodies; feminine male bodies) known within heterosexual
culture to be tragic and ugly. My first girlfriend, for instance, was
a chain-smoking, weathered-looking butch dyke, with calloused
hands and the mouth of a sailor. She reminded me, in her mood
and appearance, of the Kenickie character from the movie *Grease*.
Try as my straight friends might to force me to view her through
the lens of heteronormativity ("but you know you could get a really *beautiful* woman, don't you?" and "if you are going to be with
women, why wouldn't you want to be with one who was attractive
and feminine?"), I was completely enchanted. She was hot despite
and because she was ugly to the straight world.

One absurdly reductive account often imposed on me by mainstream lesbian and gay activists is that I simply discovered I was
bisexual, and that this had been true all along. But to tell the story
that way elides the fact that what drew me to queer life was not
vaginas, or a "constant craving" for women, to invoke the lesbian
torch song, but the promise of a life outside the predictable constraints of heteronormativity. And it certainly wasn't the fantasy
of settling down with a lovely wife. Instead, I felt what José Muñoz
calls "queerness's pull," a longing to escape the gender and sexual
order as it is, and to be among others looking into the distant
queer horizon, where sex itself could become something as yet
unimagined. I discovered that the object of my desire was not a
person or even a class of people (like women or men), but queer
spaces, queer ideas, and queer possibilities.[3] In many ways, the

particular bodies with which I interacted were the vessels, delicious and significant as they were, that carried me toward this larger object of my desire. I discovered I was neither straight nor gay nor lesbian nor bisexual—I was queer.

You can picture, then, the disconnect that occurs when well-meaning straight people wax poetic about how I had no choice about my lesbian constitution, congratulate me on being brave enough to come out of the closet despite what a hard life it is to be gay, and declare that "love is love" or "all love is the same" and that hence, they can see I am "just like any heterosexual person." Or when wait staff at restaurants compliment my genderqueer partner and me for being "such beautiful ladies, such a beautiful couple." Or when straight women, several minutes into a rant about their husbands or boyfriends, gesture at alliance with me by bemoaning their presumably unchangeable heterosexuality with a dramatic sigh: "Oh I *wish* I could be a lesbian. I'd probably be a lot happier." Or when gay and lesbian organizations presume that I am their constituency, that I owe them my money or volunteer hours in exchange for all the work they have done to normalize me and improve my public image. And, more to point of this book, you can imagine the disconnect a queer like me will feel when straight people dismiss their homosexual encounters as meaningless simply because they were unexpected, drunken, raunchy, or casual.

It is not that I am unfamiliar with the prevailing gender and sexual ideology that leads to these assumptions. It is that what I would like to say in response is unfathomable to most people—that I signed on to, and cultivated, queerness in my life; that I find both heterosexual and mainstream gay culture distasteful and often pitiable; that my partner and I are not ladies and we don't want our relationship described as beautiful; that if you think you would be happier as a dyke you could and should be one; that I don't want a good public image (at least not the kind for which the mainstream gay and lesbian movement is striving); and that it is precisely because queerness refuses normalization that is meaningful to me and to other queers. The subversion is where the romance lies.

I do not mean to suggest that my specific coming-of-age story or my particular erotic proclivities are generalizable to all queers. Rather, my story represents one example from within a collective queer experience of departure from *both* straight and homonormative structures of romance and desire. To spell out what is perhaps obvious, the now widely popular narrative of gay love—the "same love" that is felt by straights but shared between people with ostensibly matching genitals and chromosomes—may seem innocuous enough, but in fact it forecloses our capacity to see the crucial differences between, for instance, the sexist and all-too-scripted straight culture I fled, the mainstream gay culture waiting to normalize and validate me, and the defiant queer culture I found I actually desired. To account for the queerness of someone like me, but also for the straightness of men who have long engaged in not-gay sex with men, the dividing line between normal and queer sexuality is not most productively viewed as a biological one. Instead, it is a cultural one, one in which straightness—and increasingly homonormative gayness—is marked by a fetish for the normal and the sanitized, while queerness directs its loving and lusting collective gaze at precisely the bodies and ways of life disavowed by straights as ugly and failed.

Masculinity, "No Choice," and Misogyny

As we think about points of difference and similarity between the discourses that circulate around straight and gay men's homosexual activity, we see that the logic of "no choice" is a centerpiece of both. Gay men, we are told, are born gay, bound by their homosexual biology. Straight men, we are told, are bound by circumstances (hazing and initiation, institutional deprivation, developmental rites of passage, etc.) requiring that they make intimate contact with other men's bodies. Given that masculinity is normally imbued with extraordinary agency, it is worth noting that in the case of homosexuality, men's sexual agency drops out of the equation almost completely. Any homosexuality that happens to a man is, by biology or circumstance, out of his control. Such is not quite the belief about women, whose sexuality, at least in postmodernity, is thought to be influenced by more agentic forces like "curiosity" (hence the much greater popularity of the term "bi-curious" for women than for men).

Given that male agency is prized in almost every other realm, what function is served by the cultural investment in viewing male homosexuality as beyond men's control? This is where a feminist analysis is desperately needed, and is still largely absent from "born this way" debates. Bringing feminist history to bear here reveals that patriarchy and rape culture have long relied on the view that men are more subject to their animal instincts than women, and that they are at the mercy of unstoppable sexual urges and fixed sexual natures. This understanding of male biology absolves men of responsibility for rape, shifting blame to women whose presumably more agentic, receptive, and flexible sexuality should enable them to avoid unwanted sex. Still today, sexuality is a realm in which flexibility, choice, and curiosity are feminizing, while masculinity and maleness remain the domains of rigidity and hardwiring.

As sociologist Vera Whisman documented in her prescient 1995 book *Queer by Choice*, it is men, both gay and straight, who take greatest offense at the idea that gay and straight identifications are cultural phenomena, subject to a vast and dynamic field of structural, cultural, and experiential contingencies. Beliefs about the difference between male and female sexuality—with men invested in viewing their sexuality as rigid and subject to biological phenomena—not only bolster the gender binary, but sustain the hetero/homo binary as well. For the most part, homosexual sex is believed to be utterly unthinkable for heterosexual men, though just below the surface of this belief, we see that the unflinching power of male heterosexuality appears again and again in justi-fications of straight men's *homosexual* behavior. Throughout the twentieth century, it was precisely straight men's desperate, in-flexible, and unstoppable need for sex with women that was be-lieved to propel them to have sex with male substitutes, such as in cases in which women sex partners were purportedly unavail-able. Similarly, gay men's homosexuality has been constructed as fundamentally non-negotiable, with women and their bodies often cast as repulsive, and the mere thought of sex with women nauseating. For instance, gay men's decades-long use of the mi-sogynistic term "fish" to refer to women (in reference to the scent of the vagina) expresses this repulsion, reducing women to the body part imagined as the ultimate object of straight male de-sire. Tellingly, despite the common accusation that lesbians are "man-haters," dykes have no corollary term to describe their dis-gust with penises or any other part of men's bodies. In the case of the term "fish," as with other elements of gay male culture, it is difficult to untangle expressions of misogyny from expressions of exclusive homosexuality, or the presumably visceral gay male experience of the hetero/homo binary.

In this context, I want to propose that the conflation of gay-ness and queerness, and the misperception of queerness as a physiology rather than a cultural affiliation and political stance, is arguably as much about sexism and misogyny as it is about hetero- and homonormativity. Though the prevailing logic is that men, like animals, are subject to their hardwired sexual impulses, the vitriol that gay men have recently directed at critics of the "born this way" campaign suggests that something more than sexual instinct is at stake. When women, like the actress Cynthia Nixon, dare to suggest that they arrived at queerness by some path other than a congenital predisposition, gay men doth protest too much. A couple of years ago, I wrote a blog post arguing for a more constructionist view of sexual desire (old news for those of us who study gender and sexuality). The post was widely read, and while gay men were not its only critics, they were the only readers who used their disagreement as an occasion to call me an "idiot," a "fucking whore," and a "stupid cunt," and to write voluminous, mansplaining comments questioning my intellectual credentials.

Some kinder gay male critics cited Lisa Diamond's work and pointed out that both my story and their story could be true at the same time, because I am a woman (with relational, flexible sexuality) and they are men (with innate and immutable sexual orientations.) But there is another reading, a feminist reading, that elevates us from this sort of "gay men are from Mars, lesbians are from Venus" approach, which is to consider that the cultural and structural stakes of taking up legitimizing biological accounts of sexuality are different for men than they are for women. Without embarking on a detailed account of the very different cultural associations and consequences assigned to male and female homosexuality since the emergence of the sexual binary, I note here that one of the dominant associations with male homosexuality is femininity and, concomitantly, the apparently tragic abdication of male power. Female homosexuality has also been conflated with cross-gender identification, or "trying to be a man," but under patriarchy and its glorification of men, this striving for manhood—even when lesbians are perceived as wanting, but failing, to achieve it—is imbued with a kind of logic and potency not extended to male homosexuality. Hence, it stands to reason that recasting homosexuality as a biological imperative, to the extent that it diffuses the claim that gay men have "chosen" to give up their masculinity or male power, has greater legitimizing potential for men than it does for women. This, and many other nonbiological factors, may help account for gay men's persistent attachment to the idea that their homosexuality, just like the homo- and heterosexuality of straight men, is fundamentally out of their control.

Returning to Whisman's arguments in *Queer by Choice*—she notes that when public opinion favors the idea that sexual orientation is hardwired, this produces not only a silencing effect for people who cultivate, evolve into,[4] or "choose" queerness, but also a shoring up of "exclusionary male-dominated gay politics." Whisman calls for serious consideration of "chosen homosexuality as one way of making gay and lesbian political organizing more radical, democratic, and egalitarian."[5] Bringing us back to the question of heterosexuality, we might also ask what a renewed attention to noncongenital, defiant queerness means for straight people generally, and for straight men engaged in not-gay sex particularly? Certainly to imagine that queerness is an option for all people—to consider that anyone could, technically, choose to get off the tired, beaten path of heterosexuality or homonormativity and relocate him- or herself among the freaks and perverts, among the leather daddies and the fat dykes in San Francisco ravenously filling each other's orifices with organic squash—is to highlight that most straight-identified people are "straight" not because they don't ever want to have a same-sex encounter, but because, in their view, queer modes of homosexual relating do not constitute an appealing way of life. Because their allegiance, ultimately, is to normativity.

In sum, I have argued in this book that homosexuality is a ubiquitous feature of white heterosexual men's lives; it is not incongruent with white heteromasculinity, but part of what produces it. My hope is that three basic points can be taken away from this investigation, reshaping how we think about heterosexuality. The first point is that we have not focused enough attention on the vast array of sexual activities that constitute male heterosexuality. If we are to believe the significant but relatively invisible body of research on male sexuality, we find that acts of kissing, touching, jerking, licking, and penetrating men are not limited to gay and bisexual-identified men's lives nor to desperate situations in which straight men are denied access to female sex partners. In fact, these activities appear to thrive in hyper-heterosexual environments, such as fraternities, where access to sex with women is anything but constrained. What sets these scenes apart from those we might call "gay" are not the specific sex acts involved (such as male fingers in male anuses, for instance), but the cultural narratives that circulate around these acts.

Second, it is precisely because male and female heterosexuality incorporate many kinds of homosexual contact that we must push back against theories of exclusive sexual orientations and hardwired sexual natures. From a queer perspective, the major flaw in the bio-evolutionary science of sexual orientation is that it purports to study how people become heterosexual or homosexual as if it is evident what these terms mean. But taking seriously the ubiquity of homosexuality (not gay identity, but homosexual activity) raises some very basic and yet still unanswered questions about precisely what or who we are looking for when we are looking to the body for evidence of congenital heterosexuality or homosexuality.

A third and last central point of this book is that white male heterosexuality, in particular, draws on the resources of white privilege to circumvent homophobic stigma and to assign heterosexual meaning to homosexual activities. Men of color, on the other hand, quickly fall subject to misrecognized and hypersurveilled categories like "the down low." To be clear, my aim is not to suggest that we should incorporate white men into the down low. Instead, I have suggested that we extend to all men, both white men and men of color, the possibility that male sexualities are as fluid as female sexualities—and that all sexualities are shaped by a complex nexus of structural, cultural, and psychic forces.

Sincerely Queer

Beyond these basic points, I hope to have drawn attention to the dynamic and underexplored relationship among heteronormative, homonormative, and queer engagements with homosexual sex. I have done this in the service of calling for an even deeper and more sincere embrace of queer erotic worlds, which we might view as the truest objects of queer longing.

As I mentioned earlier, straights want and need non-straights, both gay and queer, to be sincere about our homosexuality so as to amplify the frivolity of their homosexuality. Dovetailing with biological narratives that speak to our authenticity, the primary way we are called upon to perform our sincerity is to narrate our queerness as an expression of romantic love, rather than a political critique of gender and sexual normativity. Despite the title of this chapter, I am not actually proposing we take a stand against gay love in and of itself, but that we take a stand against the forces attempting to erase queerness and reduce all non-straight homosexuality to romantic, couple-centered love. What a sad state of affairs when the couple, and not queer collectivity, becomes the focus of our thinking about queerness. It is hard to imagine another social movement—the feminist movement, the civil rights movement—in which the couple could so easily become the unit of analysis (even when, as in the feminist movement and civil rights movements, domestic and sexual relationships are important issues at hand).

But while I suggest that we throw romantic, couple-centered love out the window of queer politics, I am not certain that we should do the same with sincerity. How might we mine the notion of sincerity for its transgressive, queer potential? Within hetero-masculinity, homosexual sex is not gay when it is meaningless and inconsequential, brought on by coercion, or when it takes the form of homophobic play-acting, daredevil heroics, or radical art. Emptied of romantic meaning, the emphasis of not-gay homosexuality is placed instead on naughty and ephemeral homosexual sex acts. One way to intervene in this co-optation of defiant homosexual sex is to recenter sex acts themselves, rather than centering gay/lesbian identity or gay/lesbian couples in discourses about the meaning of queer life. We might express, with all queer sincerity, our attachments not to the identitarian and/

or romantic meaning of our sex acts, but to the ways that collective queer sex acts—those passed down through generations of queer bar patrons, kink enthusiasts, pornographers, sex workers, commune dwellers, sex educators, and others—are what incite our feelings of love, longing, and romance, not especially or only for our sex partners, but for our tribe. We might explain to straights that there is no queer sexuality without the queer commons. My partner and I, for instance, have been together for ten years and we know that our sexual relationship is palpably incomplete when isolated for too long from the place of its origin: public queer space—namely, the queer bar. It is in that space, where both of our genders have a wholly different meaning than they do anywhere else, and where our shared fetish for insubordinate bodies and genders finds its best outlet, that our "sex life" comes to life.

In many ways, straight white men's homosexual encounters look remarkably like the kind of queer collective sexuality I am describing here: communal, public, kinky, and defiant. But while straight white men use these features as evidence of the meaninglessness of homosexual encounters, or as signal of their true loyalty to heterosexual normalcy, we queers know that these features are the lifeblood of queer difference, to be cherished, preserved, and treated with reverence and sincerity.

NOTES

Chapter 1. Nowhere without It

1 See #53 from "The Complete List" of things bros like on broslikethissite.com, July 23, 2009, http://www.broslikethissite.com/2009/07/53-hazing.html.

2 Descriptions of the elephant walk vary somewhat, though adhere to the same basic theme. In Michael Kimmel's *Guyland: The Perilous World Where Boys Become Men* (New York: Harper Perennial, 2008), he describes the ritual as follows: "[The pledges] are then told to strip naked and stand in a straight line, one behind the other. . . . Each pledge is ordered to reach his right hand between his legs to the pledge standing behind him and grab that guy's penis, then place his left hand on the shoulder of the guy in front of him. (You have to bend over to make this work). Forming a circle, they walk around the basement for several minutes, in what is known as the 'elephant walk.' . . . These snapshots capture typical events that are taking place at colleges and universities across America" (96–97). Similarly, users of urbandictionary.com describe the elephant walk as follows: "[It is] often used for hazing where a group of guys form a straight line and grab the erect cock of the guy in back of them with one hand and put their thumb in the sphincter of the guy in front of them, then they walk in a circle" (http://www.urbandictionary.com/define.php?term=elephant+walk, accessed June 10, 2004).

3 For a brief review of this literature, see John F. DeCecco and David A. Parker's *Sex, Cells, and Same Sex Desire: The Biology of Sexual Preference* (New York: Routledge, 1995), 12–13. See also Jeffrey Escoffier, "Gay for Pay: Straight Men and the Making of Gay Pornography," *Qualitative Sociology* 26, no. 4 (2003): 531–555, for a genealogy of the term "situational homosexuality."

4 In one documented case in 1999, the University of Vermont hockey team was disbanded by the university for requiring new recruits to "parade in an elephant walk." See CBS News, "College Hazing under Fire," 2000, http://www.cbsnews.com/2100–201_162–179106.html.

5 Laurie Essig, "Heteroflexibility," Salon.com, November 15, 2000,

http://www.salon.com/2000/11/15/heteroflexibility/; Leila Rupp and Verta Taylor. "Straight Girls Kissing," *Contexts* 9, no.3 (Summer 2010): 28–32.

6 Essig, "Heteroflexibility."

7 Jeffrey Kluger, "Girls Kissing Girls: Explaining the Trend," TIME.com, September 15, 2010, http://healthland.time.com/2010/09/15/girls-kissing-girls-whats-up-with-that/.

8 Rupp and Taylor, "Straight Girls Kissing," 28–32.

9 Ibid.

10 In Lisa Diamond's *Sexual Fluidity: Understanding Women's Love and Desire* (Cambridge: Harvard University Press, 2008), she argues that the evolutionary function of proceptive desire is reproduction, and therefore our ancestors' proceptive desires were likely to be heterosexual in orientation while their receptive desires had no gender orientation. In this quite heteronormative model, occasional same-sex arousability—greater in women than in men—is part of the human condition, while more fixed homosexual "orientations" stem from a later "alteration in the intrinsic gender coding of proceptive desire" (210–211).

11 Eric Anderson, "'Being Masculine Is Not about Who You Sleep With . . .': Heterosexual Athletes Contesting Masculinity and the One-Time Rule of Homosexuality," *Sex Roles: A Journal of Research* 58, no. 1–2 (2008): 104–115.

12 See Laura Hamilton, "Trading on Heterosexuality: College Women's Gender Strategies and Homophobia," *Gender & Society* 21 no. 2 (2007): 145–172, for an empirical account of this practice.

13 Anderson, "'Being Masculine," 109.

14 Ibid.

15 Eric Anderson, "I Kiss Them Because I Love Them: The Emergence of Heterosexual Men Kissing in British Institutes of Education," *Archives of Sexual Behavior* 41, no. 2 (2012): 421–430.

16 Ritch Savin Williams and Kenneth Cohen, "Mostly Straight, Most of the Time," Good Men Project.com, November 3, 2010, http://goodmenproject.com/featured-content/mostly-straight/?utm_content=bufferfdb4f&utm_medium=social&utm_source=facebook.com&utm_campaign=buffer.

17 See, for instance, Michael Bartos, John McLeod, and Phil Nott, *Meanings of Sex Between Men* (Canberra: Australian Government Publishing Service, 1993); and Amanda Lynn Hoffman, "'I'm Gay, For Jamie': Heterosexual/Straight-Identified Men Express Desire to Have Sex with Men" (M.A. thesis, San Francisco State University, 2010). Thank you to David Halperin for pointing me in the direction of this research.

18 Steven Zeeland, *Sailors and Sexuality Identity: Crossing the Line between "Straight" and "Gay" in the U.S. Navy* (New York: Harrington Park Press, 1995), 5.

19 Diamond, *Sexual Fluidity*, 2.

20 Diamond acknowledges significant evidence pointing to male sexual fluidity, but has stated that "in general, the degree of fluidity in women appears substantially greater than in men, though we do not yet have enough data to fully evaluate this possibility. More rigorous investigation of fluidity in male sexuality . . . has begun

to receive some attention and will likely be a fascinating area of future research" (ibid., 11–12). As this book is going to press, Diamond is reported to have revised her position about the relative fixity of male sexual desire. At the February 2014 Sexuality Preconference for the Society for Personality and Social Psychology, Diamond delivered a paper titled "I Was Wrong! Men are Pretty Darn Sexually Fluid, Too!" According to the *New York Times*, the paper summarized preliminary findings from a survey of 394 people—including gay men, lesbians, bisexual men and women, and heterosexual men and women (Benoit Denizet-Lewis, "The Scientific Quest to Prove Bisexuality," March 20, 2014, http://www.nytimes.com/2014/03/23/magazine/the-scientific-quest-to-prove-bisexuality-exists.html?_r=0). These new findings, and how Diamond reconciles them with her previous claims about longstanding bio-evolutionary differences between female and male sexuality, have not yet been published.

21 Lest we imagine that young straight women's sexual contact with women always takes romantic, seductive, and noncoercive forms that differ fundamentally from those of straight men, we need only look to cases of sorority hazing rituals. In one reported hazing exercise, young women were required to take off their bras and have their breasts ranked by their "sisters"; in another, a young woman was required to either take a hit of cocaine or penetrate herself with a dildo in front of her sisters. See "Sorority Hazing Increasingly Violent, Disturbing," ABC News, February 17, 2010, http://abcnews.go.com/Health/Wellness/sorority-hazing-increasingly-violent-disturbing-college-campus/story?id=9798604&page=2.

22 Lilian Faderman, *Odd Girls and Twilight Lovers: A History of Lesbian Life in America* (New York: Columbia University Press, 1991).

23 Peggy McIntosh, "White Privilege and Male Privilege: A Personal Account of Coming to See Correspondences through Work in Women's Studies," in Richard Delgado and Jean Stefancic, eds., *Critical White Studies: Looking behind the Mirror* (Philadelphia: Temple University Press, 1997), 291.

24 See Aida Hurtado, *The Color of Privilege: Three Blasphemies on Race and Feminism* (Ann Arbor: University of Michigan Press, 1997), for a rich account of the processes by which dominant groups preserve their unmarked, normative status.

25 C. Riley Snorton, *Nobody Is Supposed to Know: Black Sexuality on the Down Low* (Minneapolis: University of Minnesota Press, 2014), 3, 25

26 See Keith Boykin, *Beyond the Down Low: Sex, Lies, and Denial in Black America* (New York: Carroll & Graf, 2005); Patricia Hill Collins, *Black Sexual Politics: African Americans, Gender, and the New Racism* (New York: Routledge, 2005); J. L. King, *On the Down Low: A Journey Into the Lives of "Straight" Black Men Who Sleep with Men* (New York: Harmony, 2004).

27 Boykin, *Beyond the Down Low*; Collins, *Black Sexual Politics*; King, *On the Down Low*.

28 Collins, *Black Sexual Politics*, 207.

29 Rafael Diaz, *Latino Gay Men and HIV: Culture, Sexuality, and Risk Behavior* (New York, Routledge, 1997).

30 Jeffrey Q. McCune, "'Out' in the Club: The Down Low, Hip-Hop, and the Architexture of Black Masculinity," *Text and Performance Quarterly* 28, no. 3 (2008): 298–314. Thanks to Mark Broomfield for drawing my attention to McCune's dazzling analysis.

31 Snorton, *Nobody Is Supposed to Know*.

32 Boykin, *Beyond the Down Low*; see also M. Alfredo González, "Latinos On Da Down Low: The Limitations of Sexual Identity in Public Health," *Latino Studies* 5 no. 1 (2007): 25–52.

33 See Janet Jakobsen and Ann Pellegrini's introduction to *Secularisms* (Durham, NC: Duke University Press, 2008), in which they argue that despite rising claims to secular universality in the United States, U.S. secularism remains deeply tied to white Protestantism.

34 Ruth Frankenberg "Mirage of an Unmarked Whiteness," in Birgit Brander Rasmussen et al., eds, *The Making and Unmaking of Whiteness* (Durham, NC: Duke University Press, 2001), 75.

35 Ibid., 76–77.

36 Judith Butler, *Gender Trouble: Feminism and the Subversion of Identity* (New York: Routledge, 1990); Jonathan Ned Katz, *The Invention of Heterosexuality* (New York: Plume, 1996); James Dean *Straights: Heterosexuality in Post-Closeted Culture* (New York: New York University Press, 2014); Chrys Ingraham, *Thinking Straight: The Power, Promise and Paradox of Heterosexuality* (New York: Routledge, 2004).

37 Judith Butler. *The Psychic Life of Power: Theories of Subjection* (Palo Alto, CA: Stanford University Press, 1997).

38 In using the term "disidentification," I mean to highlight straight men's disavowal of their homosexual attachments, including their cultivated blindness to, or ignorance of, the sexual desire that may drive their persistent efforts to touch one another's bodies. Fetishized narratives about adventure, male bonding, humiliation, resilience, and so forth not only empty gay meaning from straight men's homosexual activities, but often empty these activities of any sexual meaning at all. This way of thinking about disidentification differs from José Esteban Muñoz's use of the term in the dazzling book *Disidentifications: Queers of Color and the Performance of Politics* (Minneapolis: University of Minnesota Press, 1999), wherein Muñoz describes the ways that performance artists of color consciously rework, or disidentify with, white supremacist, heteronormative, and misogynistic representations in order to give these representations new meaning, and in so doing, to envision new queer public spheres. Thinking about Muñoz's use of the term in relation to a more psychoanalytic application yields an important distinction: There is little evidence to suggest that straight men engaged in not-gay homosexual sex are consciously rescripting homosexuality for any sort of long-range political effect; they are not hoping to change the public landscape of sexual meaning or to make sexual fluidity more possible for us all, or even for themselves. Instead, straight men arguably take these heteronormalizing narratives at face value, unconscious of the reparative work such narratives accomplish. Hence, the project at hand is to bring these narratives and their

effects to light, including their effects for the queer counterpublics at the heart of Muñoz's analysis.

39 Sara Ahmed, *Queer Phenomenology: Orientations, Objects, Others* (Durham, NC: Duke University Press, 2006).

40 Ibid., 100 (emphasis in the original).

41 David Halperin, *How to Be Gay* (Cambridge, MA: Belknap Press, 2014)

42 Hamilton, "Trading on Heterosexuality."

43 Thank you to Margaux Cowden and the students at Williams College for helping me articulate this point in such succinct terms.

44 Building on Michael Warner's term "heteronormativity," which refers to all of the ways that heterosexuality is taken for granted in both cultural and institutional life, historian Lisa Duggan coined the term "homonormativity" (see *The Twilight of Equality* [New York: Beacon Press, 2004]) to draw attention to what is now taken for granted about gay identity and culture—namely, that what lesbians and gay men want most is access to mainstream institutions (like marriage and the military) and a private, respectable, domestic existence.

45 Katz, *Invention of Heterosexuality*, 108.

46 F. Newport, "Americans Remain More Likely to Believe Sexual Orientation Due to Environment, Not Genetics," *Gallop Poll Monthly*, July 25, 1998, 14–16; L. Marvin Overby, "Etiology and Attitudes: Beliefs about the Origins of Homosexuality and Their Implications for Public Policy," *Journal of Homosexuality* 61 no. 4 (2014): 568–587.

47 DeCecco and Parker, *Sex, Cells, and Same Sex Desire*; Rainer Herrn "On the History of Biological Theories of Homosexuality," cited in ibid.

48 The sociobiological premise is exemplified in pro-gay discourse by the now well-worn refrain: "No one would *choose* a life of homophobic discrimination; hence, homosexuality is biological in origin; and hence, you must accept me because I cannot change." Consider, for also, the rapid speed at which Lady Gaga's 2011 hit song "Born This Way" became America's new gay anthem.

49 Diamond, *Sexual Fluidity*, 198.

50 Aaron Belkin, "Spam Filter: Gay Rights and the Normalization of Male–Male Rape in the United States Military," *Radical History Review* 100 (2008): 180–185.

51 CJ Pascoe, *Dude You're a Fag: Masculinity and Sexuality in High School* (Berkeley: University of California Press, 2007).

Chapter 2. Bars, Bikers, and Bathrooms

1 The sexual binary relies, after all, on a male/female dichotomy in which people are attracted either to "the same" or "the other" sex (or "both sexes")—a schema not only simplistic in its understanding of sexual desire, but of gender expression as well.

2 As George Chauncey explains in *Gay New York: Gender, Urban Culture, and the Making of the Gay Male World, 1890–1940* (New York: Basic Books, 1994), "Even the third category 'bisexuality' depends for its meaning on its intermediate position on the axis defined by those two poles (heterosexuality and homosexuality)" (13).

3 Offering a full account of this development is beyond the scope of this project. For more of this history, see Michel Foucault, *The History of Sexuality, Volume I: An Introduction* (New York: Vintage, 1978); Jonathan Ned Katz, *The Invention of Heterosexuality* (New York: Plume 1996); Jennifer Terry, *An American Obsession: Science, Medicine, and Homosexuality in Modern Society* (Chicago: University of Chicago Press, 1999); and Hanne Blank, *Straight: The Surprisingly Short History of Heterosexuality* (New York: Beacon, 2012).

4 Katz, *The Invention of Heterosexuality*, 84

5 Ibid., 92

6 Blank, *Straight*.

7 By the early twentieth century, an identity-based sexual binary had solidified within the dominant institutions of Europe and the United States. However, this way of thinking about sexuality hardly characterizes how sexuality was—and continues to be—understood around the globe, or even, to use George Chauncey's phrase, "in the city streets" of the United States. Globally, some sexual systems attribute less meaning to the gender of sexual partners than to the social context in which the sex occurs, such as whether money is exchanged (see the 1995 documentary film *Shinjuku Boys* by Kim Longinotto and Jano Williams), whether accepted kinship structures are being observed (see Gloria Wekker, *The Politics of Passion: Women's Sexual Culture in the Afro-Surinamese Diaspora* [New York: Columbia University Press, 2006]), or whether participants are penetrative, receptive, or both (see Lionel Cantú, Nancy Naples, and Salvador Vidal-Ortiz, *The Sexuality of Migration: Border Crossings and Mexican Immigrant Men* [New York: New York University Press, 2009]). In cultures in which multiple genders are recognized, the notion of a homo/hetero binary—itself dependent on a male/female binary—is largely incomprehensible (see Karen Yescavage and Jonathan Alexander, "Muddying the Waters: How Bisexuality and Transgenderism Problematize Binary Constructs of Sexuality, Gender, and Sex," in Abby Ferber et al., eds. *Sex, Gender, and Sexuality: The New Basics* [New York: Oxford University Press 2009]). And, as discussed in the later sections of this chapter, many working- class men, in both cities and rural areas, drew a different line between "queer" and "normal" sex practices than did medical and legal authorities.

8 Blank, *Straight*, 49

9 See Terry's *An American Obsession* and Siobhan Somerville's *Queering the Color Line: Race and the Invention of Homosexuality in American Culture* (Durham, NC: Duke University Press, 2000) for detailed accounts of the intersections of scientific efforts aimed at measuring racial differences and those aimed at identifying and measuring sexual difference.

10 Racial segregation and the racial and economic context of psychotherapy contributed to the representation of whites as the most visible, early examples of homosexuals.

11 See Terry, *An American Obsession*, and Somerville, *Queering the Color Line*.

12 See Roderick Ferguson, *Aberrations in Black: Toward a Queer of Color Critique* (Minneapolis: University of Minnesota Press, 2003); David Roediger, *Working*

toward Whiteness: How America's Immigrants Became White (New York: Basic Books, 2005); Karen Brodkin, *How Jews Became White Folks and What that Says about Race in America* (New Brunswick, NJ: Rutgers University Press, 1998).

13 Mary Wollstonecraft, *A Vindication of the Rights of Woman* (New York: Dover, 1996 [1792]).

14 Emma Goldman, *The Traffic in Women* (New York: Times Change Press, 1971 [1910]).

15 Daniel Boyarin, *Unheroic Conduct: The Rise of Heterosexuality and the Invention of the Jewish Man* (Berkeley: University of California Press, 1997). Quotation taken from back matter.

16 Chauncey dedicates one chapter to African American communities in New York, though white immigrant men are at the center of his analysis. Chauncey also notes that Jewish men were less likely to immigrate to the United States alone; instead, many brought their families, resulting in relatively more interaction between men and women in Jewish neighborhoods.

17 Not all men in gay life viewed themselves as effeminate, though the work of drawing distinctions between different kinds of gay men was largely an internal, rather than external project. As Chauncey explains, "the men who viewed themselves as part of a distinct category of men primarily on the basis of their homosexual interest rather than their womanlike gender status usually called themselves *queer* . . . . They might use queer to refer to any man who was not "normal," but they usually applied terms such as *fairy, faggot,* and *queen* only to those men who dressed or behaved in what they considered to be a flamboyantly effeminate manner. They were so careful to draw such distinctions in part because the dominant culture failed to do so" (*Gay New York*, 15–16).

18 Ibid., 27 (emphasis added). For an additional and fascinating account of conflicting assessments of what constituted "queer" sexuality in the early twentieth-century United States, see Chauncey's essay "Christian Brotherhood or Sexual Perversion? Homosexual Identities and the Construction of Sexual Boundaries in the World War One Era," *Journal of Social History* 19 no. 2 (1985): 189–211. Describing the 1919 Newport Naval Training scandal, which involved homosexual sex among sailors and police decoys, Chauncey explains that "even when witnesses agreed that two men had engaged in homosexual relations with each other, they disagreed about whether both men or only the one playing the 'woman's part' should be labeled as 'queer.' More profoundly, they disagreed about how to distinguish between a 'sexual' and a 'nonsexual' relationship; the navy defined certain relationships as homosexual and perverted which the ministers claimed were merely brotherly and Christian" (189).

19 The normalization of sex between straight men and fairies hardly meant that straight men held fairies in high esteem. Chauncey makes a compelling case that straight men related to fairies in ways similar to "whores" and other "impure" women, subjecting both to sexual assault and generally violent treatment. Straight men's sexual "needs" were imagined to trump all else, including the gender of their sex partners.

20 Chauncey, *Gay New York*, 65.

21 Ibid., 22.

22 Ibid., 21–22.

23 Thank you to Robert Crouch for pointing me in the direction of the Hells Angels.

24 "The History of the Hells Angels," The History Channel, http://www.youtube.com/watch?v=uQqI_IU7wDI.

25 Ibid.

26 Hunter S. Thompson, *Hells Angels: The Strange and Terrible Saga of the Outlaw Motorcycle Gangs* (New York: Ballantine, 1972), 114.

27 Ibid., 114–115.

28 Ibid., 115.

29 Ibid., 253.

30 David Lamble, "The Original Gonzo Journalist: Alex Gibney on Hunter S. Thompson," *Bay Area Reporter*, July 3, 2008, http://www.ebar.com/arts/art_article.php?sec=film&article=521.

31 Ibid.

32 Thompson, *Hell's Angels*, 254.

33 Ibid., 86.

34 Laud Humphreys, *Tearoom Trade: Impersonal Sex in Public Places* (New York: Aldine, 1970), 11 (emphasis in original).

35 Ibid., 105.

36 More generally, racial segregation of public facilities, such as bathrooms, was not outlawed until 1964 with the passage of the Equal Rights Act. De facto segregation continued for many years after.

37 Humphreys, *Tearoom Trade*, 6.

38 Ibid., 115.

39 Ibid., 11.

40 A glory hole is a hole in the dividing wall between bathroom stalls. It is used by men to engage in oral sex or to observe sexual activities in the adjacent stall, while maintaining a degree of anonymity.

41 John Howard, *Men Like That: A Southern Queer History* (Chicago: University of Chicago Press, 2001), xviii.

42 Hinson quoted in ibid., 258.

43 Ibid., 263.

44 Hinson later divorced his wife and became involved in gay and lesbian projects before his AIDS-related death in 1995.

45 Howard, *Men Like That*, 267.

46 Mrs. Preston Dampeer, quoted in ibid., 267.

47 Ibid., 266.

48 Ibid., 276.

49 Eve Shapiro, "Straight Indiscretions or Queer Hypocrites: Public Negotiations of Identity and Sexual Behaviour," in Sally Hines and Yvette Taylor, eds., *Sexualities: Past Reflections, Future Directions* (London: Palgrave, 2012), 109.

50 "Minister: Haggard 'Completely Heterosexual,'" *USA TODAY*, March 1, 2007, http://usatoday30.usatoday.com/news/religion/2007–02–06-haggard-sex-allegation_x.htm.

Chapter 3. Here's How You Know You're Not Gay

1 Lesbian, Gay, Bisexual, Transgendered, Queer, Questioning, Intersex, Asexual, Allies, and Pansexual.

2 Marvin Overby, "Etiology and Attitudes: Beliefs about the Origins of Homosexuality and Their Implications for Public Policy," *Journal of Homosexuality* 61, no. 4 (2014): 568–587.

3 Amy Stone and Jane Ward, "From 'Black People Are Not a Homosexual Act' to 'Gay Is the New Black': Mapping White Uses of Blackness in Modern Gay Rights Campaigns in the United States," *Social Identities* 17, no. 5 (2011): 605–624.

4 Human Rights Campaign, "Herman Cain Believes Being Gay Is a Choice," October 4, 2011, http://www.hrc.org/press-releases/entry/herman-cain-believes-being-gay-is-a-choice.

5 Gael Fashingbauer Cooper, "Cynthia Nixon: I'm Gay by Choice," NBC News, January 24, 2012, http://entertainment.nbcnews.com/_news/2012/01/24/10226838-cynthia-nixon-im-gay-by-choice.

6 See Suzanna Danuta Walters, *The Tolerance Trap: How God, Genes, and Good Intentions Are Sabotaging Gay Equality* (New York: New York University Press, 2014), 116–117, for additional discussion of this incident.

7 Rebecca Jordan-Young, *Brain Storm: The Flaws in the Science of Sex Difference* (Cambridge: Harvard University Press, 2010), 5.

8 In *Between Men: English Literature and Male Homosocial Desire* (New York: Columbia University Press, 1985), Sedgwick argues that "not only must homosexual men be unable to ascertain whether they are to be the objects of 'random' homophobic violence, but no man must be able to ascertain that he is not (that his bonds are not) homosexual" (88–89).

9 Anne Fausto-Sterling, *Sexing the Body: Gender Politics and the Construction of Sexuality* (New York: Basic Books, 2000); Jordan-Young, *Brain Storm*.

10 Jordan-Young, *Brain Storm*.

11 Terrance J. Williams et al., "Finger-Length Ratios and Sexual Orientation," *Nature* 404 (2000): 455–456. For a concise deconstruction of this study, see Peter Hegarty, "Pointing to a Crisis? What Finger Length Ratios Tell Us about the Construction of Sexuality," *Radical Statistics* 83 (2003): 16–30.

12 Benedict Carey, "Straight, Gay, or Lying? Bisexuality Revisited," *New York Times*, July 5, 2005, http://www.nytimes.com/2005/07/05/health/05sex.html?pagewanted=all.

13 Most people who participate as research subjects in such studies are adults who already identify as lesbian or gay; furthermore, brain organization research often points to hormonal processes and brain attributes that have *a correlation with* homosexuality, but are not definitive indicators.

14 When I asked Kort why he used the term "straightguise" to describe men he truly believed were straight, he explained that that the play on words was "too catchy" to pass up even though it did not exactly fit his purposes.

15 Joe Kort, "Straight Guise: A New Blog," 2007, http://www.joekort.com/articles91. htm.

16 A cuckold is a man who is aroused by watching another man have sex with his wife or girlfriend, a humiliation that, in cuckold-themed pornography, frequently extends to his own submission to the sexual demands of his male rival.

17 Katy Butler, "Many Couples Must Negotiate Terms of 'Brokeback' Marriages," *New York Times*, March 7, 2006, http://www.nytimes.com/2006/03/07/health/07broke. html?pagewanted=all.

18 Brian Alexander, "Is My Man Checking Out Other Men?," NBCNews.com, June 7, 2007, http://www.nbcnews.com/id/19056588/ns/health-sexual_health/t/ my-man-checking-out-other-men/#.VI7qnkvpzwI.

19 Elizabeth Perry, "Craig Scandal Brings Issues of Sexual Identity to Light," *Washington Blade*, September 21, 2007, http://www.washblade.com/2007/9-21/ news/national/11273.cfm.

20 See http://www.joekort.com/.

21 John Money (1987), cited in Jordan-Young, *Brainstorm*, 151.

22 "Is Your Boyfriend or Husband Gay?: The Quiz," Quibblo, http://www.quibblo. com/quiz/3pXSxUR/Is-your-boyfriend-or-husband-gay; "Is Your Man Gay?" MyDailyMoment, http://www.mydailymoment.com/app/quiz/userquiz/ takequiz/148/IsYourManGay.

23 The app was subsequently pulled from the market following pressure from gay and lesbian advocacy groups. See Jason Gilbert, "'Is My Son Gay' App Hits Android Market," *Huffington Post*, September 26, 2011, http://www.huffingtonpost. com/2011/09/26/is-my-son-gay-app-android-market_n_981939.html.

24 See Michel Foucault, *The History of Sexuality, Volume I: An Introduction* (New York: Vintage, 1978); Jonathan Ned Katz *The Invention of Heterosexuality* (New York: Plume 1996); Eve Kosofsky Sedgwick, *Epistemology of the Closet* (Berkeley: University of California Press, 2008 [1990]).

25 For examples, see Julian Carter, *The Heart of Whiteness: Normal Sexuality and Race in America, 1880–1940* (Durham, NC: Duke University Press, 2007), and Siobhan Somerville, *Queering the Color Line: Race and the Invention of Homosexuality in American Culture* (Durham, NC: Duke University Press, 2000).

26 The circumstantial reasons that gay men might participate in heterosexual institutions or sexual encounters—e.g., marry women, have sex with women—are rarely stated because homophobia and the closet are always already presumed to be motivation enough for gay men to "pose" as heterosexual. Straight men engaged in gay institutions or homosexual sex have no such obvious alibi, resulting in a greater demand for consideration of the circumstances that would lead straight men to act out of accordance with their heterosexual constitutions.

27 In their widely cited theorization of sexual scripts (see *Sexual Conduct: The Social Sources of Human Sexuality*, New York: Aldine, 1973), William Simon and John

Gagnon assert that sexual practices are not determined by biological instincts but by social roles, cues, and conditions that structure sexual desire and interaction.

28 John F. DeCecco and David A. Parker, *Sex, Cells, and Same Sex Desire: The Biology of Sexual Preference* (New York: Routledge, 1995), 12–13

29 John Money and A. Ehrhardt, "Gender Dimorphic Behavior and Fetal Sex Hormone," *Recent Progress in Hormone Research* 28 (1972): 735–763; John Money and Patricia Tucker, *Sexual Signatures: On Being a Man or a Woman* (New York: Little Brown, 1975).

30 Jeffrey Escoffier, "Gay for Pay: Straight Men and the Making of Gay Pornography," *Qualitative Sociology* 26, no. 4 (2003): 531–555.

31 Ibid., 533 (emphasis added).

32 Regina Kunzel *Criminal Intimacy: Prison and the Uneven History of Modern American Sexuality* (Chicago: University of Chicago Press, 2008); Escoffier, "Gay for Pay."

33 Fanfiction is a genre of writing in which fans of an original literary, film, or television work rewrite its plot, adhering loosely to the canonical universe established by the work's original creator. In the subset of fanfiction called "slash," the work is rewritten to place heterosexual characters in homosexual pairings.

34 Cuckold themes arguably have their roots in the stag films from the 1920 to the 1950s. As queer film historian Thomas Waugh argues in "Homosociality in the Classical American Stag Film: Off Screen, On-Screen," in Linda Williams, ed., *Porn Studies* (Durham, NC: Duke University Press, 2004), some stag plots revolved around men instructing or directing sex between another man and a woman; others centered on men discovering wives engaged in sex with other men and hence, wrestling their nude rival or engaging in other forms of extended male-male contact.

35 Kevin Burra and Curtis Wong, "Gay Political Scandals: 25 Politicians Who Have Faced Claims about Their Sexuality," *Huffington Post*, June 29, 2012, http://www.huffingtonpost.com/2012/06/29/gay-political-scandals-politicians-claims-sexuality-_n_1638201.html#slide=1161090.

36 From author's interview with Taormino, April 2008.

37 Unlike the American "elephant walk," the "soggy biscuit" has its own Wikipedia entry, which explains that "although 'soggy biscuit' is not necessarily associated with homosexuality, since the game does not require mutual masturbation or other contact, the idea and practice of the game is in keeping with the spirit of adolescent sexual exploration associated by many in the UK with public schools (UK) or private schools (Aus). Although the terminology may differ slightly, the notability of the game is such that variations on the theme are referred to in popular culture. . . . Due to the nature of the game, it is hard to find good evidence that it is ever actually played, and is not just an urban legend" (http://en.wikipedia.org/wiki/Soggy_biscuit).

38 Carrie Little Hersh, "Crossing the Line: Sex, Power, Justice, and the U.S. Navy at the Equator," *Duke Journal of Law and Policy* 9 (2002): 277–324; Aaron Belkin,

Bring Me Men: Military Masculinity and the Benign Façade of American Empire, 1898–2001 (London: Oxford University Press, 2012); Steven Zeeland, *Sailors and Sexuality Identity: Crossing the Line Between Straight and Gay in the U.S. Navy* (New York: Routledge, 1995).

39 Michael Kimmel, *Guyland: The Perilous World Where Boys Become Men* (New York: Harper Perennial, 2008), 116–117.

40 Belkin, *Bring Me Men.*

41 Zeeland, *Sailors and Sexual Identity.*

42 Joe Kort, interview with author, September 5, 2008.

43 Ibid.

44 Ibid.

45 Kimmel, *Guyland.*

46 Sedgwick, *Between Men.*

47 Jack Halberstam, *The Queer Art of Failure* (Durham, NC: Duke University Press, 2011).

48 Cathy Reback and Sherry Larkins, "Maintaining a Heterosexual Identity: Sexual Meanings among a Sample of Heterosexually-Identified Men Who Have Sex with Men," *Archives of Sexual Behavior* 39 (2010): 766–773.

49 Escoffier, "Gay for Pay."

50 CJ Pascoe, *Dude You're a Fag: Masculinity and Sexuality in High School* (Berkeley: University of California Press, 2007).

Chapter 4. Average Dudes, Casual Encounters

1 Stephan Holden, "Putting Bromance to an Erotic Test," *New York Times*, July 9, 2009, http://movies.nytimes.com/2009/07/10/movies/10hump.html?_r=0.

2 Rob Carnevale, "Humpday: Interview with Lyn Shelton," IndieLondon, undated, http://www.indielondon.co.uk/Film-Review/humpday-lynn-shelton-interview (accessed October 27, 2011).

3 Jack Halberstam, *The Queer Art of Failure* (Durham, NC: Duke University Press, 2011), 66.

4 Eric Spitznagel, "The Stars of *Jackass 3D* on God, Cancer, and Homosexuality," *Vanity Fair*, October 14, 2010, http://www.vanityfair.com/online/oscars/2010/10/the-stars-of-jackass-3d-talk-about-god-cancer-and-homosexuality.

5 There is disagreement on the web regarding the meaning of the term "str8." In some online communities, "str8" functions simply as Internet slang for "straight." It has also been used as an abbreviation for "straight" in rap lyrics. However, others, such as some of the contributors to urbandictionary.com, argue that str8 is used by "gay and bisexual men in the closet."

6 In January of 2005, research assistants and I collected and analyzed 118 personal ads, which represented all of the ads in which men who identified themselves as straight (or "str8") solicited sex with other men on Craigslist during a nine-day period (from January 6 through January 15, 2005). The following year, in 2006, I focused on the Casual Encounters section of Craigslist with the specific intent of observing how racial meanings circulated within it. In order to capture all ads

placed by straight-identified men seeking men, I searched for ads containing either the terms "'DL'" or "str8," the latter of which was more commonly used in Casual Encounters. In the Casual Encounters section of Craigslist, self-identified white men placed the majority of the ads for straight men seeking men, regardless of whether the term "str8" or "DL" was used. Men of color who used the term "DL" placed most of their ads in a different section of Craigslist: Men Seeking Men. This fact alone points to ethnoracial differences in constructions of (hetero)sexuality. Men of color who have sex with men are arguably interpellated into a "down low" subjectivity (itself a construction linked to the closet, and hence, to gay male sexuality). In contrast, the homosexual desires of white men—like whiteness itself—are relatively unmarked, enabling white straight men to bypass identitarian associations and conceptualize sex with men as an *encounter* (rather than an identity), and a *casual* encounter at that. In the second project, I analyzed all of the 125 ads placed by str8 men "seeking same" from May through July of 2006. The majority of the 125 ads I examined in this second study—71 percent to be exact—made reference to race: either to the racial identification of the person placing the ad or to a specific racial preference for a sex partner. Among the ads that mentioned race, 86 percent were placed by men who either identified themselves as white or who included a photo of themselves in which they appeared to be white (though I recognize that the latter is a flawed indicator of racial identification and that race itself is socially and historically constructed). My analysis in this chapter draws on the 243 ads I collected over both studies. Both studies received approval from the University of California Internal Review Board for the use of human subjects (although I did not contact or interview human subjects). Though Craigslist is a public site, I have made every effort to protect the anonymity of the men whose personal ads I have reproduced here. Any specific identifying information (e.g. name of a small and specific neighborhood, physical descriptions, contact information) has been removed from the ads.

7 Jane Ward, "Queer Sexism: Rethinking Gay Men and Masculinity," in Peter Nardi, ed., *Gay Masculinities* (Thousand Oaks: Sage Publications, 1999), 153–175.

8 Brandon Robinson and David Moskowitz, "The Eroticism of Internet Cruising as a Self-Contained Behaviour: A Multivariate Analysis of Men Seeking Men Demographics and Getting Off Online," in *Culture, Health & Sexuality: An International Journal for Research, Intervention and Care* 15, no. 5 (2013): 555–569.

9 Eve Sedgwick, *Between Men: English Literature and Male Homosocial Desire* (New York: Columbia University Press, 1985), 1.

10 Michael Kimmel, *Guyland: The Perilous World Where Boys Become Men* (New York: Harper Perennial, 2008).

11 Surfers commonly appeared in gay "physique magazines" of the 1950s.

12 Bakari Kitwana, *Why White Kids Love Hip Hop: Wangstas, Wiggers, Wannabes, and the New Reality of Race in America* (New York: Basic Civitas Books, 2005).

13 Ibid.

14 Geneva Smitherman, *Black Talk: Words and Phrases from the Hood to the Amen Corner* (New York: Mariner Books, 2000).

15 Benoit Denizet-Lewis, "Double Lives on the Down Low," *New York Times Sunday Magazine*, August 3, 2003, http://www.nytimes.com/2003/08/03/magazine/double-lives-on-the-down-low.html?src=pm.

16 Ibid.; Keith Boykin, *Beyond the Down Low: Sex, Lies, and Denial in Black America* (New York: Carroll & Graf, 2005).

17 Centers for Disease Control, "Topics: Down Low," http://www.cdc.gov/hiv/topics/aa/resources/qa/downlow.htm (accessed July 17, 2011).

18 Patricia Hill Collins, *Black Sexual Politics: African Americans, Gender, and the New Racism* (New York: Routledge, 2005); J. L. King, *On the Down Low: A Journey Into the Lives of "Straight" Black Men Who Sleep with Men* (New York: Harmony, 2004).

19 Collins, *Black Sexual Politics*, 207.

20 M. Alfredo González, "Latinos On Da Down Low: The Limitations of Sexual Identity in Public Health," *Latino Studies* 5, no. 1 (2007): 27 (emphasis in original).

21 Keith Boykin, "Go Tell It On the Mountain," Boykin's personal blog, December 19, 2005, http://www.keithboykin.com/arch/001709.html.

22 Ibid.

23 See, for instance, Roderick Ferguson's discussion in *Aberrations in Black: Toward a Queer of Color Critique* (Minneapolis: University of Minnesota Press, 2003) of the ways that canonical sociology has pathologized African American sexuality as both queer and hyper-heterosexual, as measured against white sexual norms. See also Lilian Faderman's discussion of white queer slumming in Harlem in *Odd Girls and Twilight Lovers: A History of Lesbian Life in Twentieth Century America* (New York: Columbia University Press, 1991).

24 C. Riley Snorton, *Nobody Is Supposed to Know: Black Sexuality on the Down Low* (Minneapolis: University of Minnesota Press, 2014); Jeffrey Q. McCune, "'Out' in the Club: The Down Low, Hip-Hop, and the Architexture of Black Masculinity," *Text and Performance Quarterly* 28, no. 3 (2008): 298–314.

25 BDSM is an acronym for "bondage and discipline, sadism and masochism."

26 Lionel Cantú, Nancy Naples, and Salvador Vidal-Ortiz, *The Sexuality of Migration: Border Crossings and Mexican Immigrant Men* (New York: New York University Press, 2009).

27 I am not referring here to the various white ethnicities in the United States (e.g., the cultural traditions of Irish, Germans, or Italians, etc.), but to the shared cultural experience of being classified as "white" and of benefitting from this classification.

28 See George Lipsitz, *The Possessive Investment in Whiteness: How White People Profit from Identity Politics* (Philadelphia: Temple University Press, 2006).

29 See R. W. Connell, *Masculinities* (Berkeley: University of California Press, 2005).

Chapter 5. Haze Him!

1 Thank you to Robin Podolsky for bringing this example to my attention.

2 A quick Google search of the term "Susie Rottencrotch" brings up numerous descriptions of the imagined figure. As described on the Marine Corps–themed blog TerminalLance.com, "All Marines know the name Susie Rottencrotch. If you

don't, *you've been doing it wrong*. It's just been a personal endeavor to imagine what she must look like–worn out and abused from years of plethoric amounts of cocks and semen filling the void of her hollow soul—well, her vagina at any rate" (http://terminallance.com/2010/07/06/terminal-lance-49-myths-and-legends/ [accessed June 26, 2014]).

3 See CJ Pascoe's discussion of the nexus of masculinity and compulsive hetero-sexuality in *Dude You're A Fag: Masculinity and Sexuality in High School* (Berkeley: University of California Press, 2007).

4 See, for example, Beth Richie, *Compelled to Crime: The Gender Entrapment of Battered Black Women* (New York: Routledge, 1995).

5 See Sut Jhally's 2007 documentary *Dreamworlds 3: Desire, Sex, and Power in Music Video*, Media Education Foundation, http://www.mediaed.org/cgi-bin/com-merce.cgi?preadd=action&key=223.

6 For instance, feminist philosopher Julia Kristeva's work on the history of philoso-phy points to a male philosophical tradition linking the filth and decay of the material body with femaleness. See Kristeva's *Powers of Horror: An Essay on Abjection* (New York: Columbia University Press, 1982).

7 See Michael Kimmel, *Angry White Men: American Masculinity at the End of an Era* (New York: Nation Books, 2013).

8 Carrie Little Hersh, "Crossing the Line: Sex, Power, Justice, and the U.S. Navy at the Equator," *Duke Journal of Law and Policy* 9 (2002): 277–324.

9 Steven Zeeland, *Sailors and Sexuality Identity: Crossing the Line between Straight and Gay in the U.S. Navy* (New York: Routledge, 1995); quotation taken from front matter.

10 In 1991, over one hundred Navy and Marine Corps officers sexually assaulted eighty-four women and seven men at the annual Tailhook Association Conference in Las Vegas. The assaults and the investigations that followed have since been referred to as the "Tailhook Scandal." Tailhook is a nonprofit fraternal organiza-tion of naval aviators. According to Steven Zeeland (private correspondence, June 19, 2014), the public exposure and scrutiny brought on by the scandal fundamen-tally transformed the culture of the Navy and Marine Corps, especially with regard to initiation rituals like crossing the line. Hence, in the early 1990s, as the demo-graphics of the military were changing (with women, gay men, and men of color enlisting in unprecedented numbers), the Tailhook Scandal functioned to curtail some of the military's sanctioned and ritualized homosexual contact. Zeeland points out, however, that these sorts of rituals also differed from ship to ship, as did the response to homosexual contact. According to Zeeland, it is likely that this remains true today, with differences in individual units determining the extent to which homosexual contact remains ritualized, and the forms this activity takes.

11 Aaron Belkin, *Bring Me Men: Military Masculinity and the Benign Façade of American Empire, 1898–2001* (London: Oxford University Press, 2012), 80. I note here that in Belkin's analysis of male-male rape at the U.S. Naval Academy, he offers alarming examples of rapes of male students and then moves into a discussion of the crossing the line ceremony. In this discussion, he uses the terms

"rape" and "bodily penetration" nearly interchangeably, without offering a guideline for how rape may (or may not) be identified within the blurry field of hazing, which is often simultaneously consensual and compelled.

12 Ibid., 94.

13 Zeeland, *Sailors and Sexuality Identity*, 57.

14 Ibid, 81.

15 Slavoj Žižek, "What's Wrong with Fundamentalism?" Lacan.com, 2005, http://www.lacan.com/zizunder.htm.

16 Jasbir Puar, *Terrorist Assemblages: Homonationalism in Queer Times* (Durham: Duke University Press, 2007), p. 112

17 Judith Kegan Gardiner, "*South Park*, Blue Men, Anality, and Market Masculinity," *Men and Masculinities* 2, no. 3 (2000): 252.

18 Ibid., 258.

19 Thank you to Peter Hennen for bringing theories of anality, especially in Judith Kegan Gardinar's work, to my attention.

20 Daniel Schulman, "Animal House in Afghanistan," MotherJones, September 1, 2009, http://www.motherjones.com/mojo/2009/09/animal-house-afghanistan.

21 "U.S. Contractor Accused of Deviant Hazing," CNN.com, September 2, 2009, http://www.cnn.com/2009/WORLD/asiapcf/09/02/afghanistan.embassy.contractors/.

22 Reportedly, wogs receive a card verifying their completion of the crossing the line ceremony, which they must present at each subsequent crossing of the equator. If they lose their card, they may be forced to re-experience the initiation ritual.

23 Text from the main page of HazeHim.com, at http://hazehim.com.

24 See websites such as BaitBuddies.com and BaitBus.com.

25 Fan comment on the Haze Him thread at JustUsBoys.com, August 26, 2010, http://www.justusboys.com/forum/threads/300356-Haze-him.

26 Michael Kimmel, *Guyland: The Perilous World Where Boys Become Men* (New York: Harper Perennial, 2008), 113–114.

Chapter 6. Against Gay Love

1 CJ Pascoe and Tristan Bridges, "Bro Porn: Heterosexualizing Straight Men's Anti-Homophobia Stances," *Huffington Post*, December 6, 2013, http://www.huffingtonpost.com/cj-pascoe/bro-porn-heterosexualizing-straight-mens-anti-homophobia-stances_b_4386206.html.

2 See Suzanna Danuta Walters, *The Tolerance Trap: How God, Genes, and Good Intentions Are Sabotaging Gay Equality* (New York: New York University Press, 2014), for a full discussion of this trend.

3 Thank you to Ann Pellegrini for helping me find some of the language to describe how queer worlds function as their own form of "object choice."

4 Thanks to my students, Jennifer DeMello and Antoine Da, for inspiring this word choice with their "Evolved This Way" t-shirts.

5 Vera Whisman, *Queer by Choice: Lesbians, Gay Men, and the Politics of Identity* (New York: Routlege, 1995), quotation taken from back matter.

INDEX

ABOUT THE AUTHOR

Jane Ward is Associate Professor of Women's Studies at the University of California, Riverside. She is the author of *Respectably Queer* (2008).

Printed and bound by CPI Group (UK) Ltd, Croydon, CR0 4YY

09/06/2025

14685794-0002